From "Perverts" to "Fab Five"

From "Perverts" to "Fab Five" tracks the dramatic change in how the American media have depicted gay people over the last half-century. Each chapter illuminates a particular media product that served as a milestone on the media's journey from demonizing homosexuals some fifty years ago to celebrating the gay community—or at least some sectors of the gay community—today.

The media, Streitmatter argues, have not merely reflected the American public's shift to a more enlightened view of gay people, but they have been instrumental in propelling that change. The book spans the breadth of communication venues. Individual chapters focus on major news stories, entertainment television programs, and mainstream motion pictures that captured the public imagination while, at the same time, sending powerful messages about gay men and lesbians. Ideal for any reader interested in the changing depiction of gay men and lesbians in the media over time, or as required reading in media courses, *From "Perverts" to "Fab Five"* challenges our very understandings of the words "public" and "media" both.

Rodger Streitmatter is a Professor and Senior Associate Dean in the School of Communication at American University in Washington, D.C. He is author of six previous books, including *Mightier than the Sword: How the News Media Have Shaped American History*, *Voices of Revolution: The Dissident Press in America*, and *Sex Sells! The Media's Journey from Repression to Obsession*. He holds a Ph.D. in American History.

From "Perverts" to "Fab Five"

The Media's Changing Depiction of Gay Men and Lesbians

Rodger Streitmatter

Routledge
Taylor & Francis Group

NEW YORK AND LONDON

First published 2009
by Routledge
270 Madison Ave, New York, NY 10016

Simultaneously published in the UK
by Routledge
2 Park Square, Milton Park, Abingdon, Oxon OX14 4RN

*Routledge is an imprint of the Taylor & Francis Group,
an informa business*

© 2009 Taylor & Francis

Typeset in Sabon by
Florence Production Ltd, Stoodleigh, Devon
Printed and bound in the United States of America
on acid-free paper by
Walsworth Publishing Company, Marceline, MO

Library of Congress Cataloging in Publication Data
Streitmatter, Rodger.
    From "perverts" to "fab five": the media's changing depiction
of gay men and lesbians/by Rodger Streitmatter.
        p. cm.
        Includes bibliographical references and index.
    1. Gay men—United States—Social conditions. 2. Lesbians—
United States—Social conditions. 3. Gay men in mass media.
4. Lesbians in mass media. 5. Gays in popular culture—United
States. 6. Mass media—United States. 7. United States—Social
conditions—1980–. I. Title.
HQ76.2.U5S87 2009
306.76′60973—dc22   2008024917

ISBN10: 0–7890–3670–3 (hbk)
ISBN10: 0–7890–3671–1 (pbk)
ISBN10: 0–203–88638–0 (ebk)

ISBN13: 978–0–7890–3670–4 (hbk)
ISBN13: 978–0–7890–3671–1 (pbk)
ISBN13: 978–0–203–88638–0 (ebk)

Contents

List of Figures   vii

Introduction   1

1 "Perverts" on the Potomac: Homosexuals Enter
   the News Arena   6

2 Stonewall Rebellion: Reporting on an Epic Event   17

3 *The Boys in the Band*: Homosexuality Comes to
   the Big Screen   26

4 *Soap*: A Gay Man Comes to TV Land   37

5 AIDS Enters the News: Reporting on the "Gay Plague"   50

6 AIDS Becomes Major News: "Now No One Is Safe"   57

7 Gays in the Military: The Debate over Lifting the Ban   65

8 Fleeting Images of Lesbians: Killing, Kissing,
   Being Chic   73

9 *Philadelphia*: "A Quantum Leap for Gays on Film"   83

10 A New Gay Man in Town: Hollywood Shifts to
    Positive Stereotypes   93

11 *Ellen*: Coming Out, On Screen and Off   104

12 *Will & Grace*: The Biggest Gay Hit in TV History   115

13 *Queer as Folk*: "An Unvarnished Treatment of Gay Life"   127

14 *Queer Eye for the Straight Guy*: The "Fab Five" as
    Gay Reality TV   137

15 Notes on Gay Visibility vs. Lesbian Visibility   146

16 *The L Word*: Lesbians Move into the Spotlight   149

17 Same-Sex Marriage: A Journalistic Love Fest   159

18 *Brokeback Mountain*: "A Breakthrough Gay Romance"   169

    Conclusion: From "Perverts" to "Fab Five"—Progress
    in Three Stages . . . and Waiting for a Fourth   179

    Notes   189
    Index   217

Figures

3.1   Michael and Donald, *The Boys in the Band*   29

4.1   Billy Crystal, *Soap*   38

6.1   Hollywood icon Rock Hudson with Elizabeth Taylor in *Giant*   58

9.1   Tom Hanks in the 1993 film *Philadelphia*   85

10.1   Rupert Everett and Julia Roberts in the 1997 blockbuster hit *My Best Friend's Wedding*   96

11.1   Ellen DeGeneres exited the closet thanks to the prompting of the openly lesbian character played by Laura Dern   106

12.1   Sean Hayes with Megan Mullally and Eric McCormack with Debra Messing, in *Will & Grace*   116

14.1   The "Fab Five" working their magic on one hapless hetero, in *Queer Eye for the Straight Guy*   138

16.1   *The L Word*   150

18.1   Jake Gyllenhaal and Heath Ledger starred as gay ranch hands in *Brokeback Mountain*   170

Introduction

Several of the country's leading newspapers published their first major articles about homosexuals in 1950. The stories printed in those elite journalistic voices routinely used the term "perverts" as a synonym for "homosexuals," with typical headlines in the single most influential of the papers, the *New York Times*, reading "Perverts Called Government Peril" and "Federal Vigilance on Perverts Asked."[1]

In the early 2000s, a TV show featuring five gay men dispensing fashion and decorating tips to a hapless straight guy was a runaway hit, prompting the nation's news media to embrace both the program and the "Fab Five," as the members of the *très gay* quintet became known. The *New York Times* not only congratulated the most flamboyant of the men for "his hysterically campy quips," but also gushed about the group as a whole, dubbing them "a league of superheroes." [2]

What a change!

The shift was so profound, in fact, that it has raised a whole series of questions.

- What factors caused the media's depiction of gay men to be transformed so radically in a mere fifty years?
- What impact did that seismic shift have on the nation's collective attitude toward people who are attracted to members of their own sex?
- Did the portrayal of lesbians follow the same route as that of gay men or did the media treat gay women differently? If there was a difference, why?
- Finally, which genre of the media—journalism, film, or TV—has been the most effective in changing the public perception of gay people?

This book answers these questions.

Specifically, each chapter illuminates a particular media product that served as a milestone on the media's journey from demonizing homosexuals some fifty years ago to celebrating gay people—or at least some categories of gay people—today.

From "Perverts" to "Fab Five" spans the breadth of communication types. The individual chapters focus on major news stories, television programs, and mainstream motion pictures that have captured the public imagination while, at the same time, sending powerful messages about gay men and lesbians.

The various messages identified and discussed ultimately support the major thesis that underpins this book:

> The media have not merely *reflected* the American public's shift to a more enlightened view of gay people, but they have been instrumental in *propelling* that change.

In other words, the media products showcased in the following chapters have played, both individually and collectively, a key role in shaping the public perception of the common characteristics of men who are sexually attracted to other men and of women who are sexually attracted to other women.

For example, before *The Boys in the Band* was released in 1970, the vast majority of Americans had never met a homosexual, or at least not one who publicly acknowledged his sexual orientation. So the characters in that groundbreaking film became the first gay acquaintances of several million moviegoers. Likewise, the most memorable line in the script, "Show me a happy homosexual, and I'll show you a gay corpse," simultaneously established in the minds of a huge number of moviegoers the idea that gay men were sad and pathetic creatures whose lives were defined by misery and self-hatred.

Fortunately, more media products soon followed in that film's footsteps. When Billy Crystal began appearing on the program *Soap* in 1977 as television's first recurring gay character, millions of viewers came to know a happy, well-adjusted, and highly likable fellow who was a productive member of society.

This getting-to-know-you process exploded in the 1990s, first with the Oscar-winning *Philadelphia* being released in the nation's movie theaters and then, in rapid succession, the TV sitcom *Ellen*, starring real-life lesbian Ellen DeGeneres, such box-office blockbusters as *The Birdcage* and *My Best Friend's Wedding*, and network television's smash hit *Will & Grace* (which won numerous Emmy Awards and, at its peak, attracted a weekly audience of a staggering 19 million viewers). By the beginning of the new millennium, cable television had taken center stage, offering programs such as *Queer as Folk*, *Queer Eye for the Straight Guy*, and *The L Word*, while the motion picture industry crossed a new threshold with *Brokeback Mountain*.

The various films and television shows differed widely in their quality and in the messages they sent, as the following chapters will show. But there is no question that, by the early years of the twenty-first century, only a small percentage of Americans could honestly say they had never met a gay person—or at least an actor who played one on TV.

Parallel to the process unfolding in the entertainment media was the one played out in the country's daily newspapers and on its nightly television newscasts. After "perverts" made their initial appearance in 1950, almost two decades passed before homosexuals returned to the news spotlight, this time when the Stonewall Rebellion erupted in 1969. This was followed, beginning in the early 1980s, by the news stories about the first cases of AIDS, initially known as "the gay plague."

The biggest news story of the next decade emerged in 1992 when President Bill Clinton proposed ending the ban against gay soldiers serving in the U.S. military. In the early 2000s, news organizations shifted their attention to covering—and simultaneously promoting—the efforts to legalize same-sex marriage.

The importance of the topics listed here evolves not just from their increasing numbers but also from their impact. For this book contends that, as media consumers have been exposed to an increasing number of movies, TV programs, and news stories about gay people during the past 50 years, those various media products have gradually, but relentlessly, made the American public more accepting of what Oscar Wilde called "the love that dare not speak its name."

The *Philadelphia Inquirer* is one of the newspapers that has written about the power of these media depictions. "Programs such as *Will & Grace*," the paper observed in 2003, "give straight viewers a chance to make friends with gays in their living rooms. It's like gay sensitivity training." The *Inquirer* went on to credit television portrayals of gay men, because they are viewed inside American homes, with being so influential that they not only help make millions of straight people become comfortable with gay people but also impel a sizable number of those viewers to support gay rights initiatives. "This is the genius of television. Gay characters have a cumulative power. They end up moving the center of public opinion."[3]

Other news organizations have made the same point. The *Los Angeles Times* observed, "Thanks to the popular media, there is now a whole generation of Americans who have grown up being comfortable with alternative lifestyles." Fox News Channel, widely considered one of the country's most conservative journalistic voices, also jumped on the media-have-changed-attitudes bandwagon, with one of its commentators saying:

> Silly sitcoms such as *Ellen* and *Will & Grace* help us overcome our prejudices against gays. Popular television shows are often respon-sible for dispelling the myths and ignorance that fuel hate and prejudice, and for providing a safe environment in which the public can be nudged toward understanding and acceptance by characters

they get to know and love within the safe environment of their favorite shows.[4]

Although it's impossible to prove a cause-and-effect relationship between media content and social change, *USA Today*, the country's largest-circulation daily, has argued that one exists vis-à-vis altering public attitudes toward gay people. "Cultural observers—both approving and disapproving—link the popularity of gay characters in the media," it stated, "with the comfort level many Americans now feel toward lesbians and gay men."[5]

While I wholeheartedly agree that the media have played an enormous role in raising the public's gay-content comfort level, I believe this phenomenon has its limitations. The final chapter in this book speaks to this reality, arguing that certain types of gay men and lesbians have been embraced far more readily—both by the media and, subsequently, by the public—than others have been. Indeed, my conclusion argues that many categories of gay people are still largely absent from the mainstream media. Additionally, I argue that the primary motivation of those who decide who is and who isn't depicted in the various media products is *not* a commitment to social change but a desire to appeal to a niche market seen as having large disposable incomes—a market that is a highly attractive audience for economic reasons.

The number of chapters in this book totals only eighteen. Restricting the list of milestones was a conscious decision on my part, as I was determined to avoid creating a mind-numbing list of names, dates, and titles that would make the reader's eyes glaze over. Instead, my goal was to focus on a relatively small number of topics so I could provide highly textured descriptions, making these various media products come alive as the vibrant attitude-changing cultural influences that they have been and continue to be.

My decision to limit the number of milestones illuminated in this book means that not *every* media product depicting gay people has been included. I don't devote chapters, for example, to the 1971 segment of *All in the Family* that broke ground as the first sitcom episode about homosexuality, or to the 1985 made-for-television film *An Early Frost*, which made history as TV's first drama about AIDS. I don't believe that either of these programs deserves to be labeled a milestone in the evolution of media depictions of gay people because each aired only one time; they pale in importance, in my opinion, when compared to *Soap*, for example, which offered viewers an example of a gay man every week from 1977 to 1981.[6]

Despite the choices I had to make while researching and writing this book, I am pleased—and unequivocally so—with the final product. My sense of satisfaction comes not only from my belief that *From "Perverts" to "Fab Five"* makes a significant contribution to American media scholarship as well as to gay and lesbian scholarship, but also because this book represents a high point in my own writing. Specifically, although I have published six previous books, none of them has reflected the aspects of my own being to the degree that this one does.

All of my previous scholarly projects have had a historical dimension, but the time frame covered in this particular book almost exactly parallels the span of my own life. In 1950 when the earliest milestone examined in these pages took place, I was one year old. Although I won't claim I was reading the *New York Times* at that early age, I certainly have vivid memories of many of the later media products chronicled here. It still sends shivers down my spine when I recall reading those initial news stories about "the gay plague" in the early 1980s, for example, just as I remember the exhilaration that many felt when Bill Clinton proposed lifting the ban on gays in the military in the early 1990s. And so, because most of the topics I've written about in this book coincide with my own life experiences, I feel as though they illuminate not only milestones in the relationship between the media and Gay America but also stages in my own evolution as a gay man.

1 "Perverts" on the Potomac
Homosexuals Enter the News Arena

It was on March 1, 1950, that several of America's leading newspapers first gave prominent coverage to the topic of homosexuality. The event that prompted the stories was a public hearing conducted by a sub-committee of the U.S. Senate. During that session, a government official mentioned that ninety-one State Department employees had been fired because they were "in the shady category." When one of the senators asked the witness to clarify exactly what he meant by that phrase, the bureaucrat fidgeted nervously for a moment—he was highly uncomfort-able talking publicly about such an unseemly topic—and then stated, almost in a whisper:

"They were homosexuals."[1]

That comment pushed the nation's elite news organizations across a historic threshold because, having been heard by several Capitol Hill reporters during the public session, it could not be ignored. Even though the newspapers feared that their readers would be offended to see the word "homosexuals" in print, the competitive nature of American journalism left the publications no choice. Each paper knew that if it opted *not* to quote the statement, it ran the risk of giving the other papers a scoop. And so a handful of the most influential news voices of the day took a step they previously had assiduously avoided.

The morning after the public hearing was by no means the last time in 1950 that the sensitive subject appeared in the country's media. The suggestion that homosexuals possibly had a hand in shaping American foreign policy prompted expressions of shock and outrage from legions of congressmen and other readers, which in turn propelled myriad more articles on the topic. Indeed, by December of 1950, news coverage of men who were sexually attracted to other men—lesbians were never mentioned in the stories—had become a recurring matter for discussion not only in major newspapers but also in the country's most widely read magazines, with the Washington-based story exploding into a full-scale national scandal widely referred to as "Perverts on the Potomac."[2]

The coverage, when looked at as a whole, communicated several negative messages about homosexuals, thereby consistently demonizing such men. Specifically, the articles portrayed "perverts" as a threat to the nation's well-being and, therefore, as entirely unacceptable for government service for three distinct reasons: they were vulnerable to blackmail, they were emotionally unstable, and they were immoral. The various newspapers and magazines also consistently depicted homosexuals as being afflicted with a nauseating disease, as being obsessed with sex, and as posing a grave danger to young boys.

Startling Revelations

To understand why homosexuals entered the news arena when they did, as well as why they were consistently vilified, requires looking at the events that made Joseph R. McCarthy a national newsmaker. In February 1950 the Wisconsin senator publicly accused State Department officials of knowingly employing members of the Communist Party. McCarthy's dramatic charges transformed him into the chief spokesman for a virulent campaign that he and other Republicans had designed to help the party regain the White House in the 1952 election.[3]

Two weeks after McCarthy launched his crusade against communists in the government, members of the Senate subcommittee called the official in charge of security for the State Department to testify before them. Desperate to show the nation's top lawmakers that he was doing his job, John Peurifoy stated that he vigorously investigated the background of any employee whose loyalty came into question. Peurifoy went on to say that his vigilance had led, in the previous three years, to 202 undesirable individuals either resigning or being dismissed. To reinforce his point, he added the reference to ridding the department of the ninety-one workers. Prompted by Senator Styles Bridges, a Republican from New Hampshire, to be more specific, Peurifoy uttered the word "homosexuals."[4]

When the newspapers that had reporters at the hearing published Peurifoy's quotation on the morning of March 1, they gave it considerable prominence. The *New York Times*, *Los Angeles Times*, and *Washington Times-Herald*, the most influential newspaper in the nation's capital at the time, all placed the story on page one. This was a first for these elite news outlets, as their previous references to homosexuality had been limited to brief news items, always on inside pages and veiled in euphemisms, that reported men being arrested by the local police for having committed what were called "indecent acts."[5]

After the coverage of the hearing, homosexuality returned to the columns of these elite newspapers, while also making its debut in one of the country's top news magazines later that spring. The event being reported this time was another session of the same subcommittee that had heard testimony from the State Department's security official, but now the witness was a man *Newsweek* magazine described as "tough old Lt. Roy E. Blick" of the District of Columbia police force. The senators wanted to know more about the homosexual population in the nation's capital, so they turned to the head of the local vice squad. "Blick described parties raided, officials high and low arrested, and ended with a real shocker," the newsweekly reported. "There are some 5,000 homosexuals in the District of Columbia, he testified, and 3,750 of them work for the government." (Blick later admitted the figures were, in fact, nothing more than guesses presented as fact.)[6]

Coverage of the two Senate hearings showed the nation's top journalists that the sky did not fall and readers did not cancel their subscriptions when they encountered stories about homosexuality—at least stories that depicted the "Perverts on the Potomac" in a stridently negative light. And so by the summer of 1950, articles on the topic began to dot the pages not only of America's most prestigious dailies but also of smaller newspapers and *Time*, the country's largest-circulation news magazine. Non-news publications also began to write about the subject, with articles soon appearing in *The New Yorker, Esquire, Coronet,* and the *Saturday Evening Post.*[7]

A particularly large number of articles were published in December when a Senate committee released the findings of a six-month study of homosexuals working in the federal government. By this point, coverage had expanded to the daily newspapers in such cities as Miami and Dallas, Chicago and Cleveland, San Francisco and Detroit. Typical of the lead paragraphs was one in the *Boston Globe* that began: "A Senate investigating group today labeled sexual perverts as dangerous security risks and demanded strict and careful screening to keep them off the government payroll." The most significant fact in the articles was that, during the previous four years, a total of 4,954 homosexuals had been removed from federal employment.[8]

Historians who assess how the media have performed with regard to a particular topic often ask the question: Were the media outlets of the time *reflecting* societal beliefs and attitudes of their day, or were those outlets *leading* society toward a new set of beliefs and attitudes? With regard to homosexuality at the midpoint of the twentieth century, the country's newspapers and magazines clearly were merely reflecting the feelings of repulsion that the vast majority of Americans felt toward men who were sexually attracted to other men. The articles they printed give no indication that the various media outlets were seeking to lead society toward a more enlightened understanding of homosexuality. Indeed, the coverage conveyed a number of highly denigrating messages about members of this reviled subgroup of society.

Terms of Derision

The hundreds of newspapers published in the United States look to the most highly respected dailies for guidance on what topics to report on, as well as what approach to take in dealing with those topics. In 1950 the *New York Times* was the country's most esteemed newspaper. And so it became the media outlet, more than any other, responsible for establi[shing] [...] [t]o start covering homosexuals in the ne[ws] [...] one of the stories should be one of con[...]

Begi[...] [...] about John Peurifoy's testimony at the [...] continuing through a dozen other pieces published during the year, the *Times* showed its disdain for homosexuals by consistently referring to them as "perverts." Among the headlines the paper's editors crafted to run above those early stories were "Perverts Called Government Peril" and "Federal Vigilance on Perverts Asked."[9]

The country's preeminent journalistic voice also communicated its derisive attitude toward homosexuals by the words in the bodies of the stories. In addition to referring to the men as "perverts," the *Times* also called them "homos" and "deviates"—without placing quotation marks around any of the words.[10]

As news organizations across the country began reporting on homosexuals, the publications repeated the derisive terms used in the *Times*. Among the headlines: "Senators Demand U.S. Bar Hiring of Sex Perverts" in the *Cleveland Plain Dealer*, "Probers Assail U.S. Hiring of Sex Perverts" in the *Chicago Tribune*, and "Sex Perverts Called Risks to Security" in the *San Francisco Chronicle*.[11]

Some publications determined that men being sexually attracted to other men represented such a horrifying threat to the social order that even the denigrating terms used in the *Times* and repeated in other papers were not sufficient. The *Miami Herald*, *Boston Globe*, and *Dallas Morning News* used the word "degenerates"; *Esquire*, the *Washington Times-Herald*, and the *New York World-Telegram* used the word "queers"; and the general-interest magazine *Coronet* referred to homosexuals as "sex aberrants" and "fairies."[12]

"They Might Be Blackmailed by Spies"

From the moment homosexuals made their first appearance in the nation's most elite newspapers, national security was a major theme of the coverage. As the *Los Angeles Times* stated in its first story, "[S]uch persons are rated bad security risks because they might be blackmailed by spies." At a time when China's fall to communism, the outbreak of the Korean War, and anti-communist witch hunts dominated the news, no accusation was more damning to a government employee than that he was a pawn of the enemy.[13]

[handwritten margin note: ① coinage of the term "pervert" to refer to gay on media in the 50s]

Numerous news articles described the blackmail scenario, which contended that if the homosexuality of a State Department employee became known to an official of another country, the American would automatically be labeled a security risk and lose his job. Specifically, the homosexual was vulnerable to blackmail threats because if an enemy agent demanded sensitive information and the "pervert" refused to provide it, the foreigner could expose the American's shameful sexual desires and thereby destroy the man's career.[14]

One curious detail related to the media coverage of homosexuals during 1950 was that, despite reference to the blackmail scenario in dozens of stories, none of the articles divulged the name of a single federal employee who had, in fact, been the victim of such a threat. Indeed, none of the stories even mentioned the name of any person who had been identified as a homosexual. As the *New York Post* explained (and in 1950 the *New York Post* was more widely respected journalistically than it is today), a "pervert" who was removed from the government payroll received the gift of anonymity in exchange for resigning rather than fighting to keep his job. "Unless he wants to face the unspeakable disgrace of letting his case become public," the *Post* wrote, "the homosexual will sign the resignation quietly. He always does."[15]

"Hysterical Queers"

As homosexuals moved into the news arena, the various publications portrayed them as emotionally unstable. Some papers and magazines communicated this weakness by describing the men as absurdly effeminate, while others characterized them as exhibiting such an extreme level of hysteria that they often became physically violent.

In 1950, the gender roles in American society were so rigid—men dominated the political and business spheres, while women were largely confined to the domestic sphere—that anyone who did not conform to the strict definitions was automatically considered a misfit. And according to the journalistic voices of the day, men who were attracted to other men most definitely fell into this category. Westbrook Pegler, a Pulitzer Prize-winning columnist whose words were published in the *New York Times* and 140 other newspapers around the country, wrote that the State Department employed so many "nances" that it was commonplace for these male employees to "call each other female names like Bessie, Maud, and Chloe," and to "write each other poetry and confidential notes so tender." Another columnist, Robert C. Ruark of the *New York World-Telegram*, described a "flagrantly homosexual" military attaché as being so confused about his gender that he "regaled strangers with teary tales about his inability to write his boyfriend every day," and other diplomats worried that he might start "wearing a hostess gown in public."[16]

It was also Ruark of the *World-Telegram* who painted one of the most dramatic portraits of the damage that a homosexual's emotional instability could cause. "Most queers exhibit a tendency to hysteria, which means they blow their tops in times of stress," Ruark began, going on to describe the series of events that could unfold when "hysterical queers" act on their compulsions. "A pervert fondles a child. The child cries. The creep blows his roof. He is panic-ridden and hysterically afraid of being caught. He throttles the child." Ruark said that actions such as these were common among homosexuals because of their inability to control either their emotions or their perverse sexual desires. The columnist went on to say that the large number of homosexuals in the State Department had led to egregious consequences for the country. "A great deal of the trouble we are in, internationally, can be laid to the tolerance of this weakness in a service which should be above reproach."[17]

"He Throws Off All Moral Restraints"

According to the laws in place in 1950, any man living in Washington, D.C., who had sexual contact with another man had committed an indecent act and would be punished with a $500 fine and six months in jail. But judging from the articles in the era's newspapers and magazines, the immorality being practiced by these men extended well beyond sex acts.[18]

One accusation was that all homosexuals were un-American. The *New York Post* stated, "Perverts are very susceptible to communism." The *Washington Times-Herald* made the same connection by running an editorial cartoon in which the president placed communists and homosexuals in the same category; in the caption, Harry Truman says to his assistants, "Report to me on the traitors and queers in my administration." The *Washington Daily News* made the linkage in its extensive coverage of a State Department employee known as "Case No. 14." (Although the paper published a dozen stories about him, it never printed his name.) During a period in American history when so much as being acquainted with a communist was sufficient grounds for a person to be fired, the paper stated that the man was "flagrantly homosexual" and that he had "extremely close connections with other individuals with the same tendencies and who were active members of communist front organizations."[19]

Disloyalty to the government was not the only type of immoral behavior that media outlets attributed to men who were sexually attracted to other men. "Once a man assumes the role of homosexual, he throws off all moral restraints and indulges in other vices," according to *Coronet*. The magazine provided a profile of one such man, identifying him not by name but as "a lanky, unshaven derelict who peddles dope." According to the article, the man set his sights on the son of "a prominent business leader whose name is familiar to millions," getting the young man drunk and then seducing him. The drug dealing "sex aberrant" then extorted thousands of dollars from the father, *Coronet* reported, by threatening to destroy the family's good reputation if his financial demands were not met.[20]

Esquire illuminated a similar category of corruption, except that the "heinous shake-down racket" that was the magazine's focus required the efforts not of a lone homosexual but of three "queers" working together. The first member of such a gang would engage a heterosexual man in conversation in a public park and then invite the guy to his apartment for a drink. Soon after they arrived, a boyish-looking homosexual would suddenly appear and throw himself onto the heterosexual man. Just as quickly, the third gang member would arrive on the scene dressed in a police uniform, and purport to arrest the heterosexual man on charges of indecent behavior with a minor. The victim was so fearful of having his life ruined that he agreed to pay the "officer" a large sum of money in exchange for his release. *Esquire* reported that homosexuals were carrying out this scam across the country, with victims including a Boston hotel owner who paid $200,000 and a Midwestern college professor who mortgaged his home to pay "the pervert hustlers" the money they demanded.[21]

"The Nauseating Disease"

The main goal of the earliest newspaper and magazine coverage was to alert the public to how "Perverts on the Potomac" were threatening not only the well-being of American foreign policy but also the national social order writ large. While exposing this danger, some of the articles also made at least some reference to *why* homosexuals had come to be the way they were—and what could be done about that shameful circumstance.

With regard to what caused a person to be attracted to members of the same sex, the publications emphasized that it was definitely not a genetic trait. "They are not born that way," the *New York Post* bluntly stated. Reporter Max Lerner went on to use layman's language to describe the contemporary thinking on the subject. "Scientists see homosexuals as cases of 'arrested psychological development.' It is like the case of a record that has got stuck somewhere." Lerner also articulated the most widely held theory as to what causes "the nauseating disease" to afflict a particular individual. "Psychoanalysts stress family relations—an overly protective mother combined with a cold and hostile father."[22]

The *Post* also tackled the question of exactly how many American men were attracted to members of their own sex. As his source, Lerner turned to *Sexual Behavior in the Human Male*, published in 1948 as the first comprehensive look at sexual practices in the United States, and generally referred to as the *Kinsey Report.* To complete the study, Dr. Alfred C. Kinsey of Indiana University had interviewed 12,000 American men, finding that, as Lerner reported, "10 percent were 'more or less exclusively homosexual' for at least three years" of their adult lives. "This percentage figure is so large that it has shocked many people," the *Post* reporter continued, but then said that the findings of his own journalistic investigation—interviews with dozens of psychiatrists and law enforcement officials—were consistent with the one-in-ten ratio.[23]

Newspapers and magazines also spoke with a single voice with regard to the form of treatment the country's homosexuals desperately needed. Typical of those statements was one published in *Time* magazine, using the medical jargon of the era. "Sexual deviation as a symptomatic disorder in both sexes is curable," the newsweekly wrote without equivocation. "Sexually aberrated individuals can be treated by psychoanalytic psychotherapy."[24]

"The Homosexual Is Always on the Prowl"

Publications reporting on "Perverts on the Potomac" did not portray their subjects merely as men who were attracted to other men but as depraved misfits who were so promiscuous that their pursuit of erotic pleasures dominated their lives. The *New York Post* wrote, "The homosexual is always on the prowl," and the *Washington Times-Herald* said, "The homosexual will go to any limit to attain his abnormal purposes."[25]

Despite these and other statements about an insatiable lust propelling these sexually obsessed men, none of the publications described the precise acts they committed. This was an era when censors refused to allow the word "pregnant" to be spoken on the television program *I Love Lucy,* even though actress Lucille Ball clearly was about to give birth; executives at CBS feared the word would conjure up, in the minds of viewers, images of a man and woman having sexual intercourse. And so when the country's news outlets spoke of sex between men, they did not use explicit terms but relied on euphemisms, all of them resolutely negative.[26]

The dozen articles in a *New York Post* series on homosexuality, published in July 1950, were bursting with such language. One story referred to sexual encounters between men as "twisted sex," and another called the bars and restaurants frequented by homosexuals "dens of iniquity." Sex between men was often referred to as "unnatural practices."[27]

On some occasions, *Post* reporter Max Lerner conveyed the unspeakable nature of homosexual sex by saying that such activity was far too offensive for any decent medium of communication to discuss, even in veiled terms. Lerner built one of his articles around an interview with Roy E. Blick of the District of Columbia vice squad. "When I came into Blick's office," the reporter told his readers, "he was in the midst of a phone conversation about homosexuals which would have been wonderful detail for a documentary, except that no one would dare put it on the screen."[28]

Some newspapers opted to give their readers a sense of the scandalous nature of male-to-male sexual activities by quoting extensively from the members of Congress who were spearheading the effort to remove such men from the government. When Rep. Arthur Miller proposed amending a bill by specifically stating that no federal funds would be appropriated to the project until it was certain that only heterosexual employees would be hired, the *Washington Times-Herald* reproduced his every word. "There are places in Washington where they [homosexuals] gather for the purpose of sex orgies, where they worship at the cesspools and flesh pots of iniquity," the *Times-Herald* quoted the Nebraska congressman as saying. "There are restaurants downtown where you find male prostitutes. They solicit business from male customers. They are pimps and undesirable characters."[29]

"A Sinister Threat to American Youth"

Many publications went beyond reporting that "perverts" were sexually obsessed and said they were also predators who had such out-of-control libidos that they coerced underage boys into having sex with them. In keeping with the language limitations of the era, the word "pedophilia" never appeared in print, but that clearly was the phenomenon the newspapers and magazines were talking about.

During the spring and summer of 1950, only a few passing references were made to the topic. The *New York World-Telegram* reported, for example, that "perverts routinely fondle children," and the *New York Post* stated that "sexual deviates find themselves so compulsively drawn to homosexual practice that they seduce and abuse boys."[30]

And then in September, *Coronet* published a blockbuster article titled "New Moral Menace to Our Youth." The eight-page piece stated pointblank: "No degenerate can indulge his unnatural practices alone. He demands a partner. And the partner, more often than not, must come from the ranks of the young and innocent." The magazine went on, in a strikingly alarmist tone, to articulate the enormous scope of what it called "a sinister threat to American youth," reporting that, "Each year, thousands of youngsters of high-school and college age are introduced to unnatural practices by inveterate seducers."[31]

The most powerful sections of the *Coronet* exposé were the profiles of young victims.

John was "a shy lad" who, when denied membership into an exclusive club at his Eastern prep school, "ran tearfully to a faculty member." The male teacher was "more than solicitous," the article stated. "He persuaded John to forget his disappointment in a whirl of new thrills—thrills which made John feel far superior to his untutored classmates." The teenager continued to have sexual encounters once the school year ended and he went home for the summer, the story stated, as he was soon arrested for indulging his "abnormal habit" with a delivery boy.[32]

Perhaps the most compelling of the profiles was of a Philadelphia youth who was only eleven years old, *Coronet* reported, when a man approached him on the school playground. "He told me that if I'd take a ride in his car, he'd buy me a whole box of candy," the boy said. The child was soon "enticed into perverted acts," the magazine continued, and for the next several weeks "the terrified lad continued to spend night-marish hours with his seducer." At the time the piece was published, the adolescent boy was under psychiatric care.[33]

After summarizing these and other individual case studies, the author of the *Coronet* article concluded with some overall observations. "The shock and mental confusion suffered by youthful victims of such sordid experiences cannot be over exaggerated," he wrote. "Psychiatric case histories bear eloquent testimony to the thousands of warped lives that follow in the wake of associations with perverts."[34]

In the First Stage

For the majority of Americans living in the twenty-first century, seeing the degree to which homosexuals were demonized in the nation's leading newspapers and magazines in 1950 is not only illuminating but also shocking.

Perhaps the single most stunning illustration of the demeaning depiction is the casual use of the term "pervert" to describe men who were sexually attra[cted to other men. That reporters] and editors, including those working for [obscured: ...nes], blithely used such a pejorative wo[rd obscured ...st]ories and in their headlines —symbolizes [obscured] this little-understood seg-ment of the [obscured] news media as well as society in general. That journalists occasionally used other derisive terms —"deviates," "homos," "degenerates," "queers," "fairies"—reinforces the point.

Another significant aspect of this early coverage is that it helps a modern-day observer of the American culture understand how a laundry list of negative stereotypes about homosexual men came to be widely accepted. In the wake of the three words "They were homosexuals" being spoken in a public session on Capitol Hill, publications communicated that men who were sexually attracted to other men were emotionally unstable, morally corrupt, obsessed with sex, and afflicted with a repre-hensible disease, many of them to such a degree that they represented a grave danger to young boys.

For those readers who are interested in case studies of the influence the media have on society, these various articles may initially cause a reader to question one of the widely held tenets of the discipline of communication: All publicity is good publicity.

This belief evolves from the argument that it is better for a particular topic to be talked about—even if it is criticized or portrayed in a negative light—than for that topic to be invisible. The prospects for a political newcomer being elected to office, for example, are generally thought to improve if his or her name becomes known to voters, even if that knowledge emerges through criticism coming from the better-known candidates. This same principle is sometimes stated as: It is better to be deplored than ignored.

After reading about how homosexuals were depicted when they were thrust into the news arena in 1950, however, it is difficult to see how they could possibly have benefited from the plethora of denigrating articles written about them. Had homosexual men not been better off hiding in the shadows than being perceived as so despicable that they were a threat to society in general and American boys in particular?

One way to gain a sense of the potential benefits of this early media treatment of homosexuals—as negative as it was—is to consider the comments of two early advocates of equal rights for American women. In 1852 when the *New York Herald*, then one of the country's largest and most influential newspapers, disparaged one of the movement's early women's rights conventions by referring to it as the "Women's Wrong Convention" that proved the country's "political and social fabric is crumbling," many activists were disheartened. But the visionary Elizabeth Cady Stanton took a different position. "Imagine the publicity given to our idea by thus appearing in a widely circulated sheet like the *Herald*," she wrote. "It will start women thinking, and men too; and when men and women think about a new question, the first step in progress is taken." Lucretia Mott, another early women's rights advocate, expressed a similar sentiment. She first acknowledged that mainstream newspapers had consistently "ridiculed and slandered us." But Mott then went on to say that she had become convinced that the press goes "through three stages in regard to reforms; they first ridicule them, then report them with comment, and at last openly advocate them. We seem to be still in the first stage."[35]

In 1950, homosexuals had entered that first stage.

2 Stonewall Rebellion
Reporting on an Epic Event

The Stonewall Rebellion was the explosive event that thrust an oppressed minority group full force into social upheaval. Men and women from earlier years had begun the effort to secure equal rights for homosexuals, but it was the defiant young people who stood tall and tough at the Stonewall Inn who announced to the nation, in no uncertain terms, that gay people would no longer hang their heads in shame and accept the second-class citizenship they previously had endured. When that small band of social revolutionaries fought back during the raid on that gritty New York City bar in June 1969, the militant phase of a social movement was ignited.

Because of the incident's unique stature in this nascent civil rights campaign, looking at how news organizations reported on the Stonewall Rebellion is an essential chapter in the history of the relationship between the media and gay people.

"Full Moon Over the Stonewall"

The Stonewall Inn was an unlikely site for an event that gay activists would come to call "the Boston Tea Party" of their revolution. With no heating or ventilation system, the place was as hot as a steam room in the summer and as cold as a tomb in the winter. It was also a breeding ground for hepatitis and other illnesses; because there was no running water behind the bar, after a customer finished a drink, the bartender merely dipped the dirty glass into a vat of stale water and then refilled it for the next guy. Despite these deficiencies, the Stonewall Inn attracted large crowds of chino-clad gay men in their late teens and early twenties because the Mafia-owned bar allowed men to dance with each other, as long as they were willing to pay exorbitant prices for watered-down drinks.[1]

June 27, 1969, differed from other summer days in New York City only because some 20,000 people, including legions of gay men, had lined up outside a midtown funeral home in the blistering heat to pay their respects to music legend Judy Garland, laid out in a baby blue casket, who had died from an overdose of tranquilizers. That emotional experience had put some Stonewall patrons in a contrary mood, but otherwise the balmy Friday night at the Greenwich Village bar began like every other one. Even the arrival of six police officers about 11 p.m. seemed routine, as gay men had become accustomed to such harassment being part of the price they paid for coming to a nightspot packed with 200 sweaty men.[2]

After the police moved the patrons into the street, a cluster of drag queens wandered over from nearby Sheridan Square, and then a growing number of passersby, many of them lesbians, also stopped to see what was going on. A few people whistled and jeered at the officers, and then some of the men who had been removed from the bar started tossing pennies at the cops. If there was a single catalyst for the mood turning angry, it was a lesbian who, when an officer shoved her into his patrol car, slid across the seat and out the opposite side, prompting another cop to grab her and slam his nightstick against her head. (The woman who may have been the catalyst for the Stonewall Rebellion has never been identified by name.) Emotions flared as the belligerent crowd, now numbering at least 1,000 strong, turned steely and started throwing rocks, beer cans, and cocktail glasses as more and more people began shouting, "Gay power!" and then, "Police brutality!" and finally, "Kill the cops!"[3]

All of these actions caught the police off guard, as their previous experience with such raids had led them to expect gay youths to remain docile when charged with underage drinking. But this time the startled officers had to retreat inside the Stonewall Inn, and then somebody squirted lighter fluid through a broken window and tossed in a match. The cops managed to douse the flames, but the increasingly defiant crowd forced them to stay inside or face a barrage of flying cans and bottles. Tension rose still higher when some of the protesters somehow pulled a parking meter out of the sidewalk and used it as a battering ram in an effort to break down the door to the bar. Police reinforcements finally arrived to save their fellow officers.

Random flare-ups not only continued for the next five nights but spread to other sections of the Greenwich Village neighborhood. Many of the skirmishes involved firebombs, or garbage cans being set on fire, and a few escalated into vandals ransacking stores owned by homophobic businessmen. By week's end, the various incidents added up to what could be rightly dubbed a rebellion: 2,000 protesters, 300 police officers, thirteen arrests, four injured cops.

The influential *New York Times* recognized the significance of the event, devoting next-day coverage to the initial raid and then publishing more stories as the nightly clashes continued. Other papers in the city followed the *Times*'s lead, with articles appearing in the *New York Daily News*, *New York Post*, and *Village Voice*.[4]

Publications outside of New York City weren't so sure what to make of homosexuals suddenly turning militant. The *Washington Post* reported on the Stonewall Inn incident right away, but other leading dailies initially ignored the event. In the weeks and months following what was soon dubbed the Stonewall Rebellion, many of those other papers and the country's major magazines tried to compensate for missing the first story by running lengthy, broad-based pieces under headlines such as "Gays Go Radical" and "A Look at Gay Power."[5]

"Queen Bees Are Stinging Mad"

The word "pervert," which had been ubiquitous in headlines and news stories in 1950, appeared only occasionally in the articles that followed the Stonewall Rebellion in 1969. While the popularity of that specific word of derision had faded, newspapers and magazines still found plenty of other ways to express their contempt for the revolutionaries who led the uprising.

Several words competed for the title of the most popular synonym for homosexuals. "Queens" was the choice in the *New York Daily News*, while "nellies" took center stage in the *New York Post*." "Fags" and "queers" appeared most often in the *Village Voice*, which dubbed the Stonewall confrontation the "fag follies" and the gay rebels the "forces of faggotry," before going on to report that "The scene was a command performance for queers."[6]

Journalistic disdain was not limited to the specific word a publication chose to describe men who were sexually attracted to other men. The *New York Daily News*—the largest-circulation newspaper in the country at the time—mockingly titled its first article "Homo Nest Raided, Queen Bees Are Stinging Mad" and reported that "queen power reared its bleached blonde head in revolt" when the men "pranced" out of the bar. The *Daily News* continued to portray gay men as objects of ridicule by describing the Stonewall Inn as a place where "the homosexual element could congregate, drink and do whatever little girls do when they get together."[7]

The nation's leading news magazines communicated their negative attitude toward homosexuals by reinforcing various offensive stereotypes. *Newsweek* began its first story by focusing on a particularly effeminate patron of the Stonewall Inn, reporting that he had "squealed" at the police and spoke in a "falsetto" voice. *Time*, in its story, offered readers a mini-profile of the typical gay man. "He may be the catty hairdresser or the lisping, limp-wristed interior decorator," the magazine wrote, adding, "Homosexuals still seem fairly bizarre to most Americans."[8]

Gay men of the day were particularly disappointed when they read the coverage in the *Village Voice*. The weekly tabloid purported to speak as an alternative voice to that of the establishment press, but its page-one article about this epic event in gay history was no more respectful than the stories appearing in other papers. The *Voice* piece—under the sneering headline "Full Moon Over the Stonewall"—described the patrons of the bar "posing and primping" as they "pranced high and jubilant in the street."[9]

"Hostile Crowd Dispersed"

At the same time that the publications highlighted details and chose language portraying the protesters as laughable, several of them simultaneously managed to depict the homosexual rebels as being so prone to violence and terrorist tactics that they represented a grave and imminent threat to civilized society.

The *New York Times* set the tone for this message with its choice of headlines for articles about the Stonewall incident, which included "Homosexuals in Revolt" and "Hostile Crowd Dispersed Near Sheridan Square." That the insurgents were out of control was also communicated through specific words and phrases the *Times* used. "Hundreds of young men went on a rampage," began the first article, while the second reported that even members of the tactical patrol force, the elite police officers who were protected by helmeted visors and bulletproof vests, were "unable to subdue the crowd."[10]

Other news organizations reinforced the *Times*'s characterization of the protesters as being more dangerous than the lawbreakers the police typically had to face. *Time* magazine reported, "The new militancy makes other citizens edgy," while *Newsweek* wrote, "Law enforcement officials see the homosexual community as a well of criminal activity."[11]

Publications that did not report on the Stonewall Rebellion until several months after it occurred also found ways to communicate that this new breed of militant homosexuals was threatening the well-being of all Americans. The *Chicago Sun-Times* flatly stated that "All homosexuals are dangerous," and a *Harper's* magazine profile of a gay man included the observation that "Elliott would murder merely for the experience of murdering." *Esquire* sent a similarly alarming message by re-creating an incident that had taken place a few days after the protests. "A crowd gathered to witness a sidewalk debate between a portly man in a white shirt and a boy in an acid-green tank top," the magazine stated. "The man seemed to be trying to speak for his Greenwich Village neighbors, but the boy would not listen. 'The hell you say!' he shouted. 'You are straight and you are my enemy!' The man looked ashen, quite frightened. Clearly, he would have liked to have escaped but feared the boy's reaction. 'Man, I'll screw your daughter,' the boy said. 'But I'll screw your *son* first!'"[12]

"A Severe Illness"

Among the stereotypes about homosexuality that had initially surfaced in the 1950 news coverage and aga‾‾‾‾‾‾‾‾‾‾‾‾‾‾‾‾‾‾‾‾‾‾‾‾‾‾69 stories was that men who were se‾‾‾‾‾‾‾‾‾‾‾‾‾‾‾‾‾‾‾‾re suffering from a mental disorder.

The *New York Times* stated as i‾‾‾‾‾‾‾‾‾‾‾‾‾‾‾‾‾‾‾‾‾g attracted to other men was "quite a severe illness." *Time* magazine reiterated that homosexuality was a mental disorder and then took the additional step of attributing the affliction to an improper relationship between parents and son. "Homosexuals are ill because they come from families where the father was either hostile, aloof or ineffectual," the newsweekly stated, "and where the mother was close binding and inappropriately intimate."[13]

Many news organizations reported that it was possible for at least some homosexuals to cure themselves of the mental disorder by undergoing extensive psychotherapy. But only the *New York Times* offered its readers specific details with regard to the likelihood of a patient succeeding in overcoming the "nauseating desires that plague his being." Specifically, the *Times* quoted a leading psychiatrist as estimating that "about one of every four homosexuals who seek psychiatric help could lead a normal life."[14]

"Dangerous Sex Is Groovy"

The message that homosexuals were obsessed with sex changed somewhat between 1950 and 1969. Publications in both time periods agreed on the basic premise, but as time went on such views came to be expressed in much more specific—and sometimes titillating—language.

Time's coverage included a mini-profile of what the magazine characterized as a typical Stonewall Inn patron. The sketch described its subject as being "addicted to the men's room in Grand Central Station" because the location allowed him to have sex with several different partners in a single afternoon. "He knows he is going to get busted by the cops," the magazine stated. "Yet he still has to go there every day."[15]

Esquire told its readers that the new breed of radical homosexuals had far more active and kinky sex lives than the men of previous generations. The magazine relied on a gay man named Jim Pasieniti as its major source. "Gay kids in their twenties don't have the hang-ups that old queens had when they were our age," the twenty-four-year-old said, "so they get bored with sex in pairs. They start getting interested in group activities or in playing around in places like the subway johns, because those places are more dangerous—they're watched by the fuzz, naturally—and therefore more of a challenge." Pasieniti paused for a moment before adding, "Dangerous sex is groovy."[16]

Harper's was among the publications that, like their 1950 counterparts, sent the message that many homosexuals lust after underage boys. Staff writer Joseph Epstein began his first-person essay on the topic by recalling an experience from much earlier in his life. "I was sixteen but looked more like twelve: small, slender, clear-skinned, long eyelashes, and soft features without a hint of a beard. I was then known as a pretty boy." Epstein next described how a middle-aged man had stared seductively at him, two afternoons in a row, through the window of the store where he was working. The teenage Epstein rebuffed the man, but the incident remained firmly lodged in his mind thirty years later. The author ended his piece with a statement that sent shivers up the spine of gay readers:

> There is much my four sons can do in their lives that might cause me anguish, that might make me ashamed of them and of myself as their father. But nothing they could ever do would make me sadder than if any of them were to become homosexual.[17]

"She Calls Herself a 'Butch Dyke'"

One development that came as part of the Stonewall coverage was the emergence of lesbians as a presence in newspaper and magazine articles. When the media had begun paying attention to "perverts" in 1950, their spotlight had been tightly focused on men; in 1969, readers were told about homosexual women as well.

Only one of the seven initial news stories that reported on the Greenwich Village confrontation made any reference to gay women being among those who resisted the police. Specifically, the *Village Voice* mentioned "a dyke"—not placing quotation marks around the word—who put up a struggle against one officer.[18]

The references to women increased significantly when other publications began playing catch-up by writing lengthy articles about the new militancy among homosexuals. A consistent theme throughout the articles was that gay women fit snugly into stereotypes.

First among the messages was that all lesbians were masculine in appearance and mannerisms. *Time* described the typical lesbian as "the 'butch,' the girl who is aggressively masculine to the point of trying to look like a man." Likewise, a mini-profile in the *San Francisco Chronicle* reported that the subject "looks like a boy," going on to report: "She calls herself a 'butch dyke.' She binds her breasts and shaves her moustache, such as it is. As we talked, she played idly with a switchblade knife, expertly flicking it open and closed."[19]

Another characteristic attributed to lesbians was promiscuity. The *Chronicle* told readers that homosexual obsession with sex was not limited to the men, observing that "In lesbian bars, there is a lot of cruising, a fair amount of one-night stands, a lot of butches who try to make it with everybody." *Time* reinforced the point by publishing a profile of two women who were living together as a couple but quoting one of them as saying, "I certainly don't think our relationship ought to be exclusive."[20]

Publications also made sure their readers knew that lesbianism was a mental disorder. The *New York Times*, for example, reported that a woman being sexually attracted to other women was not only "a severe illness" but also one that leads to other problems as well: "[T]he incidence of suicide and alcoholism is high among lesbians."[21]

"Bra Strap to Bra Strap"

Drag queens were a second category of homosexuals who entered the media spotlight in June 1969. Historians are uncertain exactly how many of the individuals who participated in the rebellion were biological males wearing wigs, makeup, and women's clothing, but there's no question that there were at least a few, and that the press attention to them was exaggerated.

The *New York Daily News* portrayed drag queens as being major players in the rebellion, stating that they "stood bra strap to bra strap against" the police. While that particular statement managed to report the action truthfully, several other details were inaccurate—though the bitterly sarcastic tone remained intact. For example, every other newspaper quoted eyewitnesses as stating that drag queens did not join the melee until well *after* the police had moved the patrons into the street, but the *Daily News* reported that the flamboyantly dressed men took a leading role in the protest from the outset. "The Queens pranced out to the street blowing kisses and waving to the crowd," the story read. "The proceedings took on the aura of a homosexual Academy Awards Night."[22]

The *Daily News* also had it wrong when identifying exactly who transformed the raid into a violent confrontation. Other papers reported that it was the young men who had been removed from the bar who first began tossing pennies at the police, but the *Daily News* gave the credit to the drag queens. "Without warning, Queen Power exploded with all the fury of a gay atomic bomb," the story stated.The article continued:

> Queens, princesses and ladies-in-waiting began hurling anything they could lay their polished, manicured fingernails on. Bobby pins, compacts, curlers, lipstick tubes and other femme fatale missiles were flying in the direction of the cops. The war was on. The lilies of the valley had become carnivorous jungle plants.[23]

The passage provides more evidence of the tabloid's disregard for accuracy, as none of the other papers—the *New York Times*, *Village Voice*, or *Washington Post*—mentioned any of the items on the *Daily News*'s list as having soared through the air on that fateful night. One media historian has said of the paper's account: "Written in an entertaining and dramatic fashion, the story evoked the days of yellow journalism, when newspapers put a premium on telling a story rather than finding the facts—or providing the truth."[24]

The First Stage, the Second Event

News stories about the Stonewall Rebellion, like the "Perverts on the Potomac" news stories that came before them in 1950, sent the public a long list of negative messages about homosexuals. Although the word "perverts" had faded in popularity, journalists continued to vilify gay people by referring to them with such derisive terms as "queens," "fags," and "queers." Most of the pejorative traits that the earlier coverage had established as typically homosexual were repeated in the later coverage as well; men who were sexually attracted to other men were again portrayed as being mentally ill, as being obsessed with sex, and as having lustful feelings toward young boys.

In addition, the events that erupted in Greenwich Village prompted the press to intensify its depiction of homosexuals as morally corrupt. In the "Perverts on the Potomac" coverage, this supposed weakness had been portrayed as a threat to American foreign policy, the federal government, and a relatively small number of young boys who were victims of the men's sexual obsession. In the stories that were published about the Stonewall Rebellion, by contrast, the consequences of this lack of morality were expanded enormously as homosexuals were depicted as possessing such a proclivity for violence that all of society was being threatened: Gay people were terrorists.

Even the two messages that might, on the surface, seem to qualify as progressive steps were not, in fact, positive ones.

With regard to women being included in the stories, their role in this epic event in the evolution of Gay and Lesbian America was woefully minimized. Numerous scholars who have chronicled the details of the Stonewall Rebellion have stated that a large number of lesbians participated in the uprising. Indeed, some of those historians have speculated that the enormously important event might never have taken place if it hadn't been for one gay woman trying to evade a police officer by sliding across the seat of his patrol car and, as a result, getting struck in the head. And yet, only one of the seven initial news accounts even mentioned lesbian participation in the rebellion, though there were numerous statements in the press about the hyper-masculine appearance of gay women, including the *San Francisco Chronicle*'s description of a woman who "looks like a boy and says she hates men" and who "binds her breasts and shaves her moustache."[25]

With regard to drag queens being included in the coverage, their role also was distorted. Scholars who have studied this historic event have documented that several men who dressed and groomed themselves as women were leaders in the dramatic act of defiance that took place outside the Stonewall Inn. The initial news coverage did not portray these men as activists or as persons of courage, however, but merely as objects of ridicule who deserved nothing more than to be laughed at, as evidenced by the *New York Daily News* describing the drag queens as standing "bra strap to bra strap" and "blowing kisses and waving to the crowd" as the "proceedings took on the aura of a homosexual Academy Awards Night."[26]

The only negative message about homosexuals that had subsided was that they were vulnerable to blackmail; this idea had been a mainstay of stories written in 1950 but was mentioned only occasionally in 1969.

And so, at the end of the 1960s, American homosexuals were most certainly still in what nineteenth-century women's rights advocate Lucretia Mott defined as the "first stage" of press coverage, with newspapers and magazines of the day continuing to ridicule and demonize them.

3 *The Boys in the Band*

Homosexuality Comes to the Big Screen

In 1970 when the motion picture industry's first major movie depicting homosexuality opened in theaters across the country, the reviews were mixed. Some critics praised the acting as excellent and the script as superb; others blasted the overall tone for being melodramatic and the camerawork for being amateurish.[1]

The only point that the reviewers seemed to agree upon was that *The Boys in the Band* was, with regard to its depiction of gay men, totally and unequivocally accurate. *Look* magazine praised the film's "honest portrayal of homosexual life," *Time* said the movie offered "a landslide of truths" about a little-known segment of the population, and *Vogue* applauded the movie for "dealing in the facts of homosexuality with candor and honesty."[2]

From the vantage point of a viewer who watches the film today, however, many of the messages that the movie communicates about gay men come directly from a list of the derogatory stereotypes that activists have spent some thirty years trying to erase from the American mind.

The Boys in the Band says, first and foremost, that gay men are unremittingly sad and pathetic creatures. That message is effectively captured in the line from the script most frequently quoted by reviewers:

"Show me a happy homosexual, and I'll show you a gay corpse."[3]

But by no means is that the only offensive statement in the film. Homosexual men also are depicted as being self-loathing, narcissistic, emotionally unstable, sexually promiscuous, and laughably effeminate.

Along with the negative messages is one that can be interpreted, depending on how closely a viewer looks, as being a progressive step in that the movie suggests that the gay male community is diverse in several ways, including with regard to race.

Happy Birthday, Harold

The plot of *The Boys in the Band*—the title comes from the phrase that singer Judy Garland used when acknowledging the male musicians who accompanied her when she performed on stage—revolves around a birthday dinner. Michael hosts the event for his friend Harold and a cluster of their fellow gay residents, all of them in their thirties, of New York City. Most of the action in the film, which originated as an off-Broadway play, takes place in the host's apartment during the meal and the party that follows.[4]

Initial scenes are lighthearted, showing the characters preparing for the evening while the upbeat tune "Anything Goes" plays in the background. The mood shifts, however, once the lasagna and birthday cake have been consumed and the gifts have been opened. After the host drinks too much scotch, he turns hostile and insists that the guests play a game. The rules require a participant to telephone the one person in his life he has truly loved and tell that person about his romantic feelings. As Michael clearly anticipated when creating the mean-spirited game, several of the gay men's objects of affection are straight men.

As if this activity doesn't create enough tension, still more is added by the fact that Michael's college roommate unexpectedly arrives. Indeed, it seems that part of the reason the host suggested the game is so that the intruder, who is married and has two daughters, will be forced to acknowledge his own latent homosexuality.

By the end of the film, the birthday party has become anything but festive, with so many verbal attacks that it's impossible to keep up with which man is calling the collective group "a bunch of faggots" or "tired old fairies" or "screaming queens," and which is screaming "Bitch!" or "Card-carrying cunt!" in whose direction. The sudden rainstorm that erupts outside is clearly a metaphor for the explosion of emotions, revelations, and verbal insults—not to mention the roommate slugging one of the guests—taking place inside the apartment.

Gay Men Are Miserable

Although the line in the dialogue about the only happy homosexual being a dead one doesn't come until late in the film, it's long before then that moviegoers are made acutely aware of the apparent sadness that pervades gay men's lives.

The dominant character in the movie is Harold. From the moment the party's guest of honor arrives, he overpowers the other men with the sheer force of his personality. Before anyone can chastise him for his tardiness, Harold announces to the host:

> What I am, Michael, is a thirty-two-year-old, ugly, pockmarked Jew fairy. And if it takes me a while to pull myself together and if I smoke a little grass before I get up the nerve to show my face to the world, it's nobody's goddamn business but my own.[5]

With that searing statement, Harold successfully pre-empts criticism from the other men while at the same time presenting the audience with a list of three key reasons why gay men are miserable: They place great value on youth, but everyone ultimately must age. They place great value on physical attractiveness, but not every man is handsome. They place great value on being accepted, but in 1970 homosexuals were social outcasts, a condition Harold effectively captures with the disparaging word "fairy."

Michael tries to penetrate the protective shield that Harold places around himself. In this effort, the host betrays the "birthday boy" by revealing an intimate secret about him. "Harold has been gathering, storing, and saving up barbiturates for the last year like a goddamn squirrel," the drunk and hostile Michael proudly announces to the other men, "all in preparation for—and anticipation of—the long winter of his *death*." The other guests are stunned into silence after hearing about Harold's suicide plan, and yet Michael still isn't finished with his attack. "But I tell you something, Hallie. When the time comes, you won't have the *guts* to do it."[6]

With those bitter words, Michael communicates that the lives of homosexuals are so unhappy—a point he'll later reiterate when he makes his statement involving gay corpses—that suicide seems like a reasonable form of escape.

Gay Men Are Self-Loathing

The bitchy comments that Michael and Harold exchange also communicate that gay men are vicious and catty, with a tendency to aim much of their venom at each other. This element in the dialogue tells moviegoers that homosexuals hate other homosexuals—including themselves.

Michael revealing that the guest of honor is saving up drugs so he can kill himself certainly qualifies as malicious, as Harold had told his friend about the plan in strictest confidence. Michael's betrayal then prompts an equally merciless attack from Harold. "You're a sad and pathetic man," he tells Michael. "You're a homosexual and you don't want to be. But there's nothing you can do to change it—not all your prayers to your God, not all the analysis you can buy." Harold pauses before making his final point, one that again sees death as the only relief for gay men. "You will always be a homosexual, Michael—until the day you die."

That statement, more than any other, establishes Harold as more powerful than Michael or any of the other characters. When the host realizes he's been outmatched, he could have conceded defeat and then retreated into silence. But, instead, he strikes out against a weaker member of the group.

As the vehicle for his assault, the host devises the telephone game. He then prods one of the guests, an African American, to make the first

Figure 1 Michael's misery and self-loathing become so intense by the end of *The Boys in the Band* that he collapses into tears and has to be comforted by Donald.

Courtesy of National General Pictures/Photofest.

phone call. When Bernard was a boy, he had a crush on the teenage son in the wealthy white family that his mother worked for as a laundress. "He never knew I was alive," Bernard tells the men at the party. "Besides, he's straight."[7]

When Michael hears these words, he knows that if Bernard telephones the man from his past, it will be a disaster. But rather than spare his friend the agony that's sure to follow, the host—getting drunker and nastier by the minute—cajoles his guest into making the call. "Go ahead, Bernard, pick up the phone," Michael says. "You know you want to. Go ahead."

Bernard then dials the phone, the mother in the white family answers, and the grown man suddenly reverts to being an inarticulate little boy. By the end of the call, Bernard is humiliated, shaking his head and asking himself, "Why did I call? Why did I do that?"

But Michael, in keeping with the movie's portrayal of gay men as cruel and vindictive, momentarily feels pleased with himself—perhaps even hating himself just a little less than usual.

Gay Men Are Narcissistic

Another unflattering characteristic that several of "the boys" exhibit is the propensity to spend huge quantities of time, effort, and money on themselves.

The importance of this message is communicated by the fact that the first image in the film is of Harold's bathroom. Indeed, the initial shot is of a towel featuring an appliquéd crown above the monogram "Princess Hal." A few feet away, royalty himself is soaking luxuriously in a tub overflowing with bubbles, surrounded by literally dozens of jars and bottles filled with creams, gels, lotions, and balms of every variety—all to pamper the aging queen.

Michael also is narcissistic. The first image of the party's host is of him rushing from one upscale New York boutique to the next, finally arriving at his apartment with half a dozen bulging shopping bags. Moviegoers learn what's inside all those packages when they see Michael struggling to decide how to dress for the party. He's certain about the fancy dress shirt and cufflinks, but choosing a sweater is more difficult. He first tries a pale gray one but then tosses it on the floor and slips on a black cashmere number that he accessorizes with a silk scarf. But then he rejects that combination as well, replacing it with another cashmere sweater, this one in red. Michael's narcissism is reinforced by the huge portrait of himself that covers one wall of his bedroom and by the fact that he never walks by a mirror without pausing to touch up his hair.

Another specimen of gay manhood who's obsessed with his appearance is introduced when a young man dressed in tight jeans and a Western-style shirt rings the doorbell. As a birthday gift, one of the guests has paid twenty dollars for the callboy to spend the night with Harold. Tex doesn't possess the talent for making witty comments that the older men have, but the lad still manages to communicate that he spends most of his daytime hours exercising at the gym so his body is as attractive as his facial features. The pretty boy's efforts pay off, as he proudly displays the combination of flat stomach and perfectly defined chest that a gay man, according to the film, either works to achieve or longs to have lying next to him in bed.[8]

Gay Men Are Emotionally Unstable

The coverage of homosexual men in the nation's newspapers and magazines in 1950 portrayed their emotional instability as a major factor in why they should not be allowed to work for the federal government. It came as no surprise, then, that the first major motion picture to focus on homosexuality also depicted this unflattering stereotype.

One guest arrives early to the birthday party because his psychiatrist has canceled their weekly appointment. And so the initial dialogue in the film is between shop-a-holic Michael and neurotic Donald. The two men have sex every Saturday night but don't have romantic feelings for each other.[9]

Donald had been prepared to share his most recent insights about himself with his shrink, so he tells them to Michael instead. "I was raised to be a failure. I was groomed for it," he begins. "Naturally, it all goes back to my parents, Evelyn and Walt." Moviegoers then hear Donald launch into details that reinforce one of the era's most common beliefs about homosexuality: Men become gay because of the combination of an overprotective mother and an absent or emotionally distant father. Donald says:

> Today I finally began to see how other pieces of the puzzle relate to them, like why I never finish anything I start—my neurotic compulsion to not succeed. Failure is the only thing with which I feel at home, because that's what I was taught at home.

When Donald takes a breath and gives Michael a chance to respond, the host agrees with his friend, telling Donald that he's merely one of legions of gay men suffering from the same kind of upbringing. "Christ," he says, "how sick analysts must get of hearing how Mommy and Daddy made their darling into a fairy!"

After that statement, Michael immediately launches into a description of his own psychological shortcomings. "I'm a spoiled brat. I flit from Beverly Hills to Rome to Acapulco to Amsterdam, picking up a lot of one-night stands." The manic host pauses for a moment, then supplies more evidence of his emotional instability. "I'm here to tell you that the only place in all those miles, the only place I've ever been happy, is on the goddamn plane."

Gay Men Are Promiscuous

When it comes to which of the characters in the film serves as the poster boy for a free-wheeling sex life, several candidates vie for the title. The fact that Tex earns his living as a callboy makes him a contender, while Harold's delight at being one of Tex's bed partners puts him in the running as well. In addition, snippets of dialogue reveal that Michael and Donald have both had numerous anonymous sexual encounters in gay bathhouses.

But the character whose sexual appetite is causing him the most problems is Larry. After having several drinks, the handsome man tells the other guests, without apology, that he's "not the marrying kind." This is a concern because one of the men, Hank, left his wife and two children two years earlier to move in with Larry and begin what he thought would be a monogamous relationship. But Hank soon learned that Larry is incapable of limiting his sex life to a single person. "I can't take all this 'Let's be faithful and never look at another person' routine," Larry says, "because it just doesn't work." Speaking for what he insists is the vast majority of gay men, he keeps talking, to the partygoers as well as to the movie-going public. "The ones who swear their undying fidelity are lying, 90 percent of them anyway. They cheat on each other constantly and lie through their teeth." That Larry and Hank have dramatically different views of a committed relationship creates one of the major conflicts in the film.[10]

Emory also pays a high price for his promiscuity. At one point during the party, he mentions that he's contracted sexually transmitted diseases several times. At other times the conversation makes reference to him having frequently been arrested on morals charges. But Emory tells his friends that he has no intention of ending his anonymous sexual encounters. "I'm going to San Francisco on a well-earned vacation," he says. "I'm going to the Club Baths, and I'm not coming out until they announce the departure of TWA one week later." So Larry seems to be on firm ground when he says, "Emory, you are the most promiscuous person I know."[11]

The motion picture company that created *The Boys in the Band* learned that many newspapers were not ready for the level of sexual frankness that the R-rated film depicted. National General developed an advertisement featuring a photo of Harold above the caption "Today is Harold's birthday," and a photo of Tex above the caption "This is his present." The long list of major dailies that refused to run the ad included the *Los Angeles Times*, *New York Daily News*, *Chicago Sun-Times*, *Boston Globe*, and *San Francisco Chronicle*.[12]

Gay Men Are Laughably Effeminate

Newspapers that had begun paying attention to homosexual men in 1950 had reported that these reprehensible creatures displayed overtly feminine mannerisms, with one nationally syndicated columnist telling his readers that the "perverts" working in the State Department routinely "call each other female names like Bessie, Maud and Chloe." Twenty years later, *The Boys in the Band* went beyond merely telling media consumers about such proclivities by presenting vivid images of them on the movie screen.[13]

Early in the film when Michael rushes from boutique to boutique, he doesn't walk in normal strides but moves in tiny steps that can best be described as mincing. Likewise, his hands are never still but constantly flutter, his limp wrists barely able to control fingers that constantly dance, one of them carrying a diamond ring the size of Ohio.

Emory is even more effeminate, a review in *New Yorker* magazine going so far as to refer to him as "Emory-Emily." Moviegoers get their first glimpse of the over-the-top character as he, dressed in a cream-colored suit, sashays down Fifth Avenue while walking his toy poodle. Viewers soon learn that the lisping Emory has prepared the main course for the birthday dinner, unashamedly calling himself "Connie Casserole" and boasting, "I'd make somebody a good wife. I could cook, I could decorate an apartment, and I could *entertain*," as he pulls a long-stemmed rose out of a vase, places it between his teeth, and continues, "Kiss me quick— I'm Carmen!"[14]

Most of the partygoers are amused by Emory's penchant for referring to his male friends by such names as "Mary" and "Bernadette," but Michael's former roommate finds the effeminate man irritating. The film never establishes if Alan is a straight man or a closeted gay one, but there's no question about his disdain for Emory; at one point he refers to the flighty man as "a Goddamned little pansy." After Emory fires off one too many campy lines, Alan yells, "Faggot!" and lunges at the nellie character, screaming, "Freak! Freak! Freak!" Several of the men then overpower the attacker, but not until after he's given Emory a bloody nose.[15]

That Michael and Emory are flamboyant doesn't mean they have a monopoly on girlish tendencies. When the 1960s dance tune "Heat Wave" comes on the stereo, Bernard and Larry leap from their chairs and pull the other gay men to their feet to form an impromptu chorus line, all of them laughing and giggling as they kick their legs high into the air as if they're the Rockettes performing on stage at Radio City Music Hall.

The Gay Community Is Diverse

One potentially positive message *The Boys in the Band* sends is that the gay community is, in several ways, diverse.

Physical attractiveness is one element that separates the men. The fidelity-challenged Larry is drop-dead gorgeous; his coal-black hair, dark brown eyes, and chiseled facial features create the kind of movie-star heartthrob that turns heads when he walks into a room, whether the occupants are men or women. The callboy Tex fares well in the looks department, too; his thick head of hair, pretty-boy face, and sculpted chest—fully visible because his shirt is unbuttoned throughout the film— combine to form a blond Adonis who draws words of admiration even from the acid-tongued Michael: "He's beautiful."

But not all the partygoers are so easy on the eyes. The pockmarks on Harold's face are so severe that all his creams and lotions can't mask the fact that he's unattractive; he's clearly a guy whose only chance of going to bed with a good-looking man is if the callboy is getting paid. Emory isn't pleasant to look at either; his jutting chin and hooked nose detract from his facial features, and no one at the party takes a look when he pulls up his shirt to reveal his naked upper body, one of them pleading with him to "spare us the sight of your sagging tits."

Other factors further contribute to the movie's depiction of a gay cross-section. Some of the men earn their livelihood in fields that could be classified as stereotypical, as one is an interior decorator and another a fashion photographer. But other of the partygoers pay the rent by working at jobs not particularly associated with gay men, including teaching high school math and working in a bookstore. Religion is another variable, Harold being identified as Jewish and Michael as Catholic. The film also shows that some gay men become involved in ongoing relationships while others don't; although Larry and Hank struggle to remain monogamous, they definitely care about each other, with several scenes showing the two men embracing and showing their mutual affection, though they're never shown kissing.[16]

The film's most obvious statement vis-à-vis diversity is the fact that one of the men is African American. Bernard's race is incorporated into the dialogue numerous times, as when the other men refer to him as "the African Queen" and "the Queen of Spades." And when the music prompts Bernard to start snapping his fingers and swaying his hips, another of the men instantly says, in a clear reference to African Americans, "They hear a drumbeat, and their eyes sparkle like Cartiers." On other occasions, Emory playfully calls Bernard "a pickaninny" and tells him to "have a piece of watermelon and shut up."

A Legendary Film

Because *The Boys in the Band* was the first major motion picture to focus specifically on homosexuals, it has been the subject of myriad discussions and analyses, with the negative assessments of the film far outnumbering the positive ones.[17]

The most frequent criticism has been that *Boys* communicated—and consequently helped to popularize—denigrating messages about gay men. Vito Russo's pioneering book *The Celluloid Closet* stated, "The film presented a compendium of easily acceptable stereotypes who spend an evening savaging each other and their way of life." Suzanna Danuta Walters's book *All the Rage: The Story of Gay Visibility in America* also focused on the movie's negative messages, saying, "*Boys in the Band* was filled with self-deprecating wit and truckloads of self-hatred." Larry Gross's *Up from Invisibility: Lesbians, Gay Men, and the Media in America* didn't limit itself to condemning specific pejorative stereotypes but argued that the motion picture was making a broader statement: "The real message of the film was that being out of the closet was dangerous to your health."[18]

A variation on that statement was communicated by the news media of the era. The *New York Times* splashed an article titled "You Don't

Have to Be One to Play One" across the front of its features section, saying it was publishing the piece because, "Everybody wants to know whether the actors are straight or not." The *Times* then told its readers that Cliff Gorman, the man who played "Emory, the pansy," was not only "very butch" in real life but also had a "beautiful wife" and dressed in a "John Wayne style." The *Times* reported that another of the actors was also heterosexual, saying, "Larry Luckinbill—he plays Hank, the school teacher—is married, too." A deafening silence was the order of the day with regard to the sexual orientation of the other seven actors in the film though, thereby establishing the tradition of the press reporting when straight actors play gay characters but failing to give specifics regarding the sexuality of gay actors who play gay characters. The policy could have been stated as: The message of the news coverage was that a gay actor being out of the closet could be dangerous to his career.[19]

Many themes in the film reinforce negative messages about homosexuals that the "Perverts on the Potomac" and Stonewall Rebellion news coverage previously had made. Among them are that members of this subgroup of American society are pathetic misfits who hate themselves, who are narcissistic, who are emotionally unstable, who are obsessed with sex, and who are laughably effeminate.

Other denigrating statements that had appeared in the earlier news stories are also referenced in the film. That homosexual men prey on boys and young men was a recurring topic in the 1950 and 1969 coverage; in *Boys*, that message is communicated through the character of the callboy Tex, who appears to be about fifteen years younger than the men at the party who lust after him. Likewise, earlier news coverage reported that many people blamed parents for their sons being homosexual; in *Boys*, that message comes in the scene where Donald criticizes his parents for how they raised him and Michael responds that many gay men have come to the same conclusion: "Christ, how sick analysts must get of hearing how Mommy and Daddy made their darling into a fairy!"

Still other negative messages that *The Boys in the Band* sends had not been present in the news coverage about homosexuals that preceded the film but would resurface in media products that followed in later decades. One example is Harold saving up barbiturates so he can kill himself, thereby communicating that homosexuals are so miserable that many of them escape from their despair by committing suicide. Another statement emerges from the fact that the film doesn't include a single unambiguously straight person or lesbian, thereby suggesting that homosexual men surround themselves with other misfits like themselves to create a world entirely separate from mainstream America.

When the one potentially positive message—that the gay community is diverse—is examined closely, it becomes clear that this aspect of the film is not, in fact, an indication of progress in the media's treatment of gay people. The most dramatic statement regarding diversity is that one of the characters is African American. While it is laudable that the movie communicates that the gay community of New York in 1970 included men of color, how Bernard is portrayed is highly problematic. First, the white men at the party repeatedly demean him by making racist statements, referring to him as "the Queen of Spades" and "a pickaninny," while also telling him to "have a piece of watermelon and shut up," with Bernard passively accepting the insults without objection. Second, after Michael prods Bernard into participating in the telephone game, the reluctant man ends up being humiliated far more than any of the other partygoers, thereby suggesting that black gay men are so lacking in intellect that they're easily manipulated by their white counterparts.

Despite the many shortcomings of *The Boys in the Band*, it definitely ranks as a milestone in the evolution of how gays have been depicted in the media. At the time the film was released, the stigma attached to a man being sexually attracted to other men was so strong that the vast majority of people who recognized such desires in themselves assiduously repressed them, which meant that most Americans had never met a gay man who openly acknowledged his sexuality. Because of the stories about "Perverts on the Potomac" and the Stonewall Rebellion, newspaper and magazine readers had begun to learn about members of this subgroup of society, but that information had been presented only in printed words.

Then came *Boys*.

For the first time, millions of moviegoers became acquainted with a group of homosexuals. Visual images are powerful, especially when viewers have no previous first-hand knowledge of the subject being featured. So the film had unprecedented impact on the public's collective knowledge about and attitudes toward homosexuals. It is highly regrettable that the media product that possessed such extraordinary potential for informing the American public about this largely invisible segment of society was dominated by negative messages. Indeed, it was fully understandable why a person leaving the theater might have been determined to do whatever was necessary to avoid crossing paths with a real-life homosexual.

4 *Soap*

A Gay Man Comes to TV Land

The other members of the family have already gathered around the breakfast table before the younger of the two sons, aged twenty-six, appears in the doorway to the kitchen. He pauses before entering the room, delicately placing his right hand on one doorjamb and then positioning just the fingertips of his left hand on the opposite doorjamb. Having now framed himself perfectly in the center of the passageway, he makes full use of the twinkle in his dark brown eyes and the dimples in his cheeks to create a smile that is the absolute definition of *impish*.

Even though the highly choreographed hand movements and scene-stealing facial expression were sufficient, on their own, to grab the attention of most television viewers, just in case anyone watching at home didn't recognize this unprecedented moment as the epic moment that it was, canned laughter was added as well. So while the character stood in the doorway grinning, his head and upper body filling the entire screen, people could be heard on the soundtrack giggling and snickering even before the first words finally came out of his mouth. He didn't speak dialogue but sang the lyrics from a Broadway show tune:

"Oh, what a beautiful morning . . ."[1]

Welcome to *Soap*.

Some observers have condemned that opening image, which aired in 1977, as sending the message that gay men are effeminate and narcissistic twits who use their limp wrists and mincing mannerisms to propel themselves into the spotlight; others have praised both the character and the series as shining such a rose-colored light on gay men that the program would remain without parallel in TV Land for the next twenty years.[2]

Whether the series is damned or lionized, there's no question that the ABC hit comedy—by the end of the first season, it ranked among the most-watched shows on television—was a milestone in the evolution of gays in the media, as it brought an openly gay man into American living rooms every week for four years, later becoming available on video as well.[3]

Figure 2
From 1977 to 1981, American television viewers welcomed a youthful Billy Crystal into their living rooms when he starred in the ABC sitcom *Soap*.

Courtesy of ABC/Photofest.

A detailed look at *Soap* begins with a description of how the nation—first journalists and then social conservatives—responded to the news that a TV network was creating such a program. The next step is to identify which gay stereotypes the show reinforced and which ones it challenged. Because of the topics that *Soap* covered, looking at the show also means considering what messages it communicated about transsexuals and about several issues relevant to the lives of gay men writ large.

Making History

From the moment the country's journalists heard the first whispers about the content of a sitcom that one of the networks was considering, they knew they had a major story on their hands. That most of the characters would be involved in illicit sexual activity—including a hunky tennis instructor having affairs with a mother and her daughter simultaneously, plus a married man repeatedly bedding his secretary—made the show newsworthy in its own right, but the most titillating of the details was that one of the main characters was to be a homosexual.

The initial article about the program's gay content, which appeared almost a year before the show premiered, reported the development in a straightforward manner. "If this situation comedy makes it into the ABC schedule," the *Washington Post* observed, "it will be a breakthrough in prime-time network television programming."[4]

However, many of the subsequent stories about *Soap* carried a decidedly critical tone. *Newsweek* titled its first piece "99 and 44/100% *Im*pure" and noted that some of the network's affiliate stations were "understandably uneasy" about the proposed series, while the *New York Times* predicted that ABC bringing a gay man into American living rooms would cause the network to "find itself coping with a public uproar."[5]

Once the network gave *Soap* the green light and announced that it was planning to broadcast the show on Tuesdays at 8:30 p.m., the news media had plenty of condemnations to report. The *New York Times* quoted a minister as saying, "By scheduling this program in prime time, ABC will be exposing children to something they really can't handle," and *Time* magazine quoted a Catholic newspaper's scathing comment about the show: "This desecration of morality is an outrage that calls for protest in the strongest terms."[6]

Opposition to *Soap* continued to escalate to the point that, by a month before the series premier, the controversy had grown into such a *cause célèbre* that it reached the front page of the most influential newspaper in the country. The *New York Times* reported that never before in the history of television had so many advertisers refused to place commercials on a program for fear that viewers would refuse to buy products associated with it. "Virtually all advertisers concede that the aversion to 'Soap,'" the *Times* stated, "was caused by an intense letter-writing campaign by religious groups that have hinted at their readiness to boycott products advertised on the show."[7]

Major news outlets then published denunciations of the program by four major religious organizations representing 138,000 churches from across the country—the National Council of Catholic Bishops, the United Methodist Church, the United Church of Christ, and the National Council of Churches. Jewish officials joined in the protest as well, with a group of rabbis accusing ABC of "sexual sensationalism." The National Federation of Decency, a group dedicated to keeping sexual content off television, conducted public demonstrations against the program in San Diego, St. Louis, Houston, Chicago, Atlanta, and ten other cities. "*Soap* is not entertainment," a federation spokesman said. "It is moral degradation and filth."[8]

By the time the half-hour program premiered in September 1977, ABC had received a stunning 56,000 protest letters, and nineteen of its 195 affiliate stations had refused to broadcast the series in their local markets. Meanwhile, all the publicity had made the entire country eager to see exactly what all the fuss was about.[9]

Reinforcing Gay Stereotypes

Soap revolved around the families of two middle-aged sisters, Jessica Tate and Mary Campbell. The audience didn't have to wait long to find out which of the dozen cast members was the most controversial, as the initial episodes were bursting with negative messages about the younger of Mary's two sons from her first marriage, Jodie Dallas.

After the grinning character in the first episode finally passes through the doorway and into the kitchen to join the rest of the family at the table, the conversation turns to breakfast cereal. Mary's husband asks the older of his two stepsons, "Why didn't you offer him," nodding toward Jodie, "some *Fruit* Loops? It'd be very appropriate." In later episodes, the term "fruit" was used in reference to the gay man numerous times. When a visitor arrives at the house, for example, the stepfather immediately tells her, "Jodie's a fruit," and again, when the gay man appears at a family dinner wearing a purple scarf, his cousin calls him a "little fruit." The program's dialogue included lots of other demeaning terms as well, from "sissy" and "homo" to "pansy" and "Tinkerbell."[10]

The negative message about homosexuality that was repeated most often came in the voiceover that preceded each weekly segment. The narrator introduces Mary Campbell by saying, "Unfortunately, life doesn't seem too crazy about her," and then says that her family "has many secrets." The language and images are timed so that at the precise moment the word "secrets" is spoken, Jodie appears on the screen, clearly communicating that having a gay man in the family is such a shameful fact that it has to be kept hidden from outsiders. (This message was sent despite the fact that the American Psychiatric Association had, in 1973, removed homosexuality from its list of mental illnesses.)

The most negative stereotype reinforced by *Soap* unfolded in the first season after the gay man's boyfriend announces that he's ending their relationship and marrying a woman. Jodie is so emotionally devastated that, within moments after the boyfriend leaves, his eyes well up with tears and he says, "It's checkout time," and then swallows several dozen sleeping pills. Although the character's attempt to kill himself fails and he soon recovers, the show's writers made sure this was one scene—and one unflattering message—that viewers wouldn't forget. When Jodie's aunt goes on trial for murder and her attorney is considering possible character witnesses, he rejects the gay man, saying, "I can't put you on the stand. You're a suicidal homosexual." On another occasion, when a new character meets Jodie, she's surprised that he's so attractive, and asks incredulously, "*You're* the suicidal homosexual?"[11]

Laughing Out Loud

In the next breath after stating that *Soap* reinforced unflattering gay stereotypes, it rightly must be pointed out that the sitcom communicated these messages—except in the segments about Jodie's attempted suicide —in the context of humor and playfulness rather than hatred and repulsion.

During the history-making debut episode, for instance, the comment from the stepfather about Fruit Loops being an appropriate cereal for Jodie is immediately followed by a surge of canned laughter. What's more, Jodie gives no indication of being offended by the comment. Indeed, he sits down next to his stepfather and smiles pleasantly while having his breakfast. When the gay man is finished, he stands up and gives his stepfather a cheerful "Bye, Burt," and a lighthearted tap on the shoulder before he leaves for work.[12]

The demeaning synonyms for "gay" that were sprinkled into the episodes were also delivered in a comedic vein. An example comes when "pansy" is used during a scene in which Jodie tells his family that a woman he slept with has become pregnant. Before announcing the news, the gay man warns his stepfather that what he's about to say is serious so he doesn't want to hear any wisecracks. Burt promises to keep his mouth shut, and he definitely tries. But when Jodie delivers the surprising news, the stepfather struggles so hard to keep his lips locked together that his cheeks puff up like a balloon, signaling that he's literally *bursting* to say something. Viewers at home added their own chuckles to the canned laughter, as Burt's over-the-top facial expression is, without question, laugh-out-loud funny. Finally, the stepfather's mouth pops open and he squeals gleefully, "I knew he wasn't a pansy!" The line is followed by still more canned laughter.[13]

Challenging Gay Stereotypes

At the same time that *Soap* used denigrating terms and sent negative messages—though usually in a humorous tone—about homosexuality, the series also made numerous positive statements.

One major force that must be credited with challenging a long list of stereotypes is the actor who played the first gay man that TV viewers came to know and love: Billy Crystal. With his curly dark hair, wiry physique, and mischievous smile, the actor put a new and highly attractive face on homosexuality, as his on-screen persona was exceedingly personable and likable. This elf-like fellow was neither sinister and threatening, like the faceless "perverts" in 1950 news stories, nor tormented and self-loathing, like the men in *The Boys in the Band*. Instead, Crystal's interpretation of a gay man was of someone who is generally happy and at ease with himself and his sexuality. "All my life I've lived a certain way," Jodie says in one episode, "and I don't want to change."[14]

Various aspects of the character also belied conventional wisdom, in the late 1970s and early 1980s, about what it meant to be a homosexual. Jodie was highly proficient in his chosen line of work, as he was depicted as possessing the drive, intellect, and creative talent to succeed as the director of TV commercials. He also was portrayed as being athletic, holding his own on the tennis court with his straight brother, and as guided by a steady moral compass, opting to "take a break" for several months after his boyfriend broke up with him rather than immediately having sex with the first guy he meets. TV Land's pioneering gay resident was also depicted as a man of honor and courage; when a much larger and stronger guy insults a female friend by calling her a "slut," the diminutive Jodie doesn't hesitate for a moment before slugging the man who'd uttered the offensive comment.[15]

Jodie Dallas's mannerisms and personal attributes were the result of a conscious effort on the part of ABC, according to an in-house memo that the *New York Daily News* surreptitiously acquired and then published. "As a gay character, his portrayal must at all times be handled without negative stereotyping," the memo stated. The purloined document also made it clear that network executives went out of their way to break gay stereotypes when they made the character's boyfriend a professional football player and then cast a real-life athlete—Olympic pole vaulter Bob Seagren—in the role. But, at the same time, ABC was only willing to go so far. "The relationship between Jodie and the football player," the memo read, "should be handled in such a manner that explicit or intimate aspects of homosexuality are avoided entirely." In other words, the two men were not allowed to have any physical contact with each other.[16]

An even bigger departure from the stereotypical gay man emerged during the second season when Jodie goes on a date with a woman and ends up having sex with her. And as often happens in the soap opera world that the program assiduously spoofed, that one-night stand leads to a pregnancy. The unprecedented plotline takes another surprising turn in the third season, as Jodie takes the mother to court in hopes of gaining custody of the child. "Whether Wendy lives with me or not," he tells the judge, "she'll know I've always wanted her and I'll always be there for her, and that's something no one can ever take away." Jodie ultimately wins the right to raise his daughter, making him not only American television's first recurring gay character but also its first gay father.[17]

Breaking the Transsexual Ice . . . Badly

Whether *Soap* did more to reinforce gay stereotypes or to shatter them is debatable, but there's no question about whether the program did or did not help increase public understanding of transsexuals: It did not.

The American medical community of the late 1970s defined a male transsexual as someone who was a man anatomically but who felt like a woman psychologically. Conflict also played a major role in the phenomenon, as virtually every transsexual of the era was wracked with so much uncertainty that the individual inevitably struggled with extreme depression.[18]

Many of the initial news stories about a gay man coming to network television—including articles in the *Los Angeles Times, San Diego Union*, and *Time* magazine—reported that ABC had announced that one of the characters was a transsexual. The network's announcement was inaccurate, however, as Jodie Dallas was in a very different situation than the one faced by individuals whose anatomical and psychological beings don't coincide.[19]

In the second episode of the series, Mary Campbell walks into her bedroom and finds Jodie wearing one of her dresses. The young man then tells his mother that he's thinking about having a sex-change operation. He's considering that drastic step not because of a crisis in his sexual identity, but merely as a practical solution to a problem in his relationship with his boyfriend. Dennis is a high-profile quarterback for a professional football team, who's not willing to go public with his homosexuality.[20]

So Jodie decides to become a woman.

Both the character's thinking and the plotline were illogical. First, if Jodie became a woman, his gay boyfriend presumably would no longer want to be romantically involved with him because the football player was sexually attracted to men, not women. Second, it might be within the realm of possibility for a man to change, for example, his hairstyle or eating habits to save a relationship, but it's entirely unrealistic for a man to do something so radical as to change his sex. Third, no reputable physician or medical institution would agree to perform a sex-change operation under the circumstances described in the series, and yet Jodie was depicted as being admitted to a hospital and coming within a few days of having the surgery.

And so the plotline gave TV viewers some highly misleading information about the factors that make someone a transsexual and the enormous amount of trauma that such an individual experiences in trying to reconcile the contradictory anatomical and psychological aspects of his life.

The sitcom approached the topic, as it did so many others, not with gravity but levity. When Mary Campbell learns that her son is considering a sex-change operation, she focuses not on how such a decision will change his life forever but on how he looks in her dress. "You wear it belted," she says with an admiring glance. "It looks much better that way."[21]

Succeeding at making an audience laugh is an admirable art, but certain subjects should remain off limits to comedy writers. In 1977 when the motivations for sex-change operations were widely misunderstood, transsexuals may have been among those subjects.

Illuminating Gay Issues

Soap taking TV viewers on a roller-coaster ride of negative and positive messages is reinforced when an observer considers that, at the same time the program was giving out inaccurate information about transsexuals, it was doing an excellent job of illuminating other topics central to the lives and experiences of gay men.

One example unfolds in an early episode when Burt Campbell expresses his feelings about the increased visibility of homosexuals. "It's hard—this gay business," the construction worker begins. "When I was growing up, 'gay' meant 'happy.' It's hard to get used to all the changes." As the words roll out of Burt's mouth, he turns to his stepson and continues, not in an angry tone but one of puzzlement.

> When you guys were in the closet, maybe it wasn't easy on you, but it was a hell of a lot easier on us. It used to be that when you walked down the street and a guy smiled at you, you smiled back. Now if you smile back, you either get arrested or you get invited dancing.

Burt ends his comments on an optimistic note. "It's hard getting used to a guy who likes guys and not girls, but I'll try."[22]

The words that came from Burt's mouth weren't unique to him, as the program's writers clearly were using him to represent the Heterosexual Everyman. His monologue provided a public airing of thoughts that were going through the minds of millions of Americans during the late 1970s, thereby contributing to a better understanding between gays and non-gays.

Another poignant topic surfaced in an episode that aired later that first season, this time in a conversation between Jodie Dallas and his older brother.

> Jodie: Face facts, Danny, I'm a homosexual.
> Danny: That's ridiculous. How can you be gay? We're brothers. Anyway, you're too good at sports.
> Jodie: Danny, have you ever seen me with a girl?
> Danny: You're not gay, you're just shy.

The straight brother then becomes more adamant in his tone.

> Danny: You are *not* gay. I don't *want* you to be gay, so you're *not* gay.

The gay brother pauses for a moment, collects his thoughts, and then continues.

Jodie:	Danny, what's the big deal? Now that you know, am I any different?
Danny:	You don't look gay.
Jodie:	I'm still me. I'm still the Jodie that plays tennis with you. I'm still the Jodie that bowls with you. I'm still the Jodie that laughs with you. I'm still the Jodie that counts on you.
Danny:	All these years, I didn't want to hear it. I didn't think I could look at you again.
Jodie:	(smiling) Well, *can* you?
Danny:	(looking at his brother) Yes.

The scene ends with the two men embracing.[23]

Many of the questions asked and answered during that touching conversation had the ring of truth for the millions of gay people who'd already acknowledged their sexuality to friends and family members. For an untold number of others, that dialogue served as a catalyst for similar real-life discussions with their loved ones.

The *Soap* Legacy

Because Jodie Dallas was TV's first recurring gay character, the scholars who previously have looked at how the media have dealt with gay content have all commented on *Soap*.

Some of the assessments have been critical. In his book *Up from Invisibility: Lesbians, Gay Men, and the Media in America*, Larry Gross condemned the program for featuring "a flamboyant gay character." And in *The Prime Time Closet: A History of Gays and Lesbians on TV*, Stephen Tropiano also was negative about the series, writing:

> The idea of a man having a sex change so he can be together with another gay man not only conflates homosexuality and trans-sexualism but also plays into the myth that, deep down, all gay men really want to be women.[24]

But comments by other scholars have been highly complimentary. In her book *All the Rage: The Story of Gay Visibility in America*, Suzanna Danuta Walters praised *Soap* as "a standout in a period of relative invisibility" because its pioneering gay character was both "non-stereotypical" and "interesting." Likewise, in the book *Alternate Channels: The Uncensored Story of Gay and Lesbian Images on Radio and Television*, Steven Capsuto applauded the series, saying, "Jodie turned out to be sweet, proud, basically non-stereotypical, and very open about his gayness. Many isolated gay and bisexual teenage viewers embraced him as a role model."[25]

In this book that focuses specifically on how the depiction of gay people has changed over time, the ABC series holds a pivotal position because it was the first major media product that sent a mixture of messages about gay men. News coverage of "Perverts on the Potomac" and the Stonewall Rebellion as well as the film *The Boys in the Band* resolutely demonized their subjects. *Soap*, by contrast, provided a balance of some negative and some positive statements.

As the program's detractors have pointed out, the suggestion that anyone would approach having a sex-change operation so casually was indefensible; the show's plotline related to this topic was illogical, and the information that was presented about men seeking sex changes was inaccurate. The series also can be criticized for its repeated use of such derogatory terms as "fruit," "homo," and "pansy"; yes, the terms were used in the context of humor rather than hatred, but the words nonetheless positioned gay men as objects of ridicule. Other negative messages were sent when Jodie Dallas's sexuality was portrayed as "a problem" for his family and when he attempted to kill himself; these plot points reinforced the statements, which *The Boys in the Band* previously had made, that gay men are emotionally unstable and that being gay dooms a person to such a life of misery that suicide may be an appealing alternative.

Among *Soap*'s positive messages were that gay men can succeed in challenging careers, can possess strong moral fiber, and can work with and otherwise interact with straight people, women as well as men, rather than isolate themselves in their own separate world—a very different message than the one *The Boys in the Band* had sent. TV Land's first gay man becoming a father and winning the right to raise his daughter moved the portrayal beyond the point of merely challenging stereotypes and propelled the character into the realm of being, in a word, remarkable. Considering the strongly pejorative messages that the media of earlier eras had sent about homosexuals, for the series to depict the character not only as a father but also as a committed and responsible father meant that a widely seen television show was telling viewers that a gay man could behave at a level of decency that any right-thinking American would approve of—a message that was, in the context of those that had come before it, nothing less than extraordinary.

The most positive of all the messages sent by *Soap* may have been one that was noteworthy because of its absence. News coverage of "Perverts on the Potomac" and the Stonewall Rebellion, along with the film *The Boys in the Band,* had all communicated that the most reprehensible aspect of homosexual men's obsession with sex was that they lusted after boys and young men. But in Jodie Dallas's four years of weekly visits into American living rooms, he never gave any indication that he was driven by his libido or that he was attracted to anyone younger than himself.

With regard to how *Soap* fit into the evolving media depiction of gay people, the series introduced three issues that would continue to be debated for decades to come as various movies and TV programs moved into the cultural landscape.

One issue was the type of physical contact that could be shown between two gay characters. *The Boys in the Band* had depicted the male couple in the film hugging each other, but ABC network executives stipulated that *Soap* had to avoid "explicit or intimate aspects of homosexuality," which meant Jodie and his boyfriend were never allowed to kiss or hug, even though they were portrayed as being in a romantic relationship. The relative freedom in *Boys* compared to the restrictions on *Soap* reflects the dramatically different standards in the two media genres. When moviegoers buy their tickets and enter a theater that is showing a film with gay content, they are tacitly agreeing to expose themselves to images of homosexuality. Parents of young children, by contrast, have limited power to control the content that their sons and daughters are exposed to when they turn on the television, at least when it comes to the major networks.

A second issue that *Soap* introduced in the late 1970s and that would repeatedly resurface in later years is best summarized with a statement that appeared in the *New York Times* during the show's second year on the air. With the series in the midst of sending many positive messages about gays, a reporter for the country's most influential newspaper sought out the individual who had created the Jodie Dallas character and was writing the weekly scripts for *Soap*. That search led to Susan Harris, a thirty-six-year-old straight woman. The *Times* profile of Harris included her response to a question about whether she thought a situation comedy could change the public's attitude toward homosexuality. "If you want to make a point about a controversial topic," she said, "it's much easier to do it in a comedy than in a drama, because a comedy is much less threatening." The significance of Harris's statement would be reinforced time and time again during the late 1990s and early 2000s, as it would be shows built on humor—most notably the blockbuster hit *Will & Grace*—that broke new ground with regard to gay visibility and, thereby, continued to raise the question of just how much influence laugh-out-loud TV programs had on the nation's collective attitude toward gays.[26]

A third issue that *Soap* raised was about straight actors in the roles of homosexual men. Some of the most successful TV shows and motion pictures containing substantial gay content have owed much of their success and influence to the straight men who starred in them, but observers have speculated if playing such roles has harmed those actors' careers. There's no question that one of the primary reasons TV's first recurring gay character drew a large audience—week after week, year after year—was that the highly personable and affable Billy Crystal was so popular. Crystal first became known to the public from his much-discussed role in ABC's controversial sitcom. From that point on, his career continued to climb upward, as he's been cast, during the past three decades, in the leading role in such successful films as *City Slickers*, *When Harry Met Sally*, and *Analyze This*; as the star of the one-man show *700 Sundays* on Broadway (for which he won a Tony); and as the host of glamorous awards programs that are telecast live around the world. Crystal "playing gay" early in his career clearly helped increase the visibility and acceptance of gay people. But that early career decision has never stood in the way of Crystal's success as a highly sought-after and consistently admired performer with a following that's been both large and loyal.[27]

Because of the time period—1977 to 1981—when *Soap* was on the air, the conclusion of this chapter is the right place to identify one of the most important forces that has helped to drive the media's changing depiction of gay people: Hollywood activism.

During the second half of the twentieth century, a series of major social movements attempted to secure equal rights for segments of American society that were consistently being oppressed. The first of the movements rose to prominence in the 1950s when African Americans demanded an end to racial segregation, and a second movement followed in the 1960s when feminists sought equal rights and opportunities. And then, in the 1970s, the continuum continued as gay activists built on the momentum of the earlier civil rights campaigns by seeking to end discrimination based on sexual orientation.

While the most memorable battlefronts in these civil rights campaigns were mass protests and marches in American cities, a parallel effort to change how the public perceived these various stigmatized groups—and, therefore, influence the public's thinking about what rights they should be granted—was being made, though more subtly, on the television screen. Nat King Cole showed 1950s television viewers, for example, that an African-American man could possess the talent and the charm to host his own musical variety program. Likewise, Mary Tyler Moore told the nation, via her sitcom in the early 1970s, that a young woman could succeed in the competitive field of television news while enjoying a fulfilling personal life—without being married. Billy Crystal can be seen as another star who also became an activist, as his depiction of Jodie Dallas communicated to the country's massive television audience that a gay man could be physically attractive, professionally successful, and so eminently likable that it was a joy to have him arrive in the nation's living rooms on a weekly basis.[28]

Crystal said in 2004:

> It was a risky role for me to take, but I took it because it gave me the chance to do something very important for gay people. I worked very hard to make my character a regular guy-next-door kind of man

who just happened to be gay. It was during a time when most people in this country thought a homosexual was weird and scary. Seeing my character on the TV screen helped them realize that being gay wasn't really strange at all. That was a huge step forward, and I'm very proud that I played a role in making it happen.[29]

5 AIDS Enters the News
Reporting on the "Gay Plague"

For most gay men, June 1981 was the beginning of a carefree summer. The country's leading gay magazine announced early in the month that bodybuilding had emerged as the pastime of choice among its readers, with bulging biceps becoming a far more accurate sign of a man's homosexuality than limp wrists had ever been. "Aspiring hunks can be seen walking around San Francisco," *The Advocate* observed, "with their gym bags—now a *de rigueur* piece of gay equipment—either going to or coming from their daily workout." The men were tightening up their abs and firming up their quads so they could pose with appropriate attitude on the beach and at the gay bars and bathhouses that had mushroomed into a $100 million industry.[1]

As that hedonistic summer continued to unfold, however, some men noticed a smattering of worrisome items buried on the inside pages of a few newspapers. The first story appeared in early June in the *Los Angeles Times*—"Outbreaks of Pneumonia Among Gay Males Studied"—and the next followed a day later in the *San Francisco Chronicle*—"A Pneumonia that Strikes Gay Men." The small number of alert readers who were growing concerned about this mysterious illness increased over the Fourth of July weekend when the *New York Times*, the country's most respected newspaper, announced "Rare Cancer Seen in 41 Homosexuals."[2]

It would be at least another year before most gay men acknowledged that a new demon was threatening them, however, and still more time would pass before they fully accepted that the most catastrophic epidemic in the history of modern medicine was attacking their community. Even though much of Gay America was slow to recognize the devastating scope of AIDS, there's no question that the nation's journalists, from the beginning, saw acquired immune deficiency syndrome as not only a medical story but also a gay story, as shown by either "gay" or "homosexual" appearing in the headline above each of those three early news items.

And so news coverage of this topic joined that of "Perverts on the Potomac" and the Stonewall Rebellion in playing a significant role in shaping the public's perception of gay men. With regard to specific messages that journalistic outlets sent, the primary one was that thousands of young men dying of a new disease did not qualify as important news because of one factor: The victims were gay. At the same time, the titans of American journalism decided the epidemic provided them with an opportunity to send their readers and viewers a highly negative message about gay men: They are promiscuous.

"The Patients Were All Homosexuals"

Doctors and medical writers first read about the new disease in a weekly bulletin that the federal government's Centers for Disease Control produced to warn the medical community about public health concerns. Copies were sent to the country's physicians, hospitals, and all news organizations that covered medical topics. The article in the bulletin stated that the disease, which was accompanied by such severe weight loss that patients looked like refugees from a concentration camp, had been found in five otherwise healthy men, adding that "The patients were all homosexuals."[3]

Only two of the nation's mainstream news organizations, print or broadcast, developed the item into a news story. The *Los Angeles Times* placed its piece on page three, and the *San Francisco Chronicle* put its version on page four.[4]

Although the disease didn't have an official name, medical experts informally referred to it as "gay-related immune deficiency." That designation had too many words for space-conscious journalists, however, so they began calling the disease the "gay plague." The news items noted that the condition was not, in fact, a single disease but a syndrome that destroyed the body's immune system and thereby made the victim susceptible to a wide variety of infections, cancers, and other illnesses that ultimately killed the patient.[5]

The first page-one story about the syndrome carried the accusatory headline "Started with Gays—Mysterious Fever Now an Epidemic." That article was published in May 1982 in the *Los Angeles Times*, announcing that 355 cases of the disease, by this time officially known as acquired immune deficiency syndrome, had been reported. The piece went on to say that 140 victims were already dead, that physicians around the country were diagnosing new cases at a rate of one per day, and that most of the victims were gay men living in New York City, San Francisco, or Los Angeles.[6]

In April 1983, *Newsweek* became the first national magazine to highlight the syndrome on its cover—at the urging of a reporter whose gay brother had become ill. Below an image of a blood-filled syringe and the single word "EPIDEMIC" ran the statement: "The Mysterious and Deadly Disease Called AIDS May Be the Public-Health Threat of the

Century." By this point, 1,300 Americans had been infected, and 489 of them were dead.[7]

In May 1983, the *New York Times* ignited a firestorm of anxiety when it reported that a study had found that AIDS could be contracted through "routine close contact." Dozens of other papers and TV stations then repeated that vague phrase, causing millions of Americans to fear—and understandably so—that they could die if they used the same bathroom or rode on the same subway car as someone who was infected. Medical experts quickly refuted the study's findings, but neither the *Times* nor other media outlets ran corrections of their earlier stories.[8]

In April 1984, news organizations across the country reported that the cause of AIDS had been identified. The stories said that researchers at the National Cancer Institute had found persuasive evidence that the human immunodeficiency virus, or HIV, infected and destroyed the white blood cells that normally help clear disease-causing microbes from the bloodstream. Stories reported that three out of every four AIDS victims were gay men.[9]

In July 1985, news outlets reported that the most recent of the 12,000 Americans to be diagnosed with AIDS was the popular actor Rock Hudson. A legion of observers would come to see the Hudson news stories as a major turning point in the news coverage, marking the end of the first stage of the relationship between AIDS and the media.[10]

At this point, four years after the first stories had appeared, the country's print and broadcast coverage of the syndrome had communicated two distinct messages about gay men.

"We Don't Want to Hear Stories about Homosexuals"

In mid-1981 when Jerry Bishop of the *Wall Street Journal* first heard that a new disease was killing otherwise healthy young men, the reporter was sure that the magnitude of the story he wrote would catapult his words onto page one. Bishop also took the time to craft a first sentence that fully communicated the urgency of the situation: "A mysterious, often fatal illness is breaking out in epidemic proportions among young homosexual men."[11]

Bishop was shocked, however, when his editors not only didn't see the revelation as front-page news but refused to run the article anywhere in the paper. "They were uncomfortable with the connection with homosexuals," he later recalled. Only after a series of heated arguments between Bishop and his editors did the article finally appear—several months later, cut to half its original length, and buried on page forty-one.[12]

Editors at the *Journal* were not unique. They merely provide one example of how the leaders of American journalism responded to AIDS when it began to surface during the early 1980s. Many scholars and journalists have since then examined how the news media performed in covering this huge gay story, and their indictments have been consistent.

James Kinsella began his book, *Covering the Plague: AIDS and the American Media*, with the statement: "At least some of the blame for the ravages of AIDS in America must lie with members of the media who refused to believe that the deaths of gay men were worth reporting." Larry Gross wrote in his book, *Up from Invisibility: Lesbians, Gay Men, and the Media in America*:

> The immediate response to the medical mystery that we know as AIDS was a deafening silence from the mainstream media. The homophobia of the press, combined with its assumption that audiences shared its bias, led it to ignore and downplay the story.

David Shaw, media reporter for the *Los Angeles Times*, made the same points: "The press reacted very slowly to AIDS. It was 'their' disease, and few editors were terribly concerned about it, not in a country still largely uncomfortable with, if not downright hostile toward, homosexuality."[13]

Many critics found particular fault with the *New York Times*, stating that the nation's most influential news organization—the one that lesser media outlets use as a model for their coverage—didn't pay adequate attention to a disease that was finding many of its victims in the New York metropolitan area. The *Times* didn't place an AIDS story on its front page until mid-1983 when the federal government's top health official held a press conference and announced that investigating the medical condition had become the number-one priority of the U.S. Public Health Service—a public event that the paper couldn't ignore. By that point, 1,500 cases had been reported and 600 people had died, with fully half of the victims being from New York City.[14]

The *New York Times* is also vulnerable to criticism because it lagged far behind the city's gay bi-weekly, the *New York Native*. In 1981 when the new illness was first reported, the *Times* had a fulltime reporting staff of 300, while the *Native* depended on an unpaid volunteer to cover medical news. And yet the *Times* didn't mention that gay men were getting sick for a full two months after the *Native* had published its first story.[15]

Even as AIDS cases mushroomed to epidemic proportions, the mainstream Goliath continued to perform poorly compared to the gay David. By the end of 1982, the *Times* had published only seven articles; by that point, the *Native* had published fifty-eight.[16]

The failure of the *New York Times* to provide adequate AIDS coverage also contributed to TV news failing to perform appropriately. In explaining why the networks made no mention whatsoever of the story until mid-1982, a CBS executive said, "Two-thirds of the stories that the networks cover are picked up from newspapers and magazines, and most of those stories run first in the *New York Times*."[17]

Homophobia was clearly a contributing factor, too. "Some journalists ignored the epidemic altogether because they did not consider the death of homosexuals relevant to the largely heterosexual audiences," wrote Edward Alwood, author of the book *Straight News: Gays, Lesbians, and the News Media*. He supported that accusation by quoting NBC's top medical correspondent, Robert Bazell, as saying that when he wanted to air a story on AIDS, network officials told him, "Look, it ain't us. We don't want to hear stories about homosexuals." Sally Holms, a senior producer at ABC, faced similar opposition from her network; when she proposed a piece about healthy gay men providing support for AIDS patients, her bosses told her that such a story would be "too soft on gays."[18]

Because of these factors, TV news was even slower to respond to the AIDS crisis than print publications were. The disease wasn't mentioned on an evening news program until Robert Bazell persuaded NBC to air a story that anchor Tom Brokaw introduced with the accusatory lead-in: "The lifestyle of some male homosexuals has triggered an epidemic of a rare form of cancer." Despite the fact that broadcasting the piece in June 1982—more than a year after the first story had appeared in the *New York Native*—meant that NBC got an egregiously late start in covering the epidemic, the competing network evening news shows didn't race to catch up. ABC waited four more months before running its first story, and CBS waited another two months after that.[19]

"You Have Sex First, Then Talk"

That the first statement about AIDS to be broadcast on television news began with a reference to "The lifestyle of some male homosexuals" is telling. For at the same time that news organizations were dragging their feet with regard to informing their readers and listeners about the "gay plague," they were eager to report that the victims had been promiscuous.[20]

The first *New York Times* story about the mysterious new illness included the statement: "Most cases involve homosexual men who have had multiple and frequent sexual encounters with different partners, as many as 10 sexual encounters each night up to four times a week." For readers who had trouble doing the math, the *Times* reported, in its second story on the topic, that a study by the Centers for Disease Control had found that "the median number of lifetime male sexual partners for homosexual men who did not have the syndrome was 524, while the comparable figure for men who had the syndrome was 1,160."[21]

Geronimo!

News organizations around the country soon followed the *Times*'s lead and either reproduced the startling figure or a rounded-off version of it. *Newsweek*: "Early victims had 1,160 different sex partners." *New York* magazine: "Homosexual AIDS patients had listed more than 1,000 sex partners." *Rolling Stone*: "One thousand one hundred and sixty! That's the median number of sexual partners the guys getting the disease have had. Can you believe that? One thousand one hundred and sixty! Good God!"[22]

In addition to printing the figure, publications often made statements communicating to their readers that there was an intrinsic connection between homosexuality and promiscuity. *Time* magazine, for instance, reported that "For many homosexuals accustomed to having many partners, staying faithful to one lover is not an option," going on to pronounce anonymous sex the signature element of gay life: "The tradition in the gay community is that you have sex first, then talk." The country's largest news magazine went on to say that promiscuity had become so much a part of gay life that some gay men—though no names were included—were committing suicide rather than giving it up.[23]

A Huge Step Backward

By 1985, some 9,000 gay men had been diagnosed as carrying HIV, and almost 4,000 of them were already dead. Adding to the heartbreak was the fact that most of the victims were young, their lives cut short while still in their twenties.

Millions of other men lived in constant fear that they, too, had been infected and that the deadly virus would reveal itself at any moment. For every gay man in the country, so much as stepping onto the bathroom scales and seeing that he weighed a pound or two less than the day before could hurl him into a state of anxiety and panic.

The epidemic of fear that accompanied the medical crisis had major impact as well. Even gay men who eluded the virus were suddenly shunned by their neighbors and co-workers, as perfectly healthy men were routinely evicted from their apartments or fired from their jobs because a frightened American public was taking desperate measures to distance itself from this deadly menace.[24]

While another repercussion of AIDS was by no means comparable to these catastrophic events, it is relevant to the subject of this book: The epidemic prompted a major setback in the evolution of how the media depicted gay men.

In the late 1970s, with the TV sitcom *Soap*, the American public had begun to be exposed to a few positive messages about gay men. But then came AIDS.

Starting with the first stories about a mysterious new disease in the summer of 1981 and continuing with increasing ferocity for the next four years, the progress that had been made was all but obliterated, as the media consistently demonized gay men. Indeed, the messages that the nation's news outlets were communicating sounded eerily reminiscent of the relentlessly negative ones that had been sent thirty years earlier. In 1950, homosexuals working for the government had been portrayed as a threat to the nation's well-being because they were unfit for public service; in the early 1980s, gay men with AIDS—as well as gay men in general—were portrayed as a threat to the nation's well-being because they were spreading the "gay plague."

The most disheartening message that the news media of the early 1980s sent was that the deaths of gay men were not important. Initial evidence of this nightmarish disregard came in how slowly the nation's news outlets responded to the AIDS epidemic. In June 1981, only two mainstream newspapers in the entire country felt that the discovery of a new disease that preyed on homosexuals was even worth mentioning, and not until May 1982 did the first mainstream newspaper decide that the continued growth of that illness—which had already killed more than 100 victims— was worthy of a front-page story. And it would be still another month after that before any of the television networks finally deemed the crisis in Gay America to be sufficiently newsworthy to merit the word "AIDS" being uttered during a newscast.

Further proof that homophobia was rampant in American journalism came in the form of the behind-closed-doors comments that decision-makers were uttering as the number of deaths continued to climb. Editors at the *Wall Street Journal* "were uncomfortable with the connection with homosexuals," so they kept the epidemic from receiving the kind of coverage it deserved; executives at NBC blocked the biggest public health story of the era from their newscasts by telling the network's top medical correspondent, "We don't want to hear stories about homosexuals."

Eventually, so many people became infected that the news organizations had no choice but to cover AIDS. But many scholars and journalism critics would ultimately argue that the major shift in both the quantity and the quality of coverage that occurred in mid-1985 wasn't a response to the large number of victims but to the fact that some of them were heterosexual.

6 AIDS Becomes Major News
"Now No One Is Safe"

From the 1950s through the early 1980s, no film or television star better personified American manhood than Rock Hudson. His square jaw and handsome facial features combined with a well-developed physique, a deep voice, and an easygoing demeanor to create the quintessential leading man. After first starring as a strapping cowboy in the classic film *Giant* opposite the glamorous Elizabeth Taylor, then shifting to a series of romantic comedies such as *Pillow Talk* with the perky Doris Day, and finally landing a recurring role on the nighttime TV soap opera *Dynasty* as the love interest of blond beauty Linda Evans, Hudson was one of the most popular actors in the country.[1]

But in July 1985 when the Hollywood legend appeared in public for the first time in several weeks, his millions of fans gasped in disbelief. The physical deterioration reflected in Hudson's haggard face and wasted frame were so radical that it was difficult to recognize him as the man whose dazzling good looks had been melting hearts for thirty years. When reporters asked the pale and drawn actor if he was ill, he initially pooh-poohed their questions, saying he'd just had a bout with the flu.[2]

But after collapsing and being flown to Paris for experimental treatment, the star finally authorized his spokesman to make an announcement that stunned the world:

"Rock Hudson has AIDS."[3]

In addition to leading the newscasts on all three television networks that night and appearing on the front pages of the nation's leading newspapers the next morning, that statement also created an indelible fault line that divided the media's AIDS coverage into two distinct phases. In the words of an editorial published in *USA Today* when the actor died two months after having acknowledged his illness, "With Rock Hudson's death, many of us are realizing that AIDS is not a 'gay plague' but everybody's problem."[4]

As for specific messages about gay men that American journalism sent during the second phase of its AIDS coverage, the most disturbing

Figure 6.1 It was not until Hollywood icon Rock Hudson, shown here with Elizabeth Taylor in *Giant*, was diagnosed with AIDS in 1985 that the news media began to give the illness the coverage it deserved.

Courtesy of Warner Bros./Photofest.

of them resulted from the dramatic increase in stories: Now that the illness was no longer perceived as a gay disease, it exploded into a major news story. This message could be interpreted, in blunt terms, as saying that gay men are not worth saving, but straight people are. Another troubling statement was that many gay men with AIDS were not victims to be sympathized with but, in fact, villains to be reviled.

During the second phase of coverage, the news media also sent a positive message. Specifically, the nation's news organizations began showcasing individuals who belonged to a fraternity that newspaper readers and television viewers had never heard of before: Gay Heroes.

Becoming a Major News Story

It's ironic that the individual whose illness and death, more than any other, caused the public to realize that AIDS was not an isolated concern confined to gay men but a major medical crisis that threatened everyone, regardless of their sexual orientation, was himself a man who routinely had sex with men. Although the news media reported extensively on Rock Hudson's long-hidden homosexuality during the second half of 1985, his status as a widely recognized celebrity was the factor that awakened the nation to the epidemic.[5]

David Shaw, media reporter for the *Los Angeles Times*, is among the many observers who acknowledged the increased media attention. "AIDS coverage in the American media can clearly be divided into two eras, two eras so strikingly different that it's almost as if it were two different diseases—pre-Hudson AIDS and post-Hudson AIDS," Shaw wrote. "After Hudson's diagnosis, AIDS was suddenly page-one news, cover-story news, network news. Everywhere."[6]

The statistics support this assertion.

"Media coverage of AIDS more than tripled in the six months after Hudson's announcement," Shaw reported. When *Time* looked at AIDS coverage over a longer period of time, the newsweekly found the increased number of articles to be even more dramatic—during the three years *before* the Hudson announcement, the stories totaled 605; during the three years *after* the announcement, the stories totaled 9,399.[7]

Observers believe it was Hudson's fame and familiarity among the American public that served as the catalyst for the increased coverage. "It was a goddamn disgrace—outrageous—that most newspapers essentially ignored the AIDS story until a celebrity became ill," said Donald Drake, who covered the medical beat for the *Philadelphia Inquirer*. "If AIDS had involved any group of people other than gays, the media would have been all over the story much sooner. There is a homophobia on the part of the American press."[8]

Hudson's illness, in addition to moving the epidemic into the news spotlight, also persuaded some editors to start reporting details about how HIV was being spread, even if doing so meant offending some readers by using terms such as "anal intercourse." The *New York Times*, which in 1987 ended its ban on the term "gay" and began allowing the word to be used as a synonym for "homosexual," was among the leaders in the shift to explicit language. "The only current hope for containing the epidemic," the paper's health columnist explained, "is to understand how the virus passes from person to person and to adopt sensible precautions to keep yourself from being infected." She then went on to tell her readers, point-blank: "Avoid anal intercourse." The *Times* also reported why this particular sexual act could be deadly. "The virus spreads more readily in anal intercourse than in vaginal intercourse," a front-page story explained, "because anal sex often involves breaks in rectal tissues, thus allowing easier entry of the virus into the bloodstream."[9]

Other papers then followed the *Times*'s lead. The *Washington Post* crossed the linguistic threshold in a story titled "Safe Sex in the Era of AIDS," and the *Los Angeles Times* referred to anal sex in an article reporting on the effectiveness of various types of condoms—those made of latex stop HIV, those made of animal products do not. The *Boston Globe* used the phrase anal intercourse in a story about the rate of new infections in San Francisco plummeting because gay men were practicing safe sex.[10]

That Hudson's announcement prompted print news organizations to use explicit terms didn't mean that their television counterparts did the same. "Four years into the AIDS crisis," James Kinsella wrote in *Covering the Plague: AIDS and the American Media*, "the network evening news programs were still avoiding clear language on how the disease was being spread." While broadcast executives remained wary of using explicit terms that might cause listeners to change to another channel, however, some reporters were coming up with creative tactics to circumvent their bosses. In 1985, ABC's George Strait set up an interview with Dr. Anthony Fauci, an AIDS expert from the National Institutes of Health. The medical correspondent knew that The Powers That Be at his network wouldn't allow a reporter to use explicit phrasing as part of his report, so he asked Dr. Fauci—before the cameras started rolling—to do it for him. The doctor cooperated and included the phrase "anal sex" as part of his taped sound bite, which the network then broadcast.[11]

Spotlighting Gay Villains

One way in which journalism manifested its fear and hatred of gay men was by providing extensive coverage of AIDS victims who also were villains. In the words of one scholar of gays and the media, the news outlets depicted gay men with the disease "as bottom-feeding snakes who spread 'the plague' irresponsibly and knowingly."[12]

TV journalists portrayed Fabian Bridges as America's worst nightmare. The wiry thirty-year-old was gaunt and frail by the time he appeared on WCCO in Minneapolis in early 1986. Bridges was broke, hungry, and dying of AIDS. To earn money, he'd become a prostitute. Although he previously had lived as a gay man, he was now willing to perform any sex act with anyone—man or woman, it didn't matter—who was willing to pay him. "I'm to the point where I just don't give a damn," he told the TV reporter. [13]

Between the summer of 1985 and when he died a year later, Bridges was the country's best-known AIDS villain. He became the subject first of the series of stories on the local Minneapolis station and later of a documentary that aired nationwide on the Public Broadcasting Service. Newspaper readers also learned about Bridges infecting dozens of sex partners, with articles about the gay man's reprehensible behavior appearing in such large-circulation dailies as *USA Today*, the *Chicago Tribune*, and the *Los Angeles Times*. The *Times* called Bridges "an awful, awful person."[14]

Magazines also vilified gay men with the disease. Journalists as well as scholars pointed to a 1985 story in *Life* as the most alarmist of the era. The piece was highlighted by the headline, in bright red letters spread across the cover: "Now No One Is Safe from AIDS," with the final word, printed much larger than the rest, measuring a full four inches high. Below the sensationalized headline were photos of a straight woman, a straight soldier in uniform, and a straight couple holding their infant son. The article identified all of them as AIDS victims.[15]

Inside the magazine, it didn't take long for the article to make it clear who was responsible for heterosexual Americans now being in jeopardy. "When first diagnosed in the U.S. four years ago, AIDS was seen mainly as a homosexual affliction," the first paragraph stated. "But infectious diseases have a way of breaking out of their pockets." In case readers still weren't clear precisely who was to blame for the epidemic spreading to new victims, that first paragraph went on to say, "The AIDS minorities are beginning to infect the heterosexual majority."[16]

Life reinforced the gay-man-as-villain theme—though the magazine always used the term "homosexual," never "gay"—later in the piece when the circumstances of the straight woman pictured on the cover were described. The thirty-four-year-old legal secretary had been infected during a year-long relationship with a man whose sexual history included sleeping with men. A photo accompanying the story showed the dying woman holding the burial urn she had selected to hold her ashes.[17]

In many instances, publications seemed so determined to cast gay AIDS patients in a negative light that they abandoned the journalistic tenet requiring statements to be attributed to a source, and instead relied on hearsay. "The gay culture is awash with rumors of unnamed victims," *Time* magazine reported, "who are purposely trying to infect as many others as possible"—with no source for the statement being given. Other times, media outlets spiced up their stories with sensationalized anecdotes that portrayed gay men as heartless. A *New York Times* piece spotlighted a man, identified only as "Chuck," who had known he was ill for more than a year but "continued to have sex with strangers and admits to encounters with dozens of men." The paper ended its mini-profile by stating that Chuck "seems genuinely surprised by the suggestion that he might tell his partners, before having sex, that he has AIDS."[18]

Celebrating Gay Heroes

At the same time that some news organizations were depicting gay men with AIDS as villains, others were shining the journalistic spotlight on men who deserved the public's respect and admiration for deeds that fully qualified as heroic.

The *Honolulu Star-Bulletin* focused on one of its own. When managing editor Bill Cox was diagnosed with AIDS, he immediately went public with his illness, determined not to contribute to the epidemic of fear and shame surrounding the disease. And so with a 1986 article titled "A Journalist with AIDS," Cox became one of the country's first newsmen to talk publicly about his illness, writing, "If we don't want to be treated as pariahs, we have to stop acting like pariahs." The story prompted letters from more than 1,000 readers, all supportive. When Cox died two years later, the *Star-Bulletin* announced the news on page one. "The death of Bill Cox dramatizes the tragedy of the AIDS epidemic," the story stated. "We have lost a dedicated professional, a thoughtful colleague and a fine human being. For his sake and our own, we must memorialize him with renewed efforts to find a cure."[19]

Several news organizations published profiles of another gay journalist and victim of the disease who had reached heroic stature. By the time the *Washington Post* interviewed Randy Shilts in 1987, the hundreds of stories he had written for the *San Francisco Chronicle* had gained him the reputation as the most knowledgeable AIDS reporter in the country. "For me, this is not just a story that's happening to 'those people,'" he told the *Post*, saying he had known at least 100 men whose lives had been taken by the disease. "I've seen the dead bodies and they're people I know." The *New York Times* reported, in its profile of Shilts, that some observers questioned whether the *Chronicle* should allow him to continue to report on the disease now that he'd been diagnosed with it, suggesting he was too close to the story. Shilts disagreed, telling the *Times*, "Our medical writer wrote about colds when he had a cold. The bottom line is professionalism."[20]

News organizations didn't limit their positive stories to individuals, as they also praised Gay America as a whole. "Within the homosexual community, sexual behavior has changed radically since the start of the AIDS epidemic," the *New York Times* reported in 1985. The article went on to say that men had learned exactly what sexual activities put them in danger and had changed their behavior accordingly, as instances of anal intercourse had dropped by 50 percent. Although it took several years before these changes in behavior resulted in a decreased rate of AIDS within the community, when that point came, the *Times* reported it. "Data over the last two years," the paper said in 1989, "suggest that the rate at which gay men get AIDS has begun to flatten out." When the epidemic was first discovered at the beginning of the decade, 100 percent of victims had been gay men, the *Times* noted, but, by the end of the decade, that figure had dropped to 60 percent.[21]

Raising Gay Visibility

It is beyond the limits of common sense to suggest that the AIDS epidemic had a "silver lining" for Gay America. To suggest that any benefit whatsoever resulted from a public health crisis that had, by the end of

1989, swollen to the point that 90,000 cases had been diagnosed among gay men—50,000 of the victims were already dead—seems highly insensitive, bordering on ghoulish.[22]

And yet scholars and journalists alike have unequivocally stated that one positive aspect of the epidemic was that it moved gay men into the national spotlight as never before. John D'Emilio, who has written several books about the history of Gay and Lesbian America, said: "AIDS posed a public health crisis that had to be looked at. What in the '70s and early '80s was a movement of a marginalized minority, through AIDS was now a national issue." And Suzanna Danuta Walters, in her book *All the Rage: The Story of Gay Visibility in America*, chronicled the increased attention that the media paid to gay people in the final decades of the twentieth century, giving much of the credit to AIDS: "The crisis bears a large responsibility for this new visibility, forcing America to reckon publicly and explicitly with a population long kept under wraps."[23]

Among news organizations, *Newsweek* was one of the journalistic voices that credited the AIDS epidemic with raising gay visibility. "It changed how the media portray homosexuality," the newsweekly said in a 2006 cover story. "Watching a generation of gay men wither and die, the nation came to acknowledge the humanity of a community it had mostly ignored and reviled."[24]

Coverage of Rock Hudson led the way, as the celebrity's death in 1985 signaled a dramatic increase in journalistic attention not only to the illness but also to men who felt sexual desires for other men. After the widely admired star unintentionally opened the door, other men followed him into the media spotlight—from Fabian Bridges as the quintessential AIDS villain to Bill Cox and Randy Shilts as men who doubled as journalists and casualties of the worst medical catastrophe in modern times. By the end of the 1980s, gay men had become the subjects of stories in virtually every news outlet in the country.

It should immediately be noted that the unprecedented level of visibility didn't extend across the gender line. The explosion of coverage moved gay men onto front pages and to the top of newscasts nationwide, but lesbians didn't join them. Just as news stories about "Perverts on the Potomac" had focused exclusively on men, so did news stories about AIDS. And so, with the exception of a few references after the Stonewall Rebellion, the American news media had still provided the public with scant information about or images of women who loved women.[25]

Other regrettable themes that had been present in the news media's earlier treatment of gay people also persisted in the stories about AIDS.

For example, just as the coverage in 1950 and again in 1969 had portrayed gay men as immoral, so did many of the stories in the 1980s. In this latest instance, it wasn't that homosexuals were doing damage to American foreign policy by working for the State Department, or threatening the safety of the general population by rioting in the streets.

Instead, this time they were portrayed as furtively infecting their sexual partners—"Now No One Is Safe," as *Life* magazine put it—by spreading a deadly virus, with at least some of the villains depicted as doing so either intentionally or without remorse.

Another theme that continued to define the news coverage of gay people was that journalists found it perfectly acceptable to use pejorative terms to describe this particular segment of the population. In 1950, the denigrating term of choice was "perverts," and in 1969 it had shifted to "queens," "fags," and "queers." As late as 1985, such leading news organizations as the *Chicago Tribune* were still referring to AIDS as the "gay plague," even though medical experts had officially named it acquired immune deficiency syndrome three years earlier.[26]

At the same time, there's no question that AIDS coverage also served as a positive milestone, in at least some respects, in the evolution of how the news media have depicted gay men.

One sign of progress was that the stories did not characterize homosexuality as a mental illness. In 1950, newspapers had described men who were sexually attracted to other men as suffering from a "nauseating disease" brought on by the combination of an overly protective mother and a distant father, and in 1969, news outlets had stated as indisputable fact that homosexuals suffered from "quite a severe illness" caused by a mother being "close binding and inappropriately intimate" and a father being "either hostile, aloof or ineffectual." In the 1980s, however, such statements no longer appeared in stories reporting on the real illness that was cutting its deadly swath across Gay America.[27]

A second sign of progress vis-à-vis journalism's treatment of gay people was manifested in the abundance of names of openly gay men that appeared in the stories. The "Perverts on the Potomac" coverage hadn't included the names of any homosexual men, and the flood of stories that appeared in the wake of the Stonewall Rebellion contained only a handful of names. By the 1980s, by contrast, the names of so many openly gay men appeared in stories that it would be impossible to count them all, with several of the news organizations characterizing at least some of those men as true heroes. As a gay man named Michael Brown stated in a story on the front page of the *New York Times*: "We're probably the most harassed and persecuted minority group in history, but we'll never have the freedom and civil rights we deserve as human beings unless we stop hiding in closets."[28]

7 Gays in the Military

The Debate over Lifting the Ban

In 1992 a candidate for president of the United States, for the first time in history, used the words *gay* and *lesbian* in numerous campaign speeches. "I have a vision, and you—the gay men and lesbians of America—are part of it," Bill Clinton told more than one crowd of supporters, who responded by waving their rainbow flags with unbridled enthusiasm. Those same men and women also opened their checkbooks to the tune of $5 million and showed up at the polls in huge numbers. The issue that, more than any other, caused gay voters to support the Democratic candidate was his promise to lift the ban that prevented homosexuals from serving in the U.S. military.[1]

Gay Americans continued to believe in the magic after Clinton won the election. They got all dressed up in tuxedos and sequined gowns to attend the first-of-its-kind Gay and Lesbian Inaugural Ball, and then they watched with their hearts pounding in excitement as the new president, a scant nine days after taking office, directed his secretary of defense to prepare a written policy that would, once and for all, end the discrimination based on sexual orientation that kept gays from serving in the armed forces.[2]

Then the flags stopped waving.

Clinton's proposal was opposed by a formidable coalition composed of all members of the Joint Chiefs of Staff and a sizable number of U.S. senators and representatives—nearly as many Democrats as Republicans. For the next several months, journalists placed the debate over lifting the ban at the top of their agenda, with the nation's leading newspapers and TV news programs providing continuous coverage of the hot-button issue.

By the end of the year, Clinton had abandoned his initial proposal and replaced it with a very different one, which Congress quickly approved. Under the "don't ask, don't tell" policy, military officials wouldn't *ask* new recruits about their sexual orientation, which meant that gay soldiers would be allowed to serve as long as they didn't *tell* anyone in the armed forces about their sexuality. The president called the new policy an "honorable compromise," but many gay activists considered it such a radical departure from his original promise that they believed the more accurate description was an "outright betrayal."[3]

News coverage of the lifting-the-ban debate wasn't limited to the reporting of facts. For at the same time that the nation's most influential journalistic voices were communicating breaking news related to the topic, they also were sending powerful messages about the men and women who stood four square at the center of the controversy.

The first of the two negative statements was that gay men are sexual predators, thereby making it unsafe for straight soldiers to be anywhere near them. Second, the presence of gay men in the military was depicted as being disruptive in so many ways that it would be impossible for the armed forces, if their ranks were officially opened to homosexuals, to function effectively.

The first of the two positive messages was that barring gay people from military service was a blatant act of discrimination and therefore unacceptable. Second, numerous journalistic voices reported that lesbians and gay men who had served in the military, without their sexual orientation being widely known, had proven that gay people could make exemplary soldiers.

Gay Men Are Sexual Predators

Various media genres that had depicted gay men in the 1970s and 1980s had been fascinated with the high value this subgroup of society placed on sex. From the promiscuity in *The Boys in the Band* to the sexual dimensions of the news coverage of AIDS, carnal activities had been prominent in the depictions. Finding an era in which sexual *aggression* had been as prominent as it became during the gays-in-the-military debate, however, required traveling all the way back to 1950 when newspapers reported that "The homosexual is always on the prowl" and "The homosexual will go to any limit to attain his abnormal purposes."[4]

In 1993, the conservative-leaning *Chicago Tribune* led the way in portraying gay men as sexual predators. An editorial titled "A Battle for the Military's Soul," for example, stated that "the vast majority of homosexuals are aggressively promiscuous." That same editorial went on to say that "homosexual men are much more likely than heterosexual men to incorporate youth into their sexual practices." Because of these factors, the *Tribune* concluded, "If the ban is lifted, parents of young soldiers will rightly fear for the safety of their children because of the tendency of homosexuals to recruit youth into their lifestyle."[5]

Television news relied on images to portray gay men as highly sexual. Because the lifting-the-ban debate emerged as a major story during the presidential campaign in early 1992 and then remained a hot topic throughout 1993, the men and women who put together the newscasts at ABC, CBS, NBC, and CNN became increasingly desperate for video footage to fill the screen as the anchors and correspondents reported the latest developments. Some clips had enlisted men marching or sitting in classrooms, but the most compelling scenes were those showing soldiers walking in and out of the communal showers they shared. While the images of young men wearing nothing but towels—their bare chests and legs exposed—were more graphically interesting than other shots, they also reinforced the idea of gay men being obsessed with sexual pursuits.

The nightly parade of half-naked soldiers became so ubiquitous by the spring of 1993 that the nation's liberal newspapers began reporting on it. The *New York Times* observed that, "For months now, Americans have been watching ominous shower shots on the nightly news." The *Los Angeles Times* went a step further and accused its TV news counterparts of promoting "the ugliest stereotypes" of gay men; by continually showing the viewing public those shower scenes, the *Times* argued, the broadcast organizations were "feeding wild, irrational fears and panic about straights and gays serving together."[6]

Gay Men Are Disruptive

A second recurring message was that gay men were problematic for so many reasons that allowing them to serve openly in the armed forces would destroy the American military's ability to protect the country. Exactly which specific aspects of being gay were the most disruptive depended on the particular news outlet at hand.

The *Chicago Tribune* saw gay men as fundamentally unfit for military service because they were emotionally unstable and morally corrupt. The negative characterizations sounded very much like those that had appeared in America's leading newspapers in 1950. To support its point about instability, the *Tribune* reported, "Gays are six times more likely to attempt suicide than heterosexuals." And to support its argument about homosexual men being immoral, the paper cited the high rate of promiscuity among gays. Because of these weaknesses in character, one *Tribune* editorial concluded, allowing homosexuals to serve in the military would threaten the country's security: "This battle is for our combat readiness and ability to defend America and its ideals. The gay ban must stand."[7]

Another specific reason the ban should remain in place, according to the *Tribune*, was that a policy change would cause enormous numbers of active-duty personnel to abandon their military careers. "Don't forget the heterosexuals in uniform," the paper cautioned. "If Clinton is willing to let gays *in*, will he be equally willing to permit service members *out* who object to the gay lifestyle?" The *Tribune* supported this argument by highlighting a quotation from a Northwestern University sociology professor who summarized the attitude of many members of the armed services with regard to homosexuality by stating, "A lot of them think it's abnormal and perverted."[8]

The *Wall Street Journal* was another of the nation's conservative-leaning journalistic voices that adamantly objected to lifting the ban on the basis that doing so would prevent the armed forces from keeping the country safe. "The military must maintain a sense of trust and mutual reliance in an environment that is often confined and stressful," one *Journal* editorial stated. "Service members live together, shower together, sleep in cramped quarters together, and—in an emergency—share blood with one another. There is no way that such arrangements would not be severely compromised by the presence of homosexuals." In case a reader wasn't clear where the country's largest-circulation daily stood on the question, the *Journal*'s editors made their position crystal clear through the headline that ran above the piece: "Keep the Military's Homosexual Ban."[9]

Fears about openly gay soldiers disrupting military operations were not confined to newspapers, as TV news outlets expressed the same concern. "If you have not lived in a barracks, you really don't know what it is like," CNN political commentator Robert Novak said soon after Clinton was elected. "And the problem is that an increasing number of policy-makers, including the president-elect, have not lived in a barracks."[10]

The other three networks sent the same message by showcasing, as part of their news reports, the comments of enlisted men who said that serving alongside homosexuals would distract them from their duties. *NBC Nightly News* aired a story in which a Navy enlisted man said, "Having a homosexual next to me—that would always be on my mind." *ABC World News Tonight* broadcast a piece in which a Marine said, "We have to take showers together, which means always looking over your shoulder to make sure some strange thing doesn't happen." And a *CBS Evening News* story included an Air Force captain saying, "You might be changing, you might be naked in your room and, for example, if there's a guy in there that's living with you that's homosexual and that's allowed to be in the military—I would be uncomfortable."[11]

Discrimination against Gays is Unacceptable

The most frequently publicized argument in favor of lifting the ban was that the military's refusal to allow homosexuals in its ranks was blatant prejudice, and therefore had to end.

The *New York Times* led the campaign. In the summer of 1992, the paper threw its support behind ending the ban with an editorial headlined "The High Cost of Military Prejudice." Preventing gay men and lesbians from wearing their country's uniform was so outrageous, the *Times* believed, that it prompted the newspaper to break with the journalistic rule against using exclamation points and to begin its editorial with the statement: "What an incredible waste of talent!" The paper went on to attach the label "ludicrous" to the arguments the military's top brass cited as justifications for barring gay people from their ranks. "The policy has destroyed thousands of careers and lives—all for no good reason," the *Times* insisted, before concluding with a hard-hitting final sentence that had been carefully crafted so the most powerful of its words was placed at the very end: "The nation simply can't afford to keep throwing away such talent through mindless prejudice."[12]

Two of journalism's most esteemed columnists—both Pulitzer Prize winners—used their positions of prominence on the *New York Times* commentary page to further the campaign. Anna Quindlen began by asking her readers, "Will we continue to support one of America's largest and best-known institutions as it engages in the rankest form of discrimination?" She then answered that rhetorical question by calling the military's expenditure of $27 million a year to investigate and discharge an average of 1,000 gay soldiers "an absurd waste of time and money," and by lambasting the ban as "codified prejudice." Columnist Anthony Lewis also started with a question: "Are homosexuals to be despised and rejected because of what they are—because of a status that nature gave them?" After stating that gays are a bona fide minority group and sexual orientation a matter of genetics rather than choice, Lewis went on to say, "All the rest of the noise around the issue—the talk about service morale and fighting effectiveness—is demonstrable humbug and bigotry."[13]

Other liberal-leaning news organizations soon joined the *Times* in throwing their editorial weight behind changing the military's policy. The *Los Angeles Times* called the ban an "anachronistic prejudice" that had to end. "Men and women cannot be banned from the military solely because they are homosexuals," the paper wrote. The *Washington Post* published a lift-the-ban commentary piece by Barry Goldwater, the arch-conservative who had been the Republican Party's nominee for president in 1964. "You don't need to be 'straight' to fight and die for your country," wrote Goldwater, who had a gay grandson. "You just need to *shoot* straight." *USA Today* first pointed out that other countries around the world—Israel, Germany, and Canada among them—allowed openly gay soldiers in their armies, and went on to argue that the United States should do the same. "Give each man or woman who wants to serve a chance," the paper asserted. "To do any less is just plain wrong."[14]

In the world of broadcast journalism, the strongest statement opposing discrimination based on sexual orientation came on the *NBC Nightly News*, with John Chancellor devoting a commentary segment to the topic as part of the evening news program. The veteran correspondent began by naming other countries that allowed gays to serve in the military, expanding on *USA Today*'s list by adding Australia, France, Italy, and

Japan. Chancellor then pointed out how dramatically differently gays were treated in this country. "In the United States, homosexuals are hunted down and kicked out of the military." After this introduction, the NBC commentator launched into a direct attack on the government's policy. "You can be punished in this country for what you *do* if you violate the law, but you're not supposed to be punished just for being what you *are*," Chancellor said. "Yet that's the centerpiece of the case against homosexuals in uniform."[15]

Gay People Can be Exemplary Soldiers

When news organizations that opposed lifting the ban discussed the issue, they focused on the potential complications of allowing gay men to serve openly in the military. By contrast, when newspapers and TV news programs that supported lifting the ban went in search of someone to show that gay people could make exemplary soldiers, they found a lesbian.

Margarethe Cammermeyer had enlisted in the U.S. Army as a nurse in the early 1960s and had built a distinguished record as she rose, like few women before her, to the rank of colonel. High points in her career included earning a Bronze Star while serving as a medic during the Vietnam War and being named U.S. Army Nurse of the Year in 1985. Cammermeyer also accomplished a great deal in her personal life, having married and raised four sons while also earning a doctorate in nursing with a specialty in neuro-science.[16]

Her career was unblemished until 1989 when she was asked, during an interview for a top-level security clearance, about her sexuality. Cammermeyer had gradually, over the years, grown aware that she was attracted to other women. The realization had led her to divorce her husband a few years earlier, and it also was the reason she stated, during the interview, "I am a lesbian." In keeping with the policy against homo-sexuals in the military, Army officials discharged her. When the fifty-year-old Cammermeyer was forced to leave the armed forces in May 1992, she and her male commanding officer both wept openly.[17]

During the debate over lifting the ban, liberal-leaning news organiza-tions told Cammermeyer's story, each with a tone of admiration. The *New York Times* described her as "one of the finest health officers in the military," and *USA Today* said her career was "stellar." A profile in the *Los Angeles Times* gushed, "Her 27-year service record is the kind that sets patriotic hearts aflutter," while an editorial in the same paper noted, "In her case, as in so many others, no claim was made that she impaired discipline, morale or conduct of the military's mission."[18]

Cammermeyer's emergence as a model soldier prompted news outlets to examine the lesbian angle of the story, which led to a startling discovery. "Women are three times as likely as men to be booted out under the ban against gays," *USA Today* reported, even though most of the concern and news coverage focused on male soldiers. As to why so many women were discharged, the paper reported that many experts on the subject were convinced that far more lesbians than gay men were serving in the armed forces.[19]

One Promise Forward, Two Realities Backward

Bill Clinton's promise to lift the ban was well intentioned but naïve. The former governor of Arkansas, who had served neither in the armed forces nor in the U.S. Congress, apparently had no idea how vehemently military leaders and Capitol Hill lawmakers opposed allowing gay men and women to wear the uniform of their country. Therefore, the neophyte president's ill-fated proposal backfired. Indeed, Clinton was not only forced to renege on his promise, but the debate over lifting the ban allowed many of the nation's news organizations to communicate some strikingly negative messages about gay people.

Some of those statements weren't surprising. That gay men were obsessed with sex, for example, had been a consistent theme in the news stories about "Perverts on the Potomac," the Stonewall Rebellion, and the AIDS epidemic. Homosexuals being immoral had been an ongoing message as well, although the specific way that accusation had been made changed over time. In 1950 U.S. foreign policy was described as being threatened, in 1969 the safety of the American people was portrayed as being at risk because gays had rioted in the streets, and in the 1980s the nation's health was reported as being in jeopardy because of the "gay plague." Now, in the early 1990s, national security was depicted as being jeopardized by gay soldiers making it impossible for the armed forces to function.

Other messages raised by the gays-in-the-military debate were ones that hadn't surfaced for several decades. When the *Chicago Tribune*, for example, pronounced gay men unfit for military service because they are "much more likely than heterosexual men to incorporate youth into their sexual practices," scholars in search of similar statements about homosexuals preying on young men had to go all the way back to the late 1960s to locate other news stories making such accusations.[20]

At the same time that right-leaning journalistic voices were highlighting these negative messages, their left-leaning counterparts were giving prominent display to two decidedly positive ones. The *New York Times* led the lift-the-ban campaign by repeatedly arguing that preventing gay people from serving in the U.S. military was entirely unacceptable because it was a blatant act of discrimination. The *Times*, in addition, was among the liberal voices that spotlighted Margarethe Cammermeyer as an example of a gay soldier who had served her country in an exemplary manner.

It was also the much-honored nurse who brought into focus the fact that the gays-in-the-military coverage was the most recent example of the media paying far more attention to gay men than gay women. That tendency was particularly dramatic with the debate over lifting the ban, as Cammermeyer was one of the few lesbians to be reported on, even though three times as many women as men had been discharged from the military because of their sexual orientation.

One final observation about the flood of news stories that followed Bill Clinton's ill-fated proposal is that the different stances taken by news organizations reflected the division within the country on the subject of homosexuality. In the midst of the debate, a poll jointly conducted by the *New York Times* and CBS News found that 80 percent of Americans said they believed that "homosexuals should have equal rights to job opportunities." That number dropped dramatically, however, when other questions about the rights of homosexuals were asked. Specifically, only 57 percent of the people responding to the survey supported "the idea of homosexuals in the military," and only 38 percent agreed that "homosexuality is an acceptable alternative life style." These findings prompted the *Times* to acknowledge a reality that it and other liberal journalistic voices did not find easy to accept: "There is still a deeply ingrained American inclination to will homosexuality out of sight and out of mind."[21]

8 Fleeting Images of Lesbians
Killing, Kissing, Being Chic

The two women, both wearing tight miniskirts, are laughing and swaying their bodies in time with the music as they leave the bar's dance floor and sit down close to each other at one of the nearby tables.

"You know, Roseanne, we ought to hang out more often," says the blonde, a wisp of her long hair falling across her soft blue eyes.

"I was thinking that, too," the brunette responds, then smirking and adding playfully, "except, next time, let's leave the *wives* at home."

After hearing those words, the blonde turns flirtatious, now sensing a chemistry with the other woman. "You read my mind," she says, placing her hand behind the brunette's head and pulling firmly to give the woman a passionate kiss.

Although that lip-lock was a mere five seconds long, it generated dozens of articles in the country's most influential newspapers. The *Washington Post* ran eight stories about it, and the *Los Angeles Times* ran eleven. What's more, the "lesbian kiss," as the entire country was soon calling it, succeeded in causing more TV viewers to tune into the ABC sitcom *Roseanne* that week than to any other show.

That prime-time smooch was a symbol of a much larger phenomenon. For it was during the early 1990s that the American lesbian made enough high-profile appearances in a sufficiently wide variety of genres—film, television, and magazines—that she can rightly be described as having finally inched her way out of the media closet.

At the same time, though, it would be misleading to say that the much-ballyhooed kiss between actresses Roseanne Arnold and Mariel Hemingway, or any of the other depictions of gay women that surfaced during this era, was so substantial that it ranked, in and of itself, as a milestone in the evolution of gay people in the media. While the various portrayals, when grouped together, can rightly be interpreted as significant, each and every one of those images was also, in a word, *fleeting*.

The first phase of the phenomenon came in 1992, when *Basic Instinct* was released, with the three Sapphic women in the film being portrayed so negatively that the protests against the movie ultimately garnered almost as much attention as the blockbuster movie itself. A second event occurred in 1994, with the kiss on *Roseanne* sitting at the center of a major controversy over just how far American TV should go in depicting public displays of affection between two women. The third phase of the fleeting-images-of-lesbians phenomenon played out on the printed page, as half a dozen of the country's leading magazines—from *Vogue* to *Newsweek*—documented a cultural trend they dubbed "lesbian chic."

Killing on the Big Screen

Basic Instinct opens with a scene showing a sexually adventurous couple in bed together. She's riding him like he's a bucking bronco, her curvaceous body fully visible but her identity obscured by her long hair falling across her face. To heighten the pleasure, the woman ties her partner's wrists to the headboard with a white silk scarf. Her technique appears to be working, as the man writhes in ecstasy. But then, at the very moment he reaches orgasm, the femme fatale grabs an ice pick and plunges it repeatedly into his neck and chest.[1]

The movie's male lead is the police detective, played by Academy Award winner Michael Douglas, who's assigned to investigate the killing. Number one among his suspects is an heiress worth $100 million, played by Sharon Stone in the role that made her a star, who had been the victim's most frequent sex partner. Another major character in the suspense thriller—the *New York Times* called *Basic Instinct* "the steamiest movie of the year"—is a police psychologist, played by Jeanne Tripplehorn, who's having an affair with the detective. A third woman in the film is the female lover of the heiress, played by Leilani Sarelle, who also becomes a suspect.[2]

As the story unfolds, moviegoers learn that the three women have a great deal in common. First, they're all young and beautiful. Second, they all have sex with women. Third, they're all murderers—one drowned her parents, one killed her male psychology professor, and one used a razor to slash the throats of her two brothers.

The combination of the second and third traits didn't set well with gay and lesbian activists. Women who loved women had been largely absent from the mainstream American media in the past, the detractors argued, so it was a major problem when a trio of them suddenly popped up in a high-profile film, and all three were killers. "What we're saying is," an unhappy lesbian told the *Chicago Tribune*, "if one in a thousand images of a gay woman is of a killer, that's fine. But if *all* the lesbians on the big screen are murderers, we object."[3]

Public protests erupted as soon as the film went into production in mid-1991. "Demonstrations against the portrayal of homosexual women as man-hating murderers started when *Basic Instinct* began filming," *Time* magazine reported. The *Los Angeles Times, Washington Post,* and *New York Times* were soon printing stories about the activists standing close to the movie's set, shouting and blowing whistles so loudly that the sound crew couldn't do its job. The publications continued to follow the development of the news story as, first, TriStar Pictures secured a restraining order to keep the demonstrators away from the set; later, when the protesters violated the order and were arrested; and subsequently, when the convicted activists paid their fines and defiantly repeated the same offenses—restraining orders be damned.[4]

Once the film was released, several news outlets said the protesters were on firm ground in denouncing how *Basic Instinct* depicted women who loved women. The *Boston Globe* began its review by saying, "Lesbian and gay groups are right to protest the way lesbians and bisexual women are portrayed in the movie. It's offensive." *Newsweek* made the same point, writing, "During filming, 'Basic Instinct' was the object of vociferous protest in the gay community for its depiction of homicidal lesbians. They weren't wrong to holler."[5]

Protesters took their hollering to the global stage by disrupting Hollywood's biggest night of the year. Michael Douglas and Sharon Stone were among the stars who had been tapped to present Academy Awards during the glamorous ceremony televised live around the world. One billion viewers watched as dozens of gay and lesbian activists joined the fans lining the red carpet, flashing signs that proclaimed "Basic Instinct Is Lesbi-Phobic!"[6]

Kissing on the Small Screen

By contrast, the protests that propelled the *Roseanne* "lesbian kiss" into the headlines didn't involve trying to stop people from seeing it, but fighting to make sure they did.

In early 1994, *Newsday* reported that ABC had taped a scene featuring a lesbian locking lips with Roseanne, the wife and mother who was the central character in the sitcom, but had now decided not to broadcast it. The Long Island daily quoted a network official as saying that he and his fellow executives had grown concerned that such racy content would violate standards of decency, particularly because the program aired at 9 p.m. when children could be watching. "A woman cannot kiss a woman," he said. "It's bad for the kids to see." The source went on to acknowledge that the decision not to air the scene was driven partly by economics, as sponsors of the sitcom surely would refuse to run ads on such a segment, causing the network to lose $1 million in revenue.[7]

Other papers quickly jumped on the story. The *New York Times* told its readers that "a kiss between two women or two men is taboo on network television." The *Boston Globe* quoted Roseanne Arnold as threatening to move her program—it consistently attracted the third largest audience of the 111 shows on network television—to CBS unless executives at ABC agreed to air the scene. "If they don't show it," she said, "another network will."[8]

Not everyone was in the pro-kiss camp. The *Washington Post* quoted the chairman of the conservative Media Research Center as saying, "If ABC allows this scene to air, it proves that the network cannot stand up to the bullying tactics of homosexual activists." The *Baltimore Sun* speculated the controversy was, in fact, a publicity stunt that ABC was orchestrating to attract a large audience for the segment.[9]

A major development in the story came when *USA Today* reported that ABC had reversed its decision. "That controversial buss between Roseanne Arnold and Mariel Hemingway," the paper stated, "will be seen on network TV after all."[10]

By no means, however, did that revelation end the controversy. The *Orlando Sentinel* reported that *Roseanne* would make TV history because it would be the first time a sitcom segment was ever preceded by an advisory statement warning parents of sexual content not appropriate for children. The *Los Angeles Times* kept on the story, too, suggesting that the network had purposely scheduled the episode during sweeps month (the period that local stations use to determine how much they can charge advertisers, based on audience size, to air a commercial in a particular time slot).[11]

Considering all the hoopla, the episode itself was anti-climactic. The plot began with Roseanne's bisexual co-worker and her girlfriend Sharon inviting Roseanne and her sister to come dancing with them at a gay bar. Roseanne accepts the offer because she wants to prove she's "cool." After all four women dance together for a few minutes, Roseanne and Sharon head for a table to take a break. Roseanne means to be sarcastic when she says the line about next time "let's leave the *wives* at home," but Sharon takes the words seriously—and responds by planting the kiss.

Viewers didn't actually see the women's lips touch, however, as the camera showed Sharon's head from the back and Roseanne's eyes expressing surprise at—and distaste for—what was happening. While the woman was still embracing her, Roseanne was shown trying to "wipe off" the kiss by rubbing her tongue on Sharon's sleeve. The entire scene at the bar lasted barely a minute, with most of the episode focusing on Roseanne working through her feelings of discomfort about homosexuality. The segment's overriding message had little to do with lesbians and much to do with a mother of three coming to grips with the fact that she's not nearly as hip as she'd like to think she is.

Most news outlets that previously had so much to say before the "lesbian kiss" were dead silent after it. The *New York Times, Boston Globe, Washington Post, Orlando Sentinel, USA Today, Newsday*—none of them uttered a single word following the broadcast. One exception was the *Baltimore Sun*, which reported, "There was no genuine controversy here. We need to quit playing with the hype machine every time its wheels start spinning out the siren call of higher ratings." The only other major paper to talk about the kiss after the fact was the *Los Angeles Times*, which admitted what the other papers were too embarrassed to say: Journalists had been duped by ABC. The *Times* went on to acknowledge that the pseudo-controversy surrounding *Roseanne* had accomplished what the network had set out to do. "The episode was the most-watched program for the week, attracting viewers in 19.8 million homes." The paper also reported that ABC had no trouble whatsoever finding companies to advertise during the episode.[12]

Becoming Chic on Magazine Pages

Between 1992 when *Basic Instinct* brought a trio of killers to the big screen, and 1994 when *Roseanne* made headlines by showing a female-to-female kiss—sort of—on the small screen, a cluster of leading magazines also decided the time was right to introduce their readers to women who love women. The specific angles of the articles varied with the publication, but the primary message was the same in all the stories: Lesbians are chic.

Mademoiselle, a magazine that targeted young women in their late teens and early twenties, got the ball rolling in 1993 with a piece titled "Women in Love." A new generation of lesbians were of the "lipstick" variety, the article reported, before going on to define that term as referring to gay women "of feminine appearance." A photo that ran with the story reinforced the point, as it showed two women in their early twenties, their hair long and flowing, as they kissed openly and joyfully while dancing at a tony Manhattan nightclub. Both highly attractive women wore short shorts and midriff-baring tops that showed off their shapely figures.[13]

Vogue picked up on the theme in the July 1993 issue, but made it clear that the preference for femininity wasn't limited to very young lesbians but extended to somewhat older women as well. Indeed, the magazine that's widely recognized as the bible of the fashion world announced that the chic lesbian in her thirties was so adept at dressing stylishly and applying makeup effectively that she'd become "America's newest cover girl." The *Vogue* piece went on to gush about how the whole country was going "gay-girl crazy," and to announce that "After years in the media closet, Lavender Jane has hit the big time."[14]

Later that year, *Cosmopolitan* documented the cultural trend with a first-person article that, like the earlier pieces in *Mademoiselle* and *Vogue*, placed feminine gay women front and center. "My long hair and dresses don't fit the image most people have of lesbians," Catherine Eaton began, "so it usually takes them a while to figure out I'm gay." In standard *Cosmo* style, the tone of the article remained upbeat, with Eaton continuing, "Gay women today are more visible than ever before, and to a large extent are becoming more accepted."[15]

Glamour, in 1994, took that angle a step further by saying that virtually every occupational field now had its share of Sapphic women. A mini-profile of an aerobics instructor described its subject as "a pretty blonde" who'd been the president of her college sorority. "She is so all-American that people have a hard time accepting her as a lesbian," *Glamour* wrote, "even though she's open about being one." None of the woman's co-workers reacted negatively when she told them about her sexuality, the article stated, and, moreover, "She was especially gratified that none of the women working at the health club had a problem sharing a locker room with her—'It was a non-issue,' she says."[16]

New York extended the new-found interest in chic lesbians to city magazines by devoting a cover story to the topic in 1993. "It's Friday night at an upscale lesbian bar on Hudson Street," the article stated. "Moving quickly through the room is Lisa Graziano, a corporate manager. She is a gorgeous brunette with a movie-star face and a soft page-boy cut." Other customers at the bar who caught the magazine writer's eye included "a sexy young woman in her early twenties. She has thick, dark, curly hair flowing into her eyes and down her back; she wears a skintight top over tight jeans. She is talking to her pretty blond lover, also in tight jeans."[17]

Newsweek pushed chic lesbians to a still higher level of visibility when it placed an image of two highly attractive twenty-something women—smiling and embracing—on its cover in June 1993, above a headline that read: "Lesbians Coming Out Strong." The magazine concentrated on reporting facts, dubbing the city of Northampton, Massachusetts, "Lesbianville, U.S.A." and stating that fully one third of the 30,000 residents were women who love women. Despite its focus on facts, the newsweekly ultimately joined the other magazines in telling its readers what 1990s lesbians looked like. The gay woman most frequently quoted in the story was Diane Morgan, who was described as "wearing her hair in a blond bob and using lipstick." Morgan's photo showed a sweet-faced young woman wearing a bracelet, several small rings, and delicate teardrop earrings.[18]

The Media-Defined Lesbian

As images of gay women exploded onto the media landscape in the early 1990s, several characteristics emerged to define the members of this subgroup of society.

The women were, first and foremost, beautiful by the classic Hollywood standard. All three actresses who appeared in major roles in *Basic Instinct* were stunning; former model Sharon Stone was particularly glamorous, but Jeanne Tripplehorn and Leilani Sarelle could also hold their own in a beauty pageant. Mariel Hemingway on the *Roseanne* episode was highly attractive as well; when the character revealed that she earned her livelihood as a stripper, no one questioned that men would pay to see her take it all off. The women in the photos accompanying the magazine stories also were consistently young and dazzling; the *Glamour* piece was illustrated by an image of Kate Haffner, a Silicon Valley sales rep whose gold earrings and perfect makeup enhanced her natural beauty. None of the women featured in any of the genres was in the least bit masculine, nor was a single one of them overweight. Likewise, none of the women had severely short-cropped hair, and none of them wore flannel shirts or work boots. In the words of *New York* magazine, "Women who love women are beautiful and sexy and impossibly stylish."[19]

Most of the media-defined lesbians also were found to be fluid in their sexuality. Although the women often were described as *lesbians*, a close examination reveals that most of them were, in fact, bisexuals. This particular characteristic was most prominent in the magazine articles. *Mademoiselle* reported that, "One of the hottest issues among lesbians of any age is bisexuality," supporting that statement with a quote from a Duke University professor who said that many female students fully expected their sexuality to "change more than once in their lifetime—sexuality is fluid."[20]

Finally, the women were portrayed as highly sexual. *Cosmo* had much to say on this topic. "Oral sex and mutual masturbation are popular among lesbians, and we like sex toys," Catherine Eaton wrote in her first-person piece. "Things like that seem less kinky after breaking the taboo of same-sex love." Eaton portrayed woman-on-woman sex as having other advantages, too. "Hetero sex all too often concludes after the man is satisfied," she wrote, "but lesbian sex focuses on the female orgasm and frequently lasts for hours."[21]

"We Love Lesbians!"—Or Do We?

In the early 1990s, gay women finally emerged from invisibility as numerous images of lesbians moved onto the media stage. In a major film and the protests it triggered, with considerable brouhaha about one of the most popular TV shows of the era, and through a stream of flattering articles in mass-circulation magazines—gay women seemed to be everywhere.

A *Washington Post* article titled "We Love Lesbians!" succeeded in capturing the moment. "America," the piece began, "come say hello to lesbians—they're hot! they're sexy! Many gay women, who have long watched their lives minimized and distorted, can hardly contain themselves over the newfound attention."[22]

Before the Sapphic sisters uncorked the champagne bottles to celebrate the breakthrough, however, they might have considered several observations relevant to the phenomenon.

First, the images were fleeting. This point is best made by the *Roseanne* episode. The prime-time kiss lasted only five seconds and, while dozens of articles appeared in the country's leading newspapers in anticipation of the big moment, the coverage abruptly ended as soon as Roseanne Arnold wiped her tongue across Mariel Hemingway's sleeve. Indeed, the much-hyped lip lock ultimately left a sour taste in the nation's collective journalistic mouth, as the papers realized they'd been snookered by ABC, falling victim to what eventually was seen as a highly successful publicity stunt. The "lesbian chic" articles reinforced the point. Although the six stories portrayed gay women in rose-colored hues, they didn't lead to ongoing coverage of women who love women. As *Vogue* magazine would later observe: "lesbians were the hula hoops of the 1990s," meaning they were written about as a short-lived novelty. Of the three sets of images of gay women, then, the only one with a lengthy shelf life was the decidedly negative one in *Basic Instinct*. The film was not only a huge hit in movie theaters but enjoyed another surge of popularity when it was released on video, telling millions of additional viewers that women who sleep with women are psychopathic killers.[23]

Second, the various depictions of lesbians were driven by economics, not a desire "to do the right thing." Media organizations are businesses, and The Powers That Be—at TriStar Pictures, at ABC television, and in the offices of the magazine publishers—glorified gay women in the early 1990s not because of an altruistic desire to serve a stigmatized minority group but because they hoped that showing gay women would be so unusual and titillating that it would pay off financially. They were right. The *Roseanne* episode drew a huge audience, and the magazines showed their readers they were in tune with a hip cultural trend. Still stronger evidence that money played a major role came from the motion picture industry's contribution to the fleeting-images-of-lesbians phenomenon. Even though the star vehicle for Sharon Stone and Michael Douglas released in 1992 included shockingly negative portrayals of gay—or bisexual—women, it was enormously profitable. *Basic Instinct* cost less than $50 million to make but grossed revenues of a stunning $353 million—the highest of any film that year. The message: If moviegoers will pay to see homicidal lesbians, Hollywood will give them homicidal lesbians.[24]

Third, the number of gay women prominently portrayed in the media between 1992 and 1994 could rightly be called an explosion, but the depictions were, in fact, limited to an extremely narrow range of women.

Yes, some gay women are beauty queens as lovely as Mariel Hemingway on *Roseanne*, and some wear gold earrings and perfectly applied makeup, as did the Silicon Valley sales rep whose photo accompanied the *Glamour* piece. But other women who love women are neither beautiful nor stylish in these conventionally feminine ways. Some have masculine mannerisms and full figures, cut their hair short and wear flannel shirts—proudly and unapologetically. Because of how the media defined lesbians when they momentarily stepped into the limelight, however, these citizens of Lesbian America were kept locked tightly inside the closet.

Fourth, looking at the particular type of gay women who were showcased and how they were presented, it seems the decision-makers behind the various media products may have been providing the lesbian content, at least partially, for the pleasure of a carefully targeted consumer audience: straight men. By the early 1990s, pornographic magazines and films were fulfilling male fantasies by featuring images of two or more beautiful women engaging in sex acts with each other. Such girl-on-girl scenes had become a staple of the porn industry, as they succeeded in sexually arousing many male viewers. *Basic Instinct* definitely contains scenes that feel as if they're from a XXX video, such as when Sharon Stone and Leilani Sarelle fondle each other and kiss each other passionately—while a mesmerized Michael Douglas watches them.[25]

With regard to the specific role that the fleeting-images-of-lesbians phenomenon played in how the media's depiction of gay people has changed over time, the only earlier content it can be compared to is the small number of references to gay women that appeared as part of the news coverage of the Stonewall Rebellion.

One message about lesbians that emerged from those stories and re-surfaced twenty-five years later was that some lesbians hate men. In 1969, a mini-profile in the *San Francisco Chronicle* had described its subject as saying "she hates men," before going on to report that "she played idly with a switchblade knife, expertly flicking it open and closed." This sort of profile sounds similar to the depiction of the women in *Basic Instinct*, with the Sharon Stone character ultimately being revealed as the woman who had plunged an ice pick into her male lover. At the same time, though, it should be noted that the lesbians-hate-men statement was limited to that single film, as it was not part of the characterization of lesbians in either the *Roseanne* episode or in the magazine articles of the early nineties.[26]

The controversial film also was the only one of the early-1990s media products that repeated another of the messages that had first emerged in the spate of articles from 1969: Lesbians are promiscuous. *Time* magazine was among the publications that had told readers, as part of the Stonewall coverage, that female homosexuals were as obsessed with sex as their male counterparts. *Basic Instinct* sent the same message, with Sharon

Stone's on-screen persona being portrayed as having had sex with at least dozens—if not hundreds—of different partners.[27]

Other messages that the Stonewall coverage had communicated about lesbians had disappeared entirely by the time Sapphic women reappeared a quarter century later. *Time* had described the typical gay woman as "the 'butch,' the girl who is aggressively masculine to the point of trying to look like a man," but not a single woman even remotely consistent with that profile was found among the decidedly feminine lesbians who walked across the media stage in the final decade of the twentieth century.[28]

Perhaps the strongest indication of how radically the media's depiction of lesbians had changed was the fact that the various products found it perfectly acceptable—without so much as raising an eyebrow—that many 1990s women were sexually attracted to other women. In the wake of Stonewall, the *New York Times* was among the publications that had pronounced lesbianism "a severe illness" that often leads to other problems: "the incidence of suicide and alcoholism is high among lesbians." Twenty-five years later when the *Washington Post* published a story headlined "We Love Lesbians!" and *Vogue* announced that the whole country had gone "gay-girl crazy," never once did any of the media products give the slightest indication that the word *lesbian* belonged in the same sentence with the word *illness*.[29]

9 *Philadelphia*
"A Quantum Leap for Gays on Film"

The flood of news stories about the protests against *Basic Instinct* included several articles focused not exclusively on that film, but interested more generally in reporting on two broader failures of the motion picture industry: "It is difficult to point to a Hollywood gay character who could be called a hero," the *Boston Globe* grumbled.[1] "None of the major film studios has made a film addressing the AIDS epidemic," the *Los Angeles Times* complained.[2] Those two criticisms were fully justified when the newspapers made them in 1992, but neither was valid a year later.

Philadelphia was not only the first big-budget Hollywood film to depict a gay man in a manifestly positive light and the first to deal with acquired immune deficiency syndrome, but it also broke ground in several other significant ways. Specifically, the highly successful drama—it cost $26 million to make and grossed more than $200 million—showed moviegoers a gay male relationship that remains strong despite major challenges, a family who loves their gay son and brother unconditionally, and a community of gay men who fully support one of their own during difficult times.[3]

For all these reasons, *USA Today* seemed to have it right when the paper crafted a headline that read: "Philadelphia, A Quantum Leap for Gays on Film."[4]

A David and Goliath Story

The movie focuses on a character *Time* magazine called a "quietly gay" attorney who's on the fast track at a prestigious Philadelphia firm until he's summarily fired when the managing partners learn that he's homosexual and has AIDS. Andy Beckett then sues the firm for wrongful termination and, after nine blue-chip attorneys in the City of Brotherly Love refuse to take the case, hires a small-time lawyer named Joe Miller to represent him. As the trial unfolds, Miller confronts both his own homophobia and that of the larger world, while his client struggles to stay alive long enough to hear the jury deliver its verdict.[5]

Much of the credit for the film's success belongs to the enormously popular actor Tom Hanks, who played the leading role so well—*People* magazine called his performance "flat-out terrific"—that he received the Academy Award for best actor. Denzel Washington added more star power to the cast as the lawyer who took the case—*Newsweek* dubbed Washington's performance "superb." Bruce Springsteen's mournful "The Streets of Philadelphia" also captured the essence of the film musically, receiving the Oscar for best song.[6]

Openly gay screenwriter Ron Nyswaner based his script on news stories about a Philadelphia attorney who told his superiors about his illness and was fired two weeks later. Like the Hanks character, that real-life AIDS patient ultimately sued his employers and won. *Premiere* magazine quoted the screenwriter as saying that he was determined to dramatize the case on the big screen because "It was a David and Goliath story that had to be told."[7]

Educating about AIDS

At the same time that *Philadelphia* chronicled a shameful act of discrimination against an ailing man, it also provided viewers with factual information about an illness that, by December 1993 when the film was released, had claimed the lives of 20,000 Americans. "The film ultimately becomes," *Time* magazine observed, "a documentary on the ravages of AIDS."[8]

One lesson viewers learn is that the disease has a devastating impact on a victim's physical being. In early scenes, the Tom Hanks character is a healthy and robust thirty-something lawyer with boundless energy. As the movie progresses, however, his body provides a dramatic visual depiction of the horrifying realities of AIDS, with one reviewer describing him as becoming, by late in the film, "a gray, weak, shrunken figure—yellow from liver failure, bald, blind in one eye and barely able to speak." Hanks lost thirty pounds and had his hair thinned dramatically during the six months of filming, and makeup artists painstakingly simulated his skin turning deathly pale while his face and chest became disfigured with unsightly lesions.[9]

The film communicates public health lessons about the illness as well. When the Denzel Washington character shakes hands with Andy Beckett for the first time, he's so frightened about having touched a person with AIDS that he races to his doctor's office. By the end of the next scene, the physician has communicated to his patient—as well as to millions of moviegoers—exactly how a person can become infected. "The HIV virus can only be transmitted," the doctor states, "through

Figure 9.1 Tom Hanks received an Academy Award for his performance as a heroic gay man with AIDS in the 1993 film *Philadelphia.*
Courtesy of TriStar Pictures/Photofest.

the exchange of bodily fluids—namely blood, semen, and vaginal secretions." This important message is reinforced when the Hanks character's parents and siblings don't hesitate to kiss him and when he cradles an infant niece in his arms, thereby helping to dispel the myth that the virus can be spread by casual contact.

Introducing a Gay Hero

Many of the moviegoers who trooped into theaters to see *Philadelphia* logically compared Andy Beckett to the characters in *The Boys in the Band*, the most prominent gay men the motion picture industry had previously offered them.

It didn't take long to see that the affable man who came to life on the big screen in 1993 was a far cry from the self-loathing drunks who had defined male homosexuality some twenty years earlier. "Andy is a wonderful fellow: chipper, supremely competent, lavishing genial respect on colleagues high and low," *Time* magazine observed. "He is young, good-looking, funny, smart, and is played with great emotional resonance by Tom Hanks, perhaps the most appealing actor working in movies today," the *Wall Street Journal* added. The summary of the character that appeared in the *Washington Post* was more succinct than the others but no less laudatory, with the paper calling Beckett "a noble gay hero."[10]

The most courageous deed that Andy Beckett performs in the film is taking his powerful law firm to court for having done something that an institution dedicated to upholding justice doesn't want to be found guilty of: being unfair to a dying man. Adding to the nobility of the character's undertaking is the fact that the only guy he can find to represent him is a personal-injury lawyer who's so desperate for clients that he sticks his business card into the hands of people on the street who are walking on crutches or have an arm in a cast. Not only does Beckett overcome the odds and win his case, but he wins very, very big—the jury awards him $5 million.

Jonathan Demme, who directed *Philadelphia*, decided to portray the main character as a hero after talking with a friend named Juan Botas, who was gay and infected with HIV. "I hadn't paid much attention to the absence of positive gay characters in movies or to the stereotypical ideas that are usually presented when they *do* appear," the Academy Award winner told *Premiere* magazine. Demme continued:

> Juan helped me understand by asking me to imagine I was twelve years old and gay, and that every time I saw someone like myself on the screen it was either as a pathetic misfit—Michael in *The Boys in the Band* comes to mind—or as the mincing, stereotypical butt of a certain type of limp-wristed humor.[11]

Showcasing a Committed Gay Relationship

Andy Beckett is not the only stereotype-shattering gay man in the film, as his long-time partner also is portrayed as having many admirable traits.

Andy and Miguel Alvarez, played by Antonio Banderas, have been in a relationship for nine years. Andy's illness severely tests the depth of Miguel's character as well as his commitment to the relationship. Many spouses, whether gay or straight, would have fled upon discovering that a partner was suffering from AIDS, but Miguel did not. Indeed, *Philadelphia* shows the handsome man, an artist and teacher by vocation, devoting huge quantities of time and energy to caring for his partner, and making sure Andy gets the treatment he needs.

Miguel's unswerving loyalty is particularly commendable in light of the fact that Andy contracted the virus during a clandestine sexual encounter at a gay porn theater. In addition, Andy continued to have sex with his partner even after the unsafe sexual liaison, thereby endangering Miguel's life. These circumstances would have destroyed many relationships—indeed, the vast majority of marriages—but the film depicts the wronged partner as remaining stalwartly loyal even as the illness gradually overwhelms the lives of both men. When Andy Beckett collapses in the courtroom near the end of the trial, Miguel Alvarez leaps over the railing and comes to the aid of his increasingly frail lover.

Reviews of the movie made special mention of how convincingly Tom Hanks and Antonio Banderas, who are both straight, portrayed one of the most memorable gay relationships in the history of motion pictures. *Premiere* wrote, "The intimate scenes between Hanks and Banderas—at one point Banderas kisses his lover's hand, slowly, seriously, one finger at a time—are notable, even among depictions of heterosexual love, for the absolute nakedness of the affection."[12]

Portraying a Loving Family

Also notable, according to many reviews, was that the members of Andy Beckett's family, without exception, showered him with unconditional love and encouragement. *Glamour* magazine called this aspect of the movie "heartwarming."[13]

That Andy's parents and siblings had a strong and unremittingly positive presence in *Philadelphia* was especially striking to theatergoers who were familiar with *The Boys in the Band*. In the 1970 film, no relatives were shown on screen, but some of the men made it clear that they blamed their parents for causing their homosexuality. *Philadelphia* communicated very different messages about the central character's family.

The scene that provides the most vivid statements regarding the family's unwavering love for Andy unfolds when, before launching what he knows will be a highly public legal case, he sits down with his relatives to get their approval for what he's about to do. "There are going to be things said at the trial," he begins, Miguel sitting at his side, "that are going to be hard for you to hear about me and my personal life. So I want to make sure it's okay with everybody." The younger brother speaks first, saying, "I think it's great that you're asking, Andy, but this is really your call."[14]

Next come the parents. "I didn't raise my kids to sit in the back of the bus," Sarah Beckett states firmly. "You get in there and you fight for your rights." The words that flow from Andy's father may be the most loving of all, as Bud Beckett is a short, bald, overweight man who looks like a guy who's spent many a night at the corner bar drinking beer and trading "fag jokes" with his working-class buddies. But his statement to his son couldn't have been more caring. "Andy, the way that you've handled this whole thing—you and Miguel, with so much courage— there's nothing anyone could say that could make us feel anything but incredibly proud of you."[15]

The few gay men and lesbians who didn't shed tears during that scene surely did so later in the film when the family members line up beside the hospital bed to say what ultimately will be their final farewells to a pitifully weak and frail Andy Beckett before he dies later that night. His older brother says, "God bless you, Andy," followed by his sister's, "See you first thing tomorrow." The younger brother is the next to stand by the bed, but he isn't able to speak, as he's too choked up to utter a single word. Then comes the father, managing a smile and the heart-breaking words, "Good night, son. I love you, Andy." And finally the moving words of a loving mother: "Good night, my angel—my sweet boy."[16]

Depicting a Community of Support

Those moviegoers who remembered *The Boys in the Band* recalled the mean-spirited game and non-stop barrage of insults that dominated the film, as one of the messages communicated by that cinematic window into homosexual life was that "friendships" were, in this community, defined by cruelty and vindictiveness. *Philadelphia*, by contrast, showed Andy Beckett's gay friends to be highly supportive of him.

Early in the film, several friends voluntarily come to the ailing man's apartment and do whatever is needed so he can work from home rather than risk having the homophobic law partners spot the lesions that have begun to appear on his face. One guy spends his days as Andy's secretary, a second makes periodic runs to the drugstore, and a third struggles to find the right makeup combination to make the sick man look healthy. These characters prompted *Vogue* magazine, in its review, to comment that "*Philadelphia* is full of new family values. It features gay characters who genuinely care for one another."[17]

Other memorable statements vis-à-vis a supportive gay community come later in the film when, as the trial nears its end, several dozen men join a smaller number of women who dress up in costumes to attend a party that Andy decides is needed to bolster Miguel's sagging spirits. Mona Lisa, Mahatma Gandhi, a can of Campbell's soup, Adam and Eve dressed only in fig leaves, a Catholic bishop in sequined sunglasses— friends respond to Andy's call and fashion exactly the kind of festive event he asked them to create. *New York* magazine's review was particularly complimentary of the scene. "The joyous bash," it observed, "is the first unashamed, uninhibited, and truly entertaining gay party I can think of in a major studio release."[18]

Shining the Spotlight on Homophobia

The most restrained costume at the party is the one worn by Denzel Washington, whose character comes grudgingly to his first gay social event, keeping his wife close to his side throughout the evening. So the homophobic lawyer makes only minimal concessions to Andy Beckett's call to play dress up, merely stapling a few sheets of office letterhead to his jacket so he becomes "a lawsuit."[19]

The Joe Miller character is critical to *Philadelphia*'s success, as millions of straight Americans can identify with him. In other words, Miller wouldn't go out and physically assault a gay man, but he's not ready to share a locker room with one either. As the *Los Angeles Times* put it, "Miller is intended as a kind of mass audience surrogate, someone who shares the fears and prejudices not always admitted in polite society." In one early scene, he tells his wife point-blank, "I don't like homosexuals," and later when he's in a bar with some male friends and the subject of gay men comes up, Miller says, "Those people make me sick."[20]

The African-American attorney initially refuses to represent Andy Beckett, not wanting to be associated with a highly publicized trial involving homosexuality and AIDS. But when Miller accidentally observes how patrons in a public library shun Beckett because they see the telltale lesions, he recognizes the similarities between discrimination based on race and discrimination based on sexual orientation. He then takes the case.

Miller brings his Straight Everyman perspective into the courtroom. Midway through the trial, the attorney abruptly asks a witness, "Are you a homosexual?" Everyone is stunned by the question, but Miller has no intention of stopping. "Answer the question," he demands, his voice growing louder and his demeanor more agitated. "Are you a *homo*? Are you a *faggot*? You know, a punk? A queen? A fairy, booty snatcher, rough rider?" Now screaming, Miller asks emphatically, "*Are you gay?*"

With the courtroom in chaos, the judge tries to calm the situation by calling Miller to the bench and insisting that he explain his outburst. The attorney responds by delivering a monologue that gives the film one of its most dramatic moments. Miller begins:

> Everybody in this courtroom is thinking about sexual orientation—you know, sexual preference, whatever you want to call it. They're thinking, 'Who does what to whom and how do they do it?' They're looking at Andrew Beckett and they're thinking about it.
>
> So let's get it out in the open, because this case is not *just* about AIDS, is it? So let's talk about what this case is really all about.

Miller then shifts to the first person, subtly acknowledging that he includes himself in the group of people he's describing. "It's about the general public's *hatred*, our *loathing*, our *fear* of homosexuals—and how that climate of hatred and fear translated into the firing of this particular homosexual."

When Miller finishes, the judge says, "In this courtroom, Mr. Miller, justice is blind to matters of race, creed, color, religion, *and* sexual orientation."

Miller then responds, "With all due respect, your honor, we don't live in this courtroom, though, do we?"

So as the trial and the movie continue, viewers not only watch Andy Beckett fight against the high-powered partners at his former law firm, they also see Joe Miller face his own—and much of America's—fear of homosexuality.

Denzel Washington told a writer for *Esquire* magazine that his character becomes, by the end of the film, somewhat more comfortable with gay people but has, by no means, been transformed. "Joe Miller's not going to be the grand marshal of any Gay Pride parade," the actor said. "We didn't want a rah-rah, everything-is-wonderful ending to the film because that's not the way it is in this country today. Many people are still very ill at ease with homosexuality."[21]

Setting a High Cinematic Standard

Numerous publications that reviewed *Philadelphia* praised the film's messages both about gay men and about AIDS. *Newsweek* wrote, "The film will open more than a few blinkered hearts," and *The New Yorker* told its readers, "*Philadelphia* will get to you, and stay there."[22]

One of the primary reasons that *Philadelphia* was such a major success—both in attracting a huge audience and in educating the public about gay men and a fatal disease—is the actor who played the main character. Tom Hanks is a major Hollywood star who appeals to moviegoers of all ages. Casting a man of Hanks's stature and popularity as a heroic gay man dying of AIDS had enormous impact. After spending two hours with Tom Hanks in the role of Andy Beckett, an untold number of moviegoers became much more comfortable the next time they saw someone who looked like he might be gay or might have AIDS.

Significant as well was the depiction of the committed relationship between Andy Beckett and Miguel Alvarez. Never before had the moviegoing public been exposed to two men who were involved in a long-term relationship of such depth. Although it could be argued that Andy's act of infidelity in the porn theater raised questions about his commitment to his partner, the fact that the couple survived that challenge as well as the devastating repercussions of a deadly disease showed that their devotion to each other was profound.

Other relationships that were illuminated in the film also provide models to which audience members could aspire. The way in which members of Andy Beckett's family stood shoulder to shoulder with him throughout both his illness and his David-versus-Goliath legal battle, and the support shown by members of the gay community for their ailing friend, were unprecedented in the history of gay people being depicted in the American media of any genre.

Philadelphia also deserves praise for its realistic and dramatic portrayal of homophobia. Denzel Washington's character in the film's early scenes offered an accurate view of the discomfort that a huge percentage of Americans felt toward homosexuality in the early 1990s, and the point he reached by the end of the movie showed viewers that it also might be possible for them to advance to a place where they, too, could treat gay people as human beings who deserved equal rights.

Yet another praiseworthy aspect of the film is what it says about the composition of Gay America. The movie doesn't include any specific references to the racial background of Antonio Banderas's on-screen persona, but moviegoers can clearly see that the handsome actor playing Miguel Alvarez is Latino. And so the movie subtly sends the message that the gay community is racially diverse.

With regard to points on which the movie is vulnerable to criticism, one major concern is the limited amount of physical contact between the Hanks and Banderas characters. Andy Beckett and Miguel Alvarez are long-time lovers, and yet they're never shown kissing on the lips. During one interview, Banderas reported that a scene with the two men in bed together had been filmed but was cut from the final version of the movie, which was rated PG-13. "We were just lying in bed talking and laughing," Banderas said. "It was so innocent that it's ridiculous to think that somebody would have been upset by it." The decision-makers at TriStar Pictures obviously disagreed and, like the ABC executives who had determined the content of *Soap*, were fearful that many viewers would be offended by images of two men having physical contact with each other.[23]

Another aspect of the film that can be considered a shortcoming is the absence of lesbian characters. When the various members of the Beckett family and the partygoers who dressed in creative costumes are all added together, they create a long list of gay men, straight men, and straight women who appeared on screen for varying lengths of time. Nowhere to be seen, however, is even one unambiguously gay woman.

Because the positive messages about gay people that *Philadelphia* sends so clearly outweigh the criticisms, the headline in *USA Today* hit the nail on the head when it praised the movie as "A Quantum Leap for Gays on Film." Indeed, the double Oscar winner marked a turning point in the evolution of the depiction of gay people in the media. For it was with the high-profile film's release in 1993 that a historian tracking the portrayals of gay people could, for the first time, point to a major media product and say that the messages being sent were overwhelmingly positive ones.

This observation begs the question: Why was such an important threshold crossed at this particular moment?

TriStar Pictures's decision to create a major motion picture about a gay man with AIDS, director Jonathan Demme's commitment to portraying the main character as a hero, and actor Tom Hanks's success at making Andy Beckett come across in a positive light were significant factors, earning them labels as "gay rights activists" in the same way that Billy Crystal deserves that label for his role in *Soap* during the late 1970s.

But perhaps another factor had even more influence.

Time may have been the first news organization to mention this particular dynamic when, in an article titled "Out of the Celluloid Closet" published in early 1992, the magazine quoted one Hollywood director as saying, "The business doesn't care what you do in bed, but it does care what you do at the box office." In other words, the bottom line in the world of motion pictures—as well as in other media genres—is, indeed, *the bottom line.*[24]

Various publications were soon expanding on the point by reporting that gay Americans were a newly discovered niche market of considerable interest to media decision-makers.

"It's the market of the decade," the *Chicago Sun-Times* announced in an article titled "Gay Households," that ran in the paper's financial section. "Many gay households have double incomes and no kids," the paper went on to say, "which dramatically increases their disposable income." Because of recent data produced by market researchers, the *Sun-Times* continued, "America's gay population is now in the limelight among an increasing number of forward-thinking businesses that want to appeal to well-heeled consumers."[25]

The *Cleveland Plain Dealer* then went the next step. After acknowledging that many same-sex couples have large disposable incomes and then saying that the nation's gay population could be as large as 18.5 million people, the paper estimated the total amount of money that Gay America was spending annually. In a sentence that was short in length but enormous in content, the *Plain Dealer* reported: "That buying power could approach $500 billion."[26]

Executives at TriStar Pictures who were in charge of deciding what movie proposals got the green light to move into production have never acknowledged that those news stories influenced their decision to make *Philadelphia*. There's no question, however, that by 1993 when the film was released, The Powers That Be both in Hollywood and in the media world writ large were beginning to realize that the combination of gay Americans with large disposable incomes plus straight people who were increasingly supportive of this particular minority group, added up to a potential audience of media consumers that was too large and had too much spending power to ignore.

10 A New Gay Man in Town
Hollywood Shifts to Positive Stereotypes

As the wedding rehearsal begins, the groom is none too pleased that an intruder has arrived. George hadn't even been invited to the formal ceremony, and yet suddenly this tall, dark, and handsome hunk has become the center of attention at this event that was supposed to be limited to a handful of family and friends. And if that isn't bad enough, now the groom's very own mother is asking George to join them for the luncheon that's scheduled to follow.

"Love to!" the guy chirps, ignoring the groom's irritated glare. George then turns on his million-watt smile, quickly checks out the mother's outfit, and adds cheerily, "Love the bag! Love the shoes! Love everything!"

Now that Mom is blushing like a schoolgirl, the groom is thinking to himself, "My God! If this guy keeps schmoozing, my mother's going to *adopt* him!"

No new members are added to the family during lunch, but George definitely wins over the entire wedding party, along with every other man, woman, and child in the restaurant. He manages to get everybody in the place, customers and staff alike, to join him in a rousing sing-a-long of the infectiously upbeat—at least when he's leading the chorus— Dionne Warwick classic "I Say a Little Prayer for You."

Hello, George—charming, fun-loving, personable, good-looking, successful, and endowed with impeccable taste and unlimited charisma.

The groom wasn't alone in being taken aback by how smoothly this new man in town had moved onto the scene in the second half of the 1990s, not only in the form of the scene-stealing gay character in the box-office hit *My Best Friend's Wedding* but all across the Hollywood landscape as a whole gaggle of gay men found their way into three popular and financially successful films.

Academy Award winner Robin Williams and gay Broadway veteran Nathan Lane started the trend in 1996 with their laugh-out-loud performances in *The Birdcage*. Kevin Kline, another Academy Award winner, and drop-dead-gorgeous Tom Selleck kept up the momentum a year later with the warm-hearted comedy *In & Out*. And finally came Rupert

Everett, the openly gay British import who stole all those scenes in 1997's *My Best Friend's Wedding*.[1]

No matter which actor was filling the role or which title was pulling fans into the theater, there was no question that the big-screen depiction of gay men had shifted dramatically from back in the day—1970, to be precise—when *The Boys in the Band* had told the media-consuming public: "Show me a happy homosexual, and I'll show you a gay corpse."

For a whole new set of unequivocally positive stereotypes had replaced the negative ones that had defined homosexuals three decades earlier. The members of this parade of gay manhood were such utterly genial and personable fellows that absolutely everyone (except that one disgruntled groom!) loved them. In addition, the men were physically attractive—either a dreamy matinee idol like Rupert Everett or a cuddly teddy bear *à la* Nathan Lane. They also shared an abundance of good taste, reflected both in how they dressed and how they decorated their homes. What's more, they were blessed with so much talent and energy that they—to a man—succeeded in their chosen occupations. And, finally, the members of this new fraternity of gay men left the sexually promiscuous ways of their predecessors behind them, as they all were either chaste or faithful to their partners.

Pulling Moviegoers into the Theater

Perhaps the fastest route to seeing how dramatically these gay men and their accompanying traits had veered from their predecessors is to consider how both the plots and the tones of the three films contrast with those of either the bitterly unpleasant *The Boys in the Band* or the heart-wrenchingly sad *Philadelphia*.

The Birdcage, from MGM Studios, became an instant classic by telling the story of a flamboyant gay couple whose pastel tranquility in the South Beach section of Miami is transformed into a comedic *tour de force* when the pair's son arrives home and announces that he's engaged to marry the daughter of an ultra-conservative member of the U.S. Senate—who's coming for dinner the next night.[2]

In & Out, from Paramount Studios, is a high-spirited comedy about a dapper Midwestern high school teacher who realizes, three days before his wedding, that maybe his fondness for bowties and Barbra Streisand add up to a different sexual orientation—surprise, surprise!—than that of all the overall-wearing, country-music-loving men in town.[3]

My Best Friend's Wedding, from TriStar Pictures, features one of the motion picture industry's first openly gay heartthrobs in a fast-paced romantic comedy about a commitment-shy woman who tries to sabotage the impending marriage of the man she loves rather than tell him directly, despite the urgings of her gay best friend, how she feels about him.[4]

The combination of laugh-filled plotlines and big-name stars caused huge numbers of moviegoers to troop off to their neighborhood multiplexes to see the three films and their line-up of highly appealing gay characters. And after the audiences sat down in their seats, they loved the *très gay* men they saw on the screen, with the *Washington Post* noting: "Mainstream audiences embraced the gay characters in 'The Birdcage,' 'In & Out' and 'My Best Friend's Wedding' with gusto." When the box-office receipts—not including the rental fees and purchase prices for the DVD versions—for the three blockbusters are added together, the total surpasses $555 million.[5]

Gay Men Are Charming

The Nathan Lane character in *The Birdcage* sets a high standard in the charm category, as he's relentlessly lovable as both a man and a woman. In one early scene, Albert is shown gliding among various shopkeepers to order items for that evening's dinner. Although he's clearly at a much higher socio-economic level than the vendors, he greets each one by name and with a compliment—"Oh, what beautiful flowers," "These chocolates—a triumph!" He cranks up the charm to an even higher level when he puts on a pink suit and pearls to become "the hostess with the mostest" to win over the senator. The homophobic politician, played to buffoonish perfection by Oscar winner Gene Hackman, is totally smitten by the Barbara Bush look-alike, smiling broadly as he announces, "This woman is a real lady, and I just love her." It's understandable why *Time* magazine said of the Nathan Lane character, "He is wildly endearing."[6]

Kevin Kline's on-screen persona in *In & Out* is called upon to dig into the reserve of goodwill he's built up over the years in Greenleaf, Indiana. In the film, after Kline's character leaves his fiancée stranded at the altar and at the same moment publicly identifies himself as a gay man, he faces the challenge of convincing his family and friends that he's not a jerk. No problem. "This town is crazy about you," the newsman played by Tom Selleck tells him. "I've interviewed everybody who lives here, and they all love you." Publications that reviewed the feel-good film spoke of the teacher's genial nature as well, with *People* magazine praising his "abundance of charm."[7]

The Rupert Everett character in *My Best Friend's Wedding* is so affable in the scenes at the wedding rehearsal and luncheon that the film's producer decided to expand his role in the flick. That decision came after a preview audience was shown an early version of the romantic comedy. "You could hear the people react to him," producer Jerry Zucker later said. "He got laughs, and he got cheers. We knew the audience would love Julia Roberts and Cameron Diaz, but it was a pleasant surprise to see how much they liked Rupert, too." Increasing the amount of time the gay character appeared on screen clearly paid off, as some reviewers praised the gay actor as the highlight of the film; *Newsweek* gushed, "*My Best Friend's Wedding* is at its funniest when Everett arrives on the scene."[8]

Gay Men Are Physically Attractive

Many of the publications that cheered the Rupert Everett character's personable ways praised the physical attributes of the actor who played him. *Newsweek* described the thirty-eight-year-old Brit as "a gorgeous creature," and the *Los Angeles Times* said his "chiseled features and sensual lips" make fans think of "a Roman god." *USA Today* didn't limit its hosannas to Everett's chiseled facial features but also sang them to his well-toned physique. The paper first commended the six-feet-four-inch actor's "gym-buffed torso" and then applauded Yves Saint Laurent's decision to hire the easy-on-the-eyes Everett to appear in the company's ads for men's cologne.[9]

The quantity of man candy was doubled in *In & Out*, as the film included two handsome and well-built actors who played gay characters—Kevin Kline as the star and Tom Selleck in a supporting role. Kline's classic profile and athletic build were particularly noticeable in

Figure 10.1 Rupert Everett starred as a gay man who gave advice to his best friend Julia Roberts in the 1997 blockbuster hit *My Best Friend's Wedding*.

Courtesy of Sony Pictures Entertainment/Photofest.

scenes showing him with the other men living in Greenleaf, where scraggly beards and beer bellies proliferated. The *New York Times* made special mention of how well the high school teacher, who also coached the track team, "filled out the tight black T-shirt he stripped down to" when he danced around his living room. Kline had serious competition in the looks department when he shared scenes with Selleck, who played a TV news reporter. His square jaw, pronounced dimples, and beefy body made Selleck one of the hunkiest actors in Hollywood during the 1990s.[10]

Positive comments about the physical attributes of the gay characters in *The Birdcage* may have been the most notable, as neither Robin Williams nor Nathan Lane would come to mind when a director was casting an actor in a role that demanded "a Roman god." And yet, several reviews of the film praised the two men's on-screen appearance. The *Washington Post* observed that "the two characters are cuddly," and *USA Today* wrote that Lane was "amiable-looking." The *New York Times* went still further in its assessment, calling Williams "devilishly debonair" and saying that Lane "has nice legs and looks good in pearls."[11]

Gay Men Have Taste

Reviews also pointed out that the couple at the center of *The Birdcage* exhibits the aesthetic sensibilities that many gay men are supposedly blessed with. The *New York Times*, for example, complimented the Williams and Lane characters for "modeling a delirious, silky wardrobe." In other words, the two middle-aged men clearly had a fondness for cheese Danishes and other rich pastries, so they wisely chose to wear loose-fitting, light-weight shirts and trousers—cream for Williams, pink for Lane—so their expanding waistlines would be less noticeable. The décor of the couple's apartment reflected their unique taste as well. South Beach's vacation motif was vividly reflected in the couple's mixing of tropical plants with African statues and a white lacquered grand piano.[12]

In & Out being set in rural Indiana required the Kevin Kline character to display his aesthetic sensibilities in very different ways than did his Florida counterparts. An early clue to the teacher's sense of style comes when he and his fiancée sit down with a snack to watch television—in his perfectly appointed Victorian home—and he not only serves the wine in elegant, long-stemmed glasses but also enhances the dining experi-ence by placing three roses in a crystal bud base. Other signs of the gay man's refined taste continue to appear as the film unfolds. The woman who operates the local bridal shop volunteers that "Howard has perfect taste"—he picked out his fiancée's wedding gown, of course. And when the Kline character and his father put on their tuxedos for the wedding, the groom is so visibly disturbed that he blurts out, with comic exaggeration, "The dry cleaners left a shine on my trousers, and my right lapel is slightly bent, and the laundry didn't use enough starch on my shirtfront. I mean, where are we—the *Ukraine!*"

Several publications that reviewed *My Best Friend's Wedding* included references to the Rupert Everett character's good taste. The *Washington Post* referred to his "exquisitely tailored arm," while the *Los Angeles Times* made the same point by describing the leading lady's gay best friend as "suave." This particular character also provides an example of the kind of caustic comments that often come from the mouths of gay men who have all the back issues of *Architectural Digest* filed away in their basement. When Everett flies from New York to Chicago in response to Julia Roberts's call for help, he walks into her hotel suite, turns up his nose, and snipes, "What a *hideous* room."[13]

Gay Men Are Successful

Rupert Everett doesn't use his refined sensibilities merely to critique hotel room décors. Indeed, the gay hottie combined his good taste and abundant charm to edit a lifestyle magazine that informs its upscale readers on what to wear, how to spend their leisure time, and at which trendy restaurants to dine. That position also makes him the envy of red-blooded American males everywhere, as the Julia Roberts character is his food critic. In other words, he oversees the work of Hollywood's reigning sweetheart. At the same time that Everett advises readers on how to enjoy the finer things in life and labors shoulder to shoulder with a beautiful young woman, he's "living large" in his own right—furnishing his apartment in Manhattan chic and flying across the country, at a moment's notice, in response to his comely friend's distress call.

Both gay characters in *In & Out* also qualify as success stories. The specific event that causes Kevin Kline to take a closer look at his sexual orientation is a former student thanking his beloved teacher, during a live television broadcast, for helping him win an Academy Award for his film portrayal of a gay soldier—and the young man telling the one billion viewers, "And he's gay!" Although those three words propel Kline into a temporary tailspin over his sexual orientation, that speech means this guy must be a terrific teacher to receive the praise of such an accomplished former student on such a momentous occasion. The Tom Selleck character is at the top of his game, too, as he's one of the handful of network news reporters who've been dispatched to rural Indiana to get the skinny on this inspirational educator.

The Robin Williams and Nathan Lane characters have much to be proud of on professional as well as personal levels, prompting the *New York Times* to describe them as "productive, well-adjusted men." Williams is a successful businessman who's built his nightclub into one of Miami's most popular destinations, while Lane is the glamorous drag queen—"the one, the only, the incomparable Starina!"—who keeps the well-heeled audiences coming back for more. At the same time that the couple has been packing the house with big spenders, the dad and quasi mom have also been raising a son. One night twenty years earlier, Williams had fathered a child, and then he and Lane assumed full parenting responsibilities, producing a young man that any parents—gay or straight—would be proud to call their own. At one point in the film, the college student acknowledges the stability that his father and Albert/Starina provided for him, telling his rock-steady father, "I'm the only guy in my fraternity who doesn't come from a broken home." It's hard to argue with the *Washington Post*'s statement that the comedy ranks as "the loopiest, most hysterical family-values movie ever made."[14]

Gay Men Are Either Chaste or Monogamous

Yet another item on the list of characteristics defining the new gay man in town, according to the three movies released in the second half of the 1990s, may have been the most significant of all. Beginning in 1950 and continuing with few interruptions for the next forty years, the media had portrayed homosexuals as promiscuous. This message changed somewhat with *Philadelphia*, but even in that film the Tom Hanks character is unfaithful to his partner on at least one occasion. In the three movies examined in this chapter, however, gay men are portrayed as being either sexless or as never straying.

In *My Best Friend's Wedding*, Rupert Everett, with his handsome facial features and well-developed physique, is the quintessential gay heartthrob, and yet he's never shown so much as in the same room with—much less in the same bed with—another man. The only physical contact between Everett and any other character in the PG-13 film comes when he plays a game of grab-the-boob with Julia Roberts, a charade orchestrated not for the sexual fulfillment of either participant but to provoke jealousy in the straight guy Roberts wants to fall for her.[15]

Kevin Kline and Tom Selleck, two more Hollywood hunks, appear to live sexless lives as well. Several scenes in *In & Out* give the impression that the two men have become a couple, but they're never shown being romantic with each other. Their single instance of physical affection isn't the least bit erotic but, instead, has moviegoers rolling in the aisles with laughter. The humor comes after Selleck tells Kline that he's gay, urges the teacher to declare his own sexuality, and then says, "You know what you need?" and instantly answers his own question by kissing Kline in such an exaggerated manner that the lip lock recipient's entire body goes limp, his feet rising off the ground as he nearly faints. The PG-13 film milks the scene for all the laughs it can get—the *Chicago Tribune* said "it was played for comedy, and it was very funny"—but the two men are never again shown touching each other.[16]

The Birdcage makes a strong statement about fidelity, as Robin Williams and Nathan Lane have been together in a monogamous relationship for twenty years. Their unblemished record of loyalty is particularly laudable in the context of the South Beach setting; the movie's various scenes are dotted with firm-bodied lads, many of whom would surely be happy to have sex with a wealthy older man who could usher them into the entertainment world. Williams and Lane are never shown in bed together or kissing each other with passion, but they occasionally exchange pecks on the cheek during the R-rated film, as would other husbands and wives who've been together for two decades.

"A New Homosexual Role Model"

A huge slice of the American public has seen *The Birdcage*, *In & Out*, or *My Best Friend's Wedding* because the films were not only shown in movie theaters but also are available on DVD and have been broadcast on both cable and network television. Indeed, because of the films' broad appeal, a goodly number of viewers have seen all three of the comedy favorites—many people have, indeed, seen them multiple times. And so this cinematic trio has provided a critical mass of media consumers with a long list of characteristics that those viewers have come to associate with being gay.

Men who love men, according to the messages in the films, are charming and affable fellows who are physically attractive, who are endowed with impeccable taste, and who enjoy unbridled success in both their professional and their personal lives. On top of all that, the millions of people who've seen these movies have come away with examples of gay men who are either chaste or sexually faithful to their partners. When all these messages are combined, they give the movie-viewing public, in the words of *Newsweek* magazine, "a new homosexual role model."[17]

That statement is misleading in one respect, as this new set of stereotypes, in fact, doesn't apply to all homosexuals—only to the men. When the characters in the three movies are viewed as a whole, they create a parade of gay *men* with positive traits, but none of the films includes a single character who is identified as a *lesbian*. In other words, these films continued the trend, begun in 1950 and rarely interrupted since then, of the American media paying an increasing amount of attention to gay males but largely ignoring their Sapphic sisters.

The movies also focus on a decidedly narrow range of men, as all five of the major gay characters showcased in the films are white, physically attractive, well educated, and securely positioned in either the middle or the upper class.

Another limitation of the films evolves from the fact that they are all designed to produce laughs, combined with the fact that some topics don't lend themselves to comic treatment. None of the three widely seen and broadly influential films followed in *Philadelphia*'s pioneering footsteps by dealing with AIDS, even though the medical crisis continued to threaten the well-being of gay men when the films were released. Ignoring the epidemic was of particular concern because a number of news organizations suggested, during that time period, that the crisis had ended. After protease inhibitors were introduced in 1996, a spate of high-profile articles—such as a *Newsweek* cover story titled "The End of AIDS?" and a *New York Times* piece labeled "When AIDS Ends"— gave the false impression that people no longer needed to be concerned about contracting HIV. In reality, the medications don't prevent people from becoming infected with the virus, or cure them if they do, although they can prolong the lives of AIDS victims. Those stories also down-played the fact that the protease inhibitors are so expensive that many Americans and an even larger proportion of people in other countries can't afford them.[18]

While these shortcomings are a concern, they don't negate the important contribution that the three popular comedies have made to the evolution of how the media have depicted gay people. After 1950's initial spurt of unremittingly negative news articles about "perverts," a widening range of media—first a motion picture and then a TV program—had begun to offer at least some glimpses of gay people, during the next four decades, that could be interpreted as somewhat positive. *Philadelphia* had then broken new ground in 1993 by offering filmgoers a set of statements about gay men that could be interpreted as flattering. The release of *The Birdcage*, *In & Out*, and *My Best Friend's Wedding* reinforced those messages. Indeed, the quantity and quality of the statements communicated in the three side-splitting movies meant that they played a highly influential role in changing what characteristics came to mind when people heard the phrase "a gay man"—for a new one clearly had arrived.

In a number of respects, the three films can be seen as humorous descendants of the heart-wrenching drama that preceded them. Through *Philadelphia*, the highly likable Tom Hanks character increased the movie-going public's comfort level with gay men; through the trio of Hollywood comedies, the irrepressibly affable on-screen personas of men such as Rupert Everett and Robin Williams did the same. Through *Philadelphia*, many theatergoers met their first committed gay couple in the form of Tom Hanks and Antonio Banderas; through *The Birdcage*, viewers came to know another couple—this pair's commitment extending to monogamy—in the form of Robin Williams and Nathan Lane. In *Philadelphia*, the parents and siblings of a gay man were shown to give their son and brother unconditional support; in *In & Out*, movie fans saw an entire town embrace a beloved gay teacher, in this instance Kevin Kline. In *Philadelphia*, theatergoers saw the gay friends of an ailing man stand by him during difficult times; in *The Birdcage*, moviegoers saw a community of gay men—young and old, buff and flabby—come together to create the idyllic world of South Beach.

Another thought about the new-gay-man-in-town phenomenon doesn't have to do with the gay characters who were portrayed in the films but with the straight actors and actresses who did the portraying. In short, the millions of Americans who saw positive depictions of gay men in these high-profile movies wouldn't have shelled out $555 million if it hadn't been for the powerhouse stars in the casts. Had the straight beauties Julia Roberts and Cameron Diaz, the straight man candy Tom Selleck, and the straight Academy Award winners Gene Hackman, Kevin Kline, and Robin Williams not accepted roles in these films that were bursting with gay content, moviegoers wouldn't have met the new gay man in town—just as many Americans wouldn't have seen *Philadelphia* if megastars Tom Hanks and Denzel Washington hadn't agreed to appear in a film about homosexuality and AIDS. Following in the activist steps taken by Billy Crystal when he brought the first recurring gay character to television in 1977 on *Soap*, then, these various stars did their part to advance gay rights by helping to introduce huge numbers of moviegoers to positive messages about gay men.

Robin Williams has spoken about a major actor's ability to advance the gay cause. Williams said in one interview:

> If I can use my celebrity status to draw people into a movie theater to see me perform as an admirable gay man and thereby make them a little more positive about gay people, why wouldn't I do it? I get to be an activist for gay rights without even having to get up on a Sunday morning and march in a parade. It's a win/win for me and for gay rights—I'm here! I'm queer! I'm making points to get into Heaven![19]

Actors aren't the only Hollywood professionals who have used their positions to advance the gay rights cause. Jerry Zucker of *My Best Friend's Wedding* said in an unusually candid moment:

> Conventional wisdom has it that producers like myself are only interested in making a profit. But the truth is that a lot of us are eager, at the same time, to make a social or political statement—as long as it doesn't detract from the integrity of the film. I felt great knowing that by expanding Rupert's time on the screen, we were also increasing the presence of a gay role model and so, in our own way, helping to support gay rights.[20]

A final point that needs to be mentioned in the conclusion of this chapter is that the factor that may or may not have been a driving force in *Philadelphia* getting made in 1993 almost certainly played a role in *The Birdcage, In & Out,* and *My Best Friend's Wedding* coming to the big screen during the second half of the 1990s. That is, there's no question that Hollywood decision-makers knew, by 1996, that gay people combined with heterosexual gay rights supporters—often referred to as "allies"—represented a large and highly attractive target audience for media products.

By the time the three comedies were released, a long list of news organizations had reported on the highly attractive buying power of the gay and lesbian market. *Advertising Age* pulled no punches, bluntly stating, "They're DINKS—consumers with double incomes and no kids." The *New York Times* jumped on the bandwagon as well, gushing, "Gays are a great marketing niche, with a collective $514 billion in yearly expendable income." The *Washington Post* made note of gay buying power, too, reporting, "The average income for gay and lesbian households is estimated at more than $55,000 a year, compared with about $40,000 a year for households in the general population." *Daily Variety* added yet another piece of marketing data of considerable relevance, stating, "When surveyed, 60% of gays and lesbians said they had gone to the movies in the past month, compared to the U.S. average of 28%."[21]

While no Hollywood decision-makers were willing to go on the record as saying there was a direct connection between, one, recent research showing that gays and their allies spend lots of money on movie tickets, and, two, major studios such as MGM, Paramount, and TriStar now being willing to make films that sent positive messages about gay men, anyone trying to figure out what factors had propelled these three gay-positive films into production has to consider economics as a prime candidate.

11 *Ellen*
Coming Out, On Screen and Off

It ranks, hands down, as the single most public exit from the closet in gay history. The *Los Angeles Times* published sixty articles about this particular coming out, the *New York Times* devoted its lead editorial to the event, and ABC's *20/20* magazine show used its network connections to nab the first TV interview with the woman of the hour. These and other journalistic behemoths raced to report—*Time* magazine called it a "national obsession"—that a thirty-nine-year-old comedian with glistening blond hair was a unique species of humanity that most media outlets had previously ignored: a lesbian.[1]

Ellen became the first program on network TV to feature a lesbian or gay character in a leading role. But Ellen Morgan acknowledging her sexuality on the sitcom at precisely the same moment that comedian Ellen DeGeneres came out in the country's leading news outlets was a milestone in other respects, too, as that double whammy of a revelation sent several noteworthy messages. The two coinciding events told the American public that Sapphic women can be physically attractive as well as uproariously funny, while also showing that the coming-out experience can be both lengthy and multi-dimensional. Finally, the question about whether or not companies would pay for commercials on the sitcom ultimately made it clear that myriad advertisers had no problem embracing gay or lesbian content—*if* doing so paid off financially.

"Yep, I'm Gay"

In September 1996, the *Los Angeles Times* published an item headlined "Stepping Out?" that stated, "Ellen Morgan, the lead character in ABC's comedy 'Ellen' starring Ellen DeGeneres, may be gearing up to reveal herself as a lesbian." The tip had been leaked by someone at the network, although no one would comment officially on its accuracy.[2]

Over the next several months, the *Times* provided ongoing coverage of the *Ellen* story. One article quoted DeGeneres as playfully telling talk-show host David Letterman that an upcoming episode "may reveal that my character is *Le-ba-neeeese*"—using her comedic talent to exaggerate the pronunciation of that final word. The paper also hyped the story beyond the entertainment section; when DeGeneres bought a house in Beverly Hills, the *Times* turned her purchase into the lead article on the front page of the Sunday real estate section under the headline: "She's Got Lots of Closet Space."[3]

In March 1997, ABC announced that, yes, *Ellen*'s lead character would, indeed, come out as a gay woman during the episode scheduled to air at 9 p.m. on April 30—at the end of sweeps month. With its scoop now confirmed, the *Times* shifted its focus to reporting the "why" of the story. Executives were frustrated, the paper reported, that ABC was at the bottom in the ratings for the year, consistently attracting a smaller audience than either CBS or NBC. *Ellen* was seen as part of the problem because the series, then in its fourth season, was averaging just 14 million viewers a week, placing it a mediocre forty-seventh among the 118 prime-time shows on the major networks. Officials were close to canceling the program but then decided the novelty of introducing TV's first lesbian just might pull in more viewers.[4]

Although the *Los Angeles Times* had published numerous articles about Ellen Morgan preparing to exit the closet, none of them quoted Ellen DeGeneres directly. Indeed, the star had repeatedly refused to talk to any news organization—an oddity in Hollywood where publicity is the coin of the realm. Two weeks before the coming-out episode aired, it became clear that the actress had been avoiding the press because she had her own scoop to reveal.[5]

DeGeneres wanted to make sure her real-life coming out took place on her own terms. And so she used exclusive interviews to announce that she was a bona fide lesbian, not just a woman who played one on TV. "Yep, I'm Gay" jumped off the cover of *Time* magazine, next to a large photo of DeGeneres, and ABC gave the actress free rein to say exactly what she wanted to say during a segment of *20/20*. "This has been the most freeing experience of my professional life," the star said. "I don't have to worry anymore about some reporter trying to find out information. I don't have anything to be scared of, which outweighs whatever else happens in my career."[6]

"A Positive Milestone"

In the history-making segment of *Ellen*, an old college friend of the main character visits Los Angeles, where the show is set, on a business trip. The guy's smart, handsome, and everything else a woman could hope to find in a man, and so Ellen Morgan can't figure out why, when he makes romantic overtures to her, she isn't interested. Even more confusing to her is that she's enormously attracted to the guy's female co-worker. The other woman, Susan, also feels the chemistry, but, when she says she's gay and assumes that Ellen is, too, the startled main character denies

Figure 11.1 The TV character played by Ellen DeGeneres, left, exited the closet thanks to the prompting of the openly lesbian character played by Laura Dern.

Courtesy of ABC/Photofest.

having any such feelings. Only after Ellen talks with her therapist the next day does she finally acknowledge her sexuality, first to herself and then to Susan.[7]

Other major players in the hour-long segment include the employees who work at the bookstore that Ellen manages. By the end of the episode, TV's newly visible lesbian has announced her sexuality not only to her co-workers but also to—in the laugh-out-loud central moment of the show—the entire Los Angeles International Airport.[8]

Reviews of the segment, which was later awarded an Emmy, were uniformly positive. The *Los Angeles Times* led the applause, calling the episode "a positive milestone" that was "very smart" and "very funny." Other publications agreed. The *Washington Post* said the segment was "well written and full of laughs," and the *Boston Globe* dubbed it "one of *the* great sitcom episodes of all time."[9]

The most remarkable of the comments appeared in the *New York Times*, as the country's most influential news organization devoted its lead editorial, on the day after the broadcast, not to national politics or the global economy but to a TV sitcom. "The 'coming out' of the title character on 'Ellen' was accomplished with wit and poignancy," the *Times* gushed, "which should help defuse the antagonism toward homosexuals still prevalent in society."[10]

A hefty slice of America was subject to that defusing, as ABC was soon boasting that 42 million viewers had watched *Ellen* that particular Wednesday night, tripling the show's typical audience.[11]

"Yep, She's Too Gay"

Consistent with its out-in-front role on the topic, the *Los Angeles Times* soon published an article headlined "So Ellen Is a Lesbian—What's the Next Step?" No one offered details on what direction the program would take, but they were definite about what the show would *not* become. "It's not going to be all about Ellen Morgan as a lesbian," DeGeneres's manager said, while an ABC staff member echoed the point, guaranteeing that, "No more than half a dozen of next season's 20 episodes will deal in any direct way with Ellen's sexuality."[12]

Both sources were wrong.

The segments immediately after the historic one had Ellen coming out to her parents and then to her boss. Subsequent plotlines had the title character supporting her new community by insisting on hiring only gay workers, going rock climbing because she's attracted to the woman leading the activity, dealing with friends who are uncomfortable with her sexuality, and helping her employees get used to saying the word "lesbian."[13]

Lots of additional Sapphic storylines erupted when the main character began dating a woman. One episode had the girlfriend's daughter reacting negatively to her mother and Ellen holding hands, and another had the star struggling with her own emotions when she meets her girlfriend's ex-partner. Several segments focused specifically on aspects of same-sex relationships such as balancing different interests, kissing someone for the first time, deciding when to have sex, and contemplating the possibility of living together.[14]

Ultimately, more significant than what was taking place on screen was what was happening in American living rooms: Fewer and fewer people were watching *Ellen*. The show was not drawing the larger audience that ABC had hoped for, but, in fact, it was losing viewers. The 14 million average before the coming-out episode had dropped to fewer than 11 million.[15]

Critics were quick to say why viewers had abandoned the series. *Time* magazine sniped that, "Instead of being integrated into the show, Ellen's homosexuality has *become* the show," and the *Chicago Tribune* opined that viewers tuned into sitcoms for "some laughs," not for "lectures about tolerance and acceptance." *Entertainment Weekly* may have provided the most succinct statement on the matter, when the magazine ran a photo of DeGeneres on its cover next to a headline reading "Yep, She's Too Gay."[16]

By March 1998, it was clear that *Ellen* would be canceled, as ABC began auditioning other sitcoms for the timeslot. The final episode was broadcast two months later.[17]

DeGeneres then sat down for a second interview on *20/20*. Asked why fifteen of the final season's twenty episodes focused specifically on the main character's sexuality, DeGeneres responded by reading aloud from letters she'd received from gay teenagers. One boy wrote, "Thank you for letting me realize that I'm not a nasty, sick person," while a girl said, "I was going to kill myself, but, because of you, I didn't." After the most visible lesbian in America stopped reading, she said, in her own words, "If I just had this one year of doing what I did on national television, I'll take that over ten more years of being on a sitcom and just being funny."[18]

Lesbians Can Be Physically Attractive

After *Ellen* left the air, the *Los Angeles Times* ran a post-mortem article arguing that no series in TV history had been more important. To justify that dramatic claim, the paper named several powerful messages the program had sent. First on the list was showing the public that lesbians "are not all macho, combat-booted, burly fireplugs with 15-inch biceps— they aren't all Arnold Schwarzenegger in a bra."[19]

Ellen DeGeneres provided the show's strongest example of an attractive gay woman. With her lustrous blond hair and blue eyes so pale they almost hypnotize the viewer, the actress fully deserved *Entertainment Weekly*'s description "adorable." Although clearly more the girl-next-door variety than a voluptuous blond bombshell, she was so physically appealing that even one of her most ardent critics, televangelist Pat Robertson, called her "an attractive actress."[20]

A second representative of gay womanhood for the millions of viewers who watched the coming-out episode was Laura Dern, who played Susan. Tall and slender with long blond hair, Dern was not only a well-regarded actress with several films to her credit, but also a woman endowed with a beautiful face and a shapely body. In fact, the *Washington Post* made specific mention of Dern's appearance in the groundbreaking *Ellen* episode, describing her as "attractive and sexy."[21]

In later episodes, other women provided more Sapphic eye candy. One plotline had both supermodel Cindy Crawford and Academy Award winner Helen Hunt taking screen tests in hopes of becoming TV's first lesbian star. Other easy-on-the-eyes actresses who appeared as guest stars included Emmy winner Julianna Margulies and va-va-voom hottie Demi Moore.[22]

An actress who defied easy classification was Anne Heche. During the mid-1990s, the pixieish blonde had been romantically involved with a long list of actors—Alec Baldwin, Johnny Depp, Steve Martin—and played the on-screen love interest of Harrison Ford and Tommy Lee Jones. So it came as quite a surprise that DeGeneres, during her public coming out, identified Heche as her lover. The attractive twosome soon became the most visible same-sex couple in the country, with dozens of papers running a photo of Heche with her arm around DeGeneres while they chatted with President Bill Clinton. In fact, though, Heche never publicly identified herself as a lesbian. She wasn't attracted to women, she said, until she met DeGeneres and instantly fell in love, admitting, "No one was more confused than me."[23]

Lesbians Can Be Funny

A second reason *Ellen* was significant, according to the *Los Angeles Times*, was that the series showed millions of television viewers that gay women are not, contrary to the prevailing opinion, humorless scolds. Indeed, Ellen Morgan and many of the other lesbian characters on the program were, the newspaper wrote, uproariously funny.[24]

Ellen DeGeneres had begun her career in stand-up comedy, gaining national attention in 1982 when she won a contest that crowned her the funniest person in America. So when she came out on national TV, she filled the high-profile episode with lots of laughs and woo-hoos.[25]

The moment viewers were waiting for was the one in which the main character acknowledges her sexuality. By the time Ellen is finally ready to tell the object of her affection that she's gay, she and Susan are both at the airport. Ellen hurries to the crowded gate, locates Susan, and begins her stumbling monologue.

"Susan, I think that maybe I'm . . .," the anxious woman begins. "I am . . . uh . . . I guess what I'm trying to say is. . . ." She's so nervous that she's gasping for breath. "This is so hard, but I think. . . . I think I've realized that I am . . ." Ellen twitches and fidgets, barely able to speak. "Why can't I just say the word?" She's so uncomfortable that she leans on the ticket agent's podium to steady herself. "Why can't I just say the truth?" She then lowers her arm and accidentally trips the switch to a microphone so that her next two words—as a complete surprise to her—are broadcast over the airport's loudspeaker system: *"I'm gay!"*

Yikes! Ellen has suddenly made her climactic statement, the one she's kept bottled up inside of herself for years, not in a soft whisper to Susan but in an amplified voice that reverberates through the entire building.

"That felt great," Ellen tells Susan, smiling broadly. "It felt great, and it felt so . . . *loud.*"

The gag showcased DeGeneres's much-anticipated words, and she played it for all its over-the-top comic effect, looking around the waiting room as dozens of people stared at her.

The Ups and Downs of Coming Out

At the same time that *Ellen* could be raucously funny, the program also could be dauntingly poignant. The emotional pain that many episodes evoked came from the fact that the series depicted, in greater depth than any media product before it, the bracing and tumultuous process of sexual awakening that is known as coming out.

Several news organizations applauded the show for its success at portraying this life-changing experience. The *Boston Globe* said, "Ellen DeGeneres and an infantry of writers, cast members, and guest stars have fairly and credibly depicted the misunderstood process of coming out." *Time* magazine echoed the point, saying, "The show is groundbreaking not only for having a gay lead character, but for having a gay lead character who is not yet entirely comfortable with her sexuality."[26]

The coming-out episode vividly illustrated the roller-coaster ride of emotions that many people go through when they first realize, on a conscious level, that they're gay. From the instant that Ellen's friend, Richard, introduces her and Susan, the chemistry between the two women is palpable. Within a matter of seconds, they're joking and laughing and finishing each other's sentences. "It's so strange," Ellen says gleefully. "It's like I'm looking into a mirror." The ride takes a dramatic dip, however, when Susan tells Ellen that she's a lesbian and then adds, "I thought you were gay, too."

That statement thrusts the befuddled Ellen into panic mode. She instinctively moves away from Susan, initially to the other side of the room and then out the door. Ellen clearly is terrified, so she subconsciously puts as much physical distance as possible between herself and Susan, who represents the sexuality that Ellen's trying to suppress. Denial comes next, with Ellen racing to Richard's hotel room and throwing herself into his bed, although the effort ultimately fails to lead her into the safe harbor of heterosexuality that she was seeking.

Ellen is next shown talking with her therapist, played by Oprah Winfrey, as the patient recounts the unsettling events from the night before and then as she expresses how desperately she wants to find someone she "clicks" with. Oprah then asks, "Has there ever been anyone you felt you 'clicked' with?" Ellen nods her head yes. Oprah continues, "And what was his name?" Ellen, filled with trepidation and yet determined to be honest, softly responds "Susan."

That scene leads to the one in the airport where Ellen trips the switch to the loudspeaker. But saying "I'm gay" that first time isn't the end of her coming-out process, as she—like most gay people—makes that same statement time and time again while receiving various responses. The roller coaster plunges downward when Ellen learns that Susan is already in a committed relationship, but then it climbs upward again when the bookstore manager comes out to her co-workers and they warmly embrace her. In a later episode, the ride plummets once more when Ellen comes out to her boss and he says he doesn't want her around his children, a statement that propels her to quit her job.[27]

Ellen Morgan's fictional coming out wasn't the only one that moved into the media spotlight. In her *20/20* interview that aired the same week as the sitcom's historic episode, Ellen DeGeneres talked about how she had recognized her sexuality twenty years earlier and had told her real-life father and stepmother, as well as close friends, about it. That story was sadder than the television version, as the frightened teenager was banished from her home because her father feared she'd be a bad influence on her younger stepsisters.[28]

The Downs and Ups of Advertisers and Gay Content

A roller-coaster ride was also an apt metaphor for the money angle of the *Ellen* phenomenon. Specifically, negative and then positive developments, from the program's perspective, surrounded the question of whether companies would pay to advertise their products on a series that showcased homosexuality.

Early coverage in the *Los Angeles Times* raised the issue. "If the program's main character identifies herself as a lesbian," the paper wrote, "religious conservatives would see it as validating the gay lifestyle, and ABC would lose advertisers." That prediction initially was proven accurate, as the Rev. Jerry Falwell's criticism of Ellen DeGeneres—the televangelist called her "Ellen De*Generate*"—prompted the Ford Motor Company to stop running commercials on *Ellen*.[29]

The who-will-advertise-and-who-will-not question continued to loom large as the airing date for the history-making episode neared. The *New York Times* quoted a leader of the conservative American Family Association as saying:

> The show is providing a one-sided view of homosexuality as a normal, natural, alternative lifestyle. The only option is to ask advertisers not to support programming that viewers feel is objectionable and to let them know that if they do, viewers will vote with their wallets the next time they are in the grocery store.

Coca-Cola and McDonald's were now refusing to sponsor *Ellen*, the paper reported.[30]

This particular roller-coaster ride's upward swing didn't happen until the night the coming-out episode aired, but, when it finally came, that change of direction was a decisive one. "The funny thing about the 'Ellen' controversy," the *Washington Post* reported, "is that sponsors didn't find it so controversial."[31]

Indeed, the list of companies that had advertised on the episode was long and wide-ranging—from Volkswagen to Calvin Klein, from Trident chewing gum to 20th Century Fox, from Bayer One-a-Day vitamins and Sony electronics to Time Warner and Burlington Coat Factory.[32]

When journalists looked for someone to explain why so many companies had been willing to defy conservatives and advertise on the show, they found the president of an ad agency that specialized in the gay market. "Everybody's always saying they're looking for a desirable demographic," Dave Mulryan told the *New York Times*. "Well, we have it."[33]

Companies clearly had bought that argument, as news stories reported that they'd been willing to pay premium prices to promote their products during the much-watched segment. Before Ellen Morgan came out, ABC had been charging $150,000 for a thirty-second ad during the program; for the historic episode, the network had upped that figure to $335,000.[34]

Most of the companies continued to advertise on the program throughout the rest of 1997 and into early 1998, although the fees they paid decreased as the show's ratings faltered. The most salient statement on the topic of *Ellen* and advertisers came in the *Los Angeles Times*'s postmortem article after the show was canceled: "Television is not motivated by good will or changing social mores, but by economics."[35]

A Milestone of Epic Proportions

Ellen ranked as a major milestone because it was the first television program to feature a gay or lesbian character in a leading role. *Soap* had broken the gays-on-TV ice in 1977, and then, two decades later, *Ellen* took the next step of promoting a gay character to the star of the show.

An assessment of how this particular media product compared to those that came before it must begin with the fact that Ellen Morgan was a lesbian. How the media treated gay people had changed enormously since 1950 when the *New York Times* published the headline "Perverts Called Government Peril," to the point where, in the 1990s, the same newspaper described the Robin Williams and Nathan Lane characters in *The Birdcage* as "productive, well-adjusted men." But that dramatic transformation had been largely limited to gay *men*.

Yes, Sharon Stone had played a pseudo-lesbian in *Basic Instinct*, and Mariel Hemingway had kissed Roseanne Arnold on a TV sitcom, but those images were not only fleeting but also plagued with problems and qualifications that made the representations of gay women less than ideal, including Stone's character being a psychopathic killer and Arnold instantly wiping Hemingway's saliva off her mouth.

Ellen Morgan, by contrast, wouldn't kill a fly and didn't hesitate to kiss her girlfriend on the lips during one episode—oh, my! What's more, Morgan wasn't played by a straight actress such as Stone or Hemingway who only acted the part of Sapphic women.

Indeed, Ellen "Yep, I'm Gay" DeGeneres left the closet in a remarkably public fashion that included a *Time* magazine cover and a much-hyped sitcom episode that 42 million people watched. DeGeneres's coming out continued with the widely published photo of her and Anne Heche embracing while the couple chatted with the president of the United States, and then week after week on the TV screen as her fictional persona illuminated what it means to be a lesbian.

Before the *Ellen* phenomenon exploded onto the cultural landscape, the only two consistent messages about lesbians that the media had communicated were that they hate men and they love sex. News coverage of the Stonewall Rebellion had made that pair of statements in 1969, and the blockbuster film *Basic Instinct* had reiterated them in 1992. But Ellen Morgan and Ellen DeGeneres obliterated both of those messages. The Ellens liked men well enough; they just didn't want to sleep with them. Likewise, neither the fictitious Ellen nor her real-life counterpart showed any signs of being promiscuous; both women had steady girlfriends, and their respective relationships appeared to be monogamous.

Because the epic coming out of Ellen Morgan and Ellen DeGeneres reinforced neither of the messages about gay women that had originated in the Stonewall coverage, the only previous milestone in the history of the media's depiction of lesbians is the spate of fleeting images in the early 1990s. Looking for consistent messages communicated by that phenomenon and by the Ellens produces three clear statements.

At the top of the list is that lesbians can be physically attractive. Sharon Stone in *Basic Instinct* and Mariel Hemingway in *Roseanne* provided gay-girl eye candy early in the decade, and Cindy Crawford, Helen Hunt, and Demi Moore were among the bevy of beautiful women who kept up the pace when they appeared on *Ellen* a few years later. Ellen DeGeneres reinforced the message, too; she's not the most glamorous woman in Hollywood, but there's no question that she qualifies as physically attractive.

A second message is that gay women can be funny. Roseanne Arnold introduced this concept with the much-ballyhooed "lesbian kiss" episode in 1994. While the comedian herself didn't portray a gay woman, the fact that a lesbian locked lips with her on the popular sitcom—one of the funniest shows of the era—made it clear that Sapphic content didn't have to be dour. That fact paved the way for the Ellens to arrive on the scene three years later to make television history by having a laugh-out-loud lesbian become the medium's first gay leading character.

A final message isn't about lesbians so much as it's about lesbian content: It can make money. The Powers That Be had their first indication that this might be the case with the back-to-back financial successes of *Basic Instinct* and the *Roseanne* segment. The big test then followed in 1997 when the news media spent considerable time speculating on how many companies would be willing to pay for commercials on a sitcom episode that revolved around a woman acknowledging her sexual orientation. A long list of advertisers ultimately agreed not only to sponsor the high-profile segment but to pay a premium price to do so. It was only when viewers turned away from the heavy-on-lesbian-content *Ellen* that advertisers did the same. In short: Depictions of lesbians have no problem finding support either from media decision-makers or from advertisers . . . as long as they bring in profits.

The fact that companies were willing to advertise on a TV series about a lesbian reinforces the point that creating media content that appeals to gay consumers—and their substantial buying power—remained a significant factor in Hollywood's decision to emphasize positive messages about gay people. As important to the decision-makers as the gay consumers themselves was the growing number of straight allies who were eager to support gay rights. This segment of the population was becoming particularly strong, by the late 1990s, among young Americans. The memories of teenagers and college-age students of the era didn't extend back to the days when the term "perverts" was synonymous with "homosexuals," or to the time when the lives of gay men were defined by misery and self-loathing as depicted in *The Boys in the Band*. Instead, youthful members of society drew their knowledge of gay people from the overwhelmingly gay-positive films *Philadelphia*, *The Birdcage*, *In & Out*, and *My Best Friend's Wedding*—and now from the TV show *Ellen*. These young allies, therefore, expected positive messages about gay people, and the media were eager to provide them.

A second factor that continued to drive the trend toward positive content was that a number of major Hollywood stars became gay activists by joining the cast of *Ellen* either for the coming-out episode or for later segments of the history-making series. Oprah Winfrey, Helen Hunt, and Demi Moore were among the names on the impressive list of celebrities who stepped up to the plate and did their part to advance the Gay and Lesbian Rights Movement.

12 *Will & Grace*
The Biggest Gay Hit in TV History

In 1994 when ABC announced that two women would lock lips on *Roseanne*, dozens of news articles erupted in the country's major newspapers. Six years later when NBC's *Will & Grace* showcased two men kissing, the reaction could be characterized by the single word: Zip.

The lack of reaction to that second kiss wasn't due to the American public having evolved to the point that it accepted two characters of the same sex being physically affectionate with each other. Instead, that non-reaction showed how adept NBC had been at avoiding controversy. "The lack of hubbub after the kiss should be attributed to the fact," *TV Guide* explained, "that *Will & Grace* concentrates more on laughs than on issues." To support its point, the magazine went on to quote one of the show's co-creators as saying, "The only thing we're trying to force down people's throats is comedy."[1]

NBC's strategy paid off—in spades—as it launched the series into the ratings stratosphere and helped *Will & Grace* become the most visible gay media product of all time. At the peak of the show's eight-year run, 19 million people were tuning in every week to see the latest episode of the laugh-out-loud comedy. Because the sitcom was so popular, it also was able to attract A-list celebrities such as Madonna, Cher, Alec Baldwin, and Academy Award winners Michael Douglas, Glenn Close, and Matt Damon as guest stars for individual episodes. Millions of viewers soon began watching the reruns, too, thereby further exposing themselves to the show's recurring messages about men who are attracted to other men.[2]

One of the sitcom's distinctive elements was that it showcased not just one gay man but a pair of them who differed from each other in numerous ways, communicating that gay men aren't all alike. Other of *Will & Grace*'s important messages were that many gay men form close bonds with straight women, many are masters of witty repartee, and many are vain and narcissistic—but endearingly so. Perhaps the show's most far-reaching statement was a subtle one that emerged gradually over time: Gay people deserve equal rights.

Figure 12.1 Central to NBC's formula for success with *Will & Grace* was to pair the two gay male characters with two straight female characters. Shown here, left to right, are Sean Hayes with Megan Mullally and Eric McCormack with Debra Messing.

Courtesy of NBC/Photofest.

Playing It Chaste

Beginning with the premier episode of *Will & Grace* in the fall of 1998, it was clear that the series would approach the topic of sexuality far differently than *Ellen* had the previous season.

That first segment revolved around Grace trying to decide how to respond to a marriage proposal from her boyfriend. She knows she's not head-over-heels in love with the guy, but, well, she's thirty years old and this is the first time she's been asked the big question. So she seeks advice from the man who's been her best friend for fifteen years. "Honey, this guy's not enough for you," Will responds. "He's not funny, he doesn't know what your favorite flower is, he's passive-aggressive—the man high-five's you after sex! If you really believed he's the one, would you be asking me?" Grace initially rejects Will's advice, buys a wedding dress, and rushes off to city hall to tie the knot. By the segment's final scene, though, she decides that her friend is right, so she doesn't go through with the wedding. Instead, she joins Will at a bar for a beer, still wearing her full-length bridal gown and matching veil.[3]

While that first episode focused on whether Grace would marry, it also contained lots of gay references. In the opening scene, Will is looking forward to watching the NBC television drama *ER* so he can drool over heartthrob George Clooney. "Sorry, babe," Grace tells him, "but George doesn't *bat for your team*," a comment that prompts Will to smile mischievously and say, "Well—he hasn't seen me *pitch*." Once Will's effeminate friend Jack is introduced, more one-liners start flying through the dialogue. When Jack says, "Most people who meet me don't know that I'm gay," Will laughs heartily and then quips, "Jack, blind and deaf people know you're gay." Jack gasps in comically exaggerated disbelief at his friend's statement and then asks Grace, "Did you know I was gay when you first met me?" Without missing a beat, Grace deadpans, "My dog knew." None of the lines is spoken with even a hint of bitterness, all of them followed by bursts of good-natured laughter from the audience.[4]

While there were plenty of gay references during that first episode, neither Will nor Jack was shown expressing affection for another man. Not even close. In the lead paragraph of a story titled "Will Plays It Chaste," the *San Francisco Chronicle* posed the rhetorical question: "After the wreckage of 'Ellen,' how does a television series handle another lead character who is gay?" And then answered: "Judging by 'Will & Grace,' with extreme caution."[5]

A close look at the early segments of *Will & Grace* bears out that point. Of the twenty episodes of *Ellen* that aired after the main character came out, fifteen focused on lesbian storylines; of the first twenty episodes of *Will & Grace*, only one focused on a gay storyline.[6]

Also central to NBC's strategy was avoiding the physical-contact issue by stating, in the first episode, that Will is taking a break from romantic involvement because his partner of seven years recently dumped him. Critics who reviewed the show had mixed reactions. The *San Francisco Chronicle* sniped that NBC had "caved in" to anti-gay pressure, but the *Los Angeles Times* gushed that *Will & Grace* had cleverly succeeded in "flying under the radar of outrage."[7]

Showing Two Stops on the Gay Male Spectrum

Early in the first episode, Jack prances into Will's apartment, a hatbox dangling from one of his noticeably limp wrists. Will looks at his friend, smirks playfully, and asks, "What's in the box, your tiara?" The next scene unfolds in Will's office. "You're my lawyer," the high-powered client begins, "so tell me: What do I have to do to buy this company?" Will's all business as he responds, in legalese: "First you've got to get something called a Hart-Scott-Rodino antitrust clearance, and then we can negotiate standstills and lockups." Through those two scenes, viewers had been told that gay men are not all the same.[8]

Indeed, one of the program's most noteworthy characteristics was that, unlike its TV predecessors *Soap* and *Ellen*, it didn't feature a solo gay character but two of them who differ from each other in numerous respects. Will dates only rarely; Jack is promiscuous. Will works at a prestigious Manhattan law firm; Jack has no consistent means of support. Will is so lacking in effeminate mannerisms that members of a focus group that previewed the first episode refused to believe he was gay; Jack is flighty, highly excitable, and over-the-top on the swishy scale.[9]

Will & Grace's initial reviews reinforced the differences between the two characters. A critique in *TV Guide* said of actor Eric McCormack's TV persona, "Will is gay, although he's so low-key about it you might not notice." Among the contrasting characterizations of Jack was one that came in a *Los Angeles Times* profile of Sean Hayes, the actor who played Jack, with the comment: "Jack is not just openly gay—he's open-24-hours-a-day gay."[10]

Articles about the two actors playing the roles made a point of exploring their sexuality. Readers of a *People* magazine piece about the man who played Will got their answer in the headline "Happily Married Eric McCormack Plays a Gay Lawyer," and again in the story itself, which reported, "he's as straight as an arrow." But the question mark continued to hover over the show's other male star. "Sean Hayes will not address the is-he-or-isn't-he speculation," *Entertainment Weekly* reported, "saying the question is too personal."[11]

Developing Close Bonds with Straight Women

Will & Grace's central focus was the relationship between a gay man and a straight woman. The *Boston Globe* praised the show for "paying homage to pure friendship between the sexes." This mutual love and support of the two title characters communicated one of the sitcom's most important messages: Gay men often develop strong bonds with straight women.[12]

The point is a significant one. In 1970 when *The Boys in the Band* gave moviegoers their first glimpse inside the world of gay men, no women appeared in the film. Some of the later chapters in the evolution of gay men and the media, such as news coverage of AIDS, excluded women as well. Because of these media products, many Americans were left with the impression that gay men want to have nothing to do with straight women. Not so on *Will & Grace*.

Feelings shared by the program's title characters were front and center in the premier episode. When Will tells Grace why she deserves someone better than the guy who's asked her to marry him, the comments aren't limited to criticism of the boyfriend. For Will also lists several of the attributes he ascribes to the neurotic and high-spirited redhead, played by Debra Messing. "You're passionate and creative and beautiful and, well, you're *perfect*," he tells her. Grace returns the favor in the final scene of the segment. When they're in the bar, she lifts her beer glass and says, wearing the broadest of smiles, "To my Will. You are my hero and my soul mate, and I'm a better woman for loving you." [13]

After that introduction, the gay man/straight woman *pas de deux* experienced various ups and downs, but the bond between the two friends remained strong. One of Grace's ups came in season seven when Will walked her down the aisle and into the arms of a handsome doctor, which was followed by the down of discovering that her husband had cheated on her. After Grace decides she'll never be able to trust her husband again, she leaves him and turns to Will for the unconditional love and comfort she knows he'll give her.[14]

Reinforcing the message that gay men often form close ties with straight women was the relationship between Will's friend Jack and Grace's assistant Karen, played by Megan Mullally. When Jack sees the buxom Karen for the first time, he exclaims, "You are *fab*ulous! Loving the boobs!" It's love at first sight for the wealthy socialite as well, who shows her approval not in words but in action. Karen pulls up her shirt and thrusts her midriff at Jack, who instantly reciprocates, allowing the couple's bare stomachs to come together in a unique—and altogether zany—gesture of friendship.[15]

Mastering the Art of Repartee

Numerous media products of the 1980s and 1990s—including *Soap, My Best Friend's Wedding*, and *The Birdcage*—communicated that many gay men are witty. But no TV show or movie raised the level of clever banter to that displayed on *Will & Grace*.

Will's humorous comments often referred to the laundry list of stereotypically gay traits that Jack exhibited. In one segment, the target was Jack's propensity for using beauty treatments. Jack: "I did a papaya salt scrub, a cucumber mask, and two shots of wheatgrass." Will: "Wow, you're a *gay salad bar!*" The witty lawyer also sometimes took aim at his friend's shallowness:

> Will: When I was a teenager, the school bully made me write his history papers.
>
> Jack: I, too, was bullied, but I'm proud to say no one ever made *me* do their homework.
>
> Will: That's because no teacher ever assigned a history paper on the rise of the leg warmer.[16]

A second category of repartee involved sexual innuendo. In one episode, Jack boasts he's an expert on dating because, "I go on literally thousands of dates per year," prompting Will to respond, "That doesn't make you an *expert*—that makes you an *escort*." Some of the sexual banter involved double-entendres that raced by so fast a listener wasn't always sure what had been said. When Jack meets an attractive naturalist, he instantly says, "So you're a birdwatcher. I bet you've seen a cockatoo" —or did he say "cock or two"?[17]

Other rapid-fire witticisms didn't fit into any particular category. In a scene in which Will's dad drops by for a visit, the son offers his father a sandwich; after Dad says, "No, thanks," Jack says, "Since you're offering, I'll have one," prompting Will to respond, "Sure, Jack, how about a *fat chance on rye?*" Another time, Grace and her boyfriend kiss in front of Jack; the gay man then scrunches up his nose in disgust and says, "What you two do behind closed doors is your business, but flaunting that lifestyle like you're doing right now—it's just plain gross."[18]

Being Vain and Narcissistic

The Boys in the Band portrayed gay men as vain, showing Michael racing from one upscale boutique to the next, looking for the perfect sweater to wear to the birthday party he's hosting that night. Michael's obsession with looking good ultimately fails, as he later tries on one expensive purchase after another but is never satisfied, bitterly tossing his rejects onto the floor. Another narcissist in the film is the man whose birthday is being celebrated, as Harold uses creams and lotions in a desperate attempt to obscure his unattractive facial features.

While the comedic *Will & Grace* also showed its two gay male leads being self-indulgent, the sitcom approached the topic far more humorously.

Jack's eagerness to show off his trim physique was one of his many endearing qualities. In one episode, he sashays into Will and Grace's apartment, turns his firm derriere toward his friends and announces, "Ladies and gentlemen, after forty-five minutes of butt-robics, I give you . . . my ass!" With a broad grin on his face, he then asks, "Anybody want to touch, feel, poke, caress?" Another time, Jack and Will are playing poker with friends. When the other guys catch Jack daydreaming when he should be showing if he has the winning hand, one of them asks impatiently, "What you got, Jack?" Suddenly pulled back into the moment, Jack smiles and says, "One pair of . . . *fabu*lous butt cheeks!"[19]

The larger-than-life character values looking good so highly that when the much more articulate Will criticizes him, Jack fights back by attacking his friend's appearance—even though Will is quite handsome. Viewers got their first taste of this running gag in the pilot when Will accuses Jack of sounding like his mother. Jack is so horrified by this insult that he pulls out all the stops to attack his friend. "I don't need this crap from you, Will," Jack screeches. "You nasty, bitter, lonely, balding man!" In another episode, the plot revolves around the two men both pursuing the same guy. When it appears that the object of their affection prefers Will to Jack, the lovable narcissist again mocks his friend's physical appearance, this time by asking Will if he's heard the latest hit being played on the radio. "It's called 'Will Is Fat,'" Jack snaps. "It's from a new album called *Will's Losing His Hair*."[20]

Promoting Gay Rights—Subtly

Major newspapers generally publish a review of a new sitcom, and then pay no more attention to it. For a program to merit any additional stories, it has to do something out of the ordinary. *Will & Grace* made such a return in 2000 because, after two years on the air, the hit comedy had begun to make some powerful—yet subtle—statements about important gay issues. "By keeping things silly," the *Los Angeles Times* reported, "the show has been able to venture into terrain that has proven problematic for other shows."[21]

The specific topic the *Times* was referring to involved the action that had caused such a ruckus when *Roseanne* had dared to provide an image of it in 1994: a same-sex kiss. In fact, *Will & Grace* not only showed a man-on-man lip lock but, at the same time, derided the TV networks for being skittish about allowing viewers to see gay people being affectionate.

In the episode, Jack tunes into a sitcom because NBC has promised that the show's two gay characters will engage in a historic kiss—"One giant step for man on mankind," Will says sarcastically. But when the big moment arrives, the camera turns away. Jack is so incensed that he persuades Will to march down to the network's offices with him to complain. When an assistant won't let the two men talk to NBC's president, they take matters into their own hands—or, more accurately, their own *lips*—by joining the line of people waiting to talk to *Today* show weatherman Al Roker and then kissing in front of a live national audience.[22]

The *Los Angeles Times* praised the episode for approaching the topic of same-sex affection in a humorous vein and thereby avoiding the attacks that conservative groups would have made if the kiss had been of the romantic variety. *Will & Grace* co-creator Max Mutchnick was a major source in the *Times* article, repeating his earlier assertion that the show wasn't trying to force gay rights issues down its audience's throat. "Nothing about Will and Jack being gay is in bold," he said. At the end of the piece, however, Mutchnick made a statement that suggested the program would address other serious issues in the future. "We're going to tell every kind of story," he said. "Just be patient. It's all coming at you."[23]

One message that came at viewers involved same-sex couples being allowed to legalize their relationships. The major storyline in an episode in season three was that Will had grown tired of Grace assuming that he'd always buy gifts for their friends in observance of a birthday or a wedding. On this particular occasion, the celebration takes place in Vermont, the only state that allowed same-sex civil unions at the time, between their friends Joe and Larry. And so, while in the foreground Will and Grace are squabbling, in the background *Will & Grace* is quietly endorsing civil unions. What's more, snippets of dialogue communicate factual information about the issue. When Grace says, "I love weddings," Will responds, "It's not a wedding but a civil union, which affords many—but not all—of the same rights as a marriage."[24]

Joe and Larry's relationship also allowed the sitcom to speak to the issue of gay couples being allowed to adopt children. This time, the primary plotline in another segment during season three was about Will and Jack spending a weekend in the Hamptons. Before the getaway, the guys are flying high with expectations—Jack screams, "It's gonna be *wild!*" But when they arrive at the couple's house, they realize the weekend will be a sedate one. "Hi, guys, great to see you," Larry whispers when greeting them. "I'd kiss you, but it's flu season." He then motions to the baby sleeping in his arms. "This is Hannah, our little pudding." Will and Jack soon learn that the other two couples invited for the weekend also have adopted babies and therefore don't risk passing germs onto the infants, don't drink alcohol, and don't stay up past 10 p.m. Despite the sacrifices to responsible parenthood, all the fathers are blissfully fulfilled. "I haven't slept in eight months," Larry tells them, smiling serenely, "but I have what I've always dreamed of—a family."[25]

A Winning Equation

A month after *Will & Grace* went on the air, *Entertainment Weekly* published a story about the program titled "When Gay Men Happen to Straight Women." One question the writer of that article asked his sources was why the series was doing so well, after *Ellen* had failed just a year earlier. The most persuasive answer came from an NBC executive who said, "It's a fundamentally different show. *Ellen* was about the journey of one character. We're in broader territory with *Will & Grace* because its focus is a relationship."[26]

Unstated but highly relevant in that answer was the fact that this particular relationship was between a gay man and a straight woman. Indeed, Will consistently took a backseat to Grace, as more plotlines revolved around the wacky interior decorator than the milquetoast attorney. The moral of the success, as stated by the *New York Times*: "The gay-straight couple proves that a gay male can appear as a main character in a sitcom on one of the big three networks only when he is safely paired with a heterosexual woman."[27]

A second major element in *Will & Grace*'s winning equation was that the actor portraying the main gay character, unlike with *Ellen*, didn't publicly announce that he was gay at the same moment that his television persona did. Indeed, numerous news stories reported that Eric McCormack is straight. This meant that viewers who enjoyed watching the show but weren't necessarily ready to embrace homosexuality in real life could take solace in the fact that the affable guy they invited into their living rooms every week wasn't really a gay man—he just played one on TV.

Another important factor in the NBC sitcom's success had nothing to do with gay content but much to do with quality. The show won the Emmy Award for best comedy as well as best comedy writing, and each of the show's four stars took home individual trophies as well. "*Will & Grace* is a rarity," *TV Guide* gushed in one of several cover stories about the series, "in that it is a fresh, sexy sitcom populated by a crackerjack team of comic actors."[28]

Economics was another facet of the program's triumph. After the coming-out episode of *Ellen* proved that many companies were willing to advertise on a gay-themed TV program as long as the show drew a large audience, *Will & Grace* took that reality to new heights by attracting a stable of sponsors for a wide range of products and services. "The novelty of showcasing gay characters week after week," the *Atlanta Journal* wrote, "counts for nothing if it doesn't go *ka-ching* financially, and that was never a problem for this popular NBC hit."[29]

Yet another relevant observation is that the popularity of *Will & Grace* was, from the beginning, enhanced by the network's strategy to make the show, as described by the *Chicago Tribune*, "an exercise in pragmatism, not polemic." Clearly learning from ABC's ill-fated experience with *Ellen*, NBC executives didn't allow their sitcom to move quickly into potentially controversial subject areas such as showing a same-sex romantic kiss. For it wasn't until *Will & Grace*'s eighth and final season that its leading man finally locked lips with a male love interest.[30]

At the same time, though, a fair-minded assessment of *Will & Grace* should not denigrate the program as, in the words of the *San Francisco Chronicle*, having "caved in" to anti-gay pressure. Ellen DeGeneres said, after her sitcom was canceled, that she had incorporated lesbian topics into her plotlines in response to letters from gay teenagers such as the boy who wrote, "Thank you for letting me realize that I'm not a nasty, sick person." If that same young man later watched *Will & Grace*, he saw a gay character who was every bit as happy, healthy, and successful as the lesbian on *Ellen*. Indeed, that teenage boy didn't see just one gay male role model, but a pair of them.[31]

The fact that fulfilled and emotionally stable gay men come in more than one variety—some steady and chaste, others flighty and promiscuous—is just one of several statements that *Will & Grace* made during its triumphant time on the air. Other important messages included that many gay men form close bonds with straight women and that a goodly number of those same fellows are masters of witty repartee as well as narcissists who work hard to look good. The most substantive message, one that emerged only after the sitcom had become well established, was that gay people deserve to be treated fairly, including having the right to legalize their relationships and to adopt children.

These specific messages shouldn't obscure the much broader contribution that the program made: It exposed an unprecedented 19 million viewers to gay men on a weekly basis. Various news organizations spoke to this topic. "There are millions of people in this country who do not know an openly gay person," the *Los Angeles Times* said. "Once a week, those people let Will and Jack into their homes, and therefore now they know two gay men." The *Philadelphia Inquirer* made the same point, saying, "Programs such as *Will & Grace* give straight viewers a chance to make friends with gays in their living rooms. It's like gay sensitivity training." The *Inquirer* went on to argue that the show not only helped make many Americans comfortable with gay men but also persuaded a sizable number of those people to support gay rights. "This is the genius of television. Gay characters have a cumulative power. They end up moving the center of public opinion."[32]

Despite *Will & Grace*'s long list of achievements, the program also is vulnerable to criticism on several counts.

At the top of the list is the fact that Will never entered the kind of long-term relationship that would have forced The Powers That Be at the network to show him displaying affection toward another man. Although NBC's strategy for avoiding controversy by not showing a gay romantic kiss in an early episode is understandable from a pragmatic point of view, the fact remains that having a smart, handsome, personable, and successful guy like Will staying single for eight years strains the limits of believability.[33]

Another concern is that while the program featured Will and Jack in starring roles and other gay men such as Joe and Larry in recurring ones, lesbians appeared in no more than half a dozen segments. And so, while *Will & Grace* represented a huge step forward vis-à-vis the visibility of gay men, the series reinforced the media's long-standing tendency to sideline gay women.[34]

Lesbians weren't the only gay people largely absent from the world created by *Will & Grace*. While Will and Jack differed from each other in significant ways, both of the characters, as well as their buddies in recurring roles, were white. It was only in the last of the eight seasons that an African-American man appeared in four episodes. As the *New York Times* pointed out, "A lot of gays are men of color, but a viewer wouldn't know that from watching this show."[35]

Will & Grace's success prompted the *Los Angeles Times* to report, in a front-page story published in 1999, on a curious dynamic related to minority groups on television:

> Thanks primarily to the blockbuster hit 'Will & Grace,' there has been a dramatic increase in the visibility of gay characters on the major networks, but it also must be acknowledged that black, Asian and Latino characters are still almost totally absent.[36]

When the *Times* sought to explain this yes-gays/no-persons-of-color phenomenon, the paper focused some of its attention on gay buying power. "One network president, who asked not to be identified, conceded that gay viewers are regarded as a key component of the young, upwardly mobile audience that networks are wooing at the expense of other minority groups," the paper reported. "Gay characters are gaining visibility in the media because decision-makers are eager to reach out to gay consumers who are seen as having lots of disposable income, while blacks and Latinos are not." The *Times* also pointed out that many liberal-leaning stars such as Madonna, Glenn Close, Matt Damon, and Michael Douglas used their appearances as guests on the show to advance gay rights. "They're eager to use their power as celebrities to attract a larger audience and thereby make more of the public comfortable with gay characters and gay issues."[37]

But the *Times* gave the most prominence to another factor that it saw as driving TV to showcase gay characters: the Gay Mafia.

"There are gays *on* television because there are gays *in* television," the paper reported. "Unlike Latinos, blacks and Asian Americans, gay people are fully integrated into the Hollywood power structure. They hold jobs from the upper ranks to the lower reaches of the industry." The *Times* found this point so significant, in fact, that it took the unusual step, in the world of journalism, of making virtually the same observation a second time later in the story: "Unlike ethnic minorities, gays are common in upper-level network and studio management and on show staffs. Show business is one of the industries in America that has a disproportionate number of gay people in it."[38]

The strongest support for the *Times*'s argument involved *Will & Grace*. Max Mutchnick, the openly gay co-creator and executive producer of the series, based the concept of the show on his personal experiences as a gay man who'd been best friends with a straight woman for several decades. "We were always a couple in every single way except the bedroom," Mutchnick said. "Save for her vagina, she'd be perfect for me." Mutchnick didn't stop with creating the series, though, as he also was relentless in pushing NBC executives to put the show on the air. "I kept faxing them the grosses from 'My Best Friend's Wedding' and 'The Birdcage,'" he said. If it hadn't been for Mutchnick's persistence, the most successful gay program in television history, the *Times* pointed out, never would have been made.[39]

Other members of what the *Times* labeled the Hollywood "Gay Mafia" were David Crane, whose production company created the NBC sitcom *Friends* and its various gay characters and story lines; Kevin Williamson, who created the WB series *Dawson's Creek* with a gay teenager as one of its central characters; and David Lee and Joe Keenan, who wrote the scripts for the numerous episodes of the NBC comedy *Frasier* that revolved around gay characters and issues.[40]

As the new millennium was about to begin, then, three major forces were working to increase positive gay content in the media: the buying power of gay Americans made them a highly attractive target audience, numerous liberal-minded Hollywood stars and other industry heavy-weights were eager to use their power to advance gay rights, and members of the Gay Mafia were committed to employing their creative talent to make sure gay characters and issues were part of the media mix.

13 *Queer as Folk*
"An Unvarnished Treatment of Gay Life"

In the first year of the new millennium, one scene in the premier episode of a groundbreaking television series made a same-sex kiss seem downright quaint.

The scene began with a handsome twenty-nine-year-old telling a baby-faced seventeen-year-old about his first experience with gay sex a dozen years earlier. When the man finishes his description, the awestruck teenager says, "I bet you were really scared." The man then responds softly, "We're all scared the first time," before gently directing the virginal youth, who's lying buck-naked among the sheets, to lean back and lift his legs into the air so the man can insert his erect penis into the boy's anus.[1]

Queer as Folk could showcase such graphic content because it aired not on a major broadcast network but on the pay-cable channel Showtime, which earns its revenue not from commercials but from subscribers who pay a monthly fee to bring its programming into their homes. So the show didn't have to worry about offending advertisers or being censored by network executives, as long as its content was sufficiently titillating to attract an audience.

And that it was. "There's never been anything like it," *USA Today* said of the program, while the *Chicago Tribune* added:

> "Queer as Folk" is a randy and often explicit exploration of the gay experience—the sort of gutsy programming that would never get past the drawing board at the networks. The place for an honest and an unvarnished treatment of gay life is Showtime.[2]

Queer as Folk's characters routinely bared their butts and exposed their genitals, while also using words that the major networks wouldn't allow. When a man at a party asks the seventeen-year-old how he spends his time, the art student says he's recently been manipulating classical form with digital imagery. Impressed by the boy's words, the man says, "So you're not just a pretty face," and Justin responds, "No, I've got a pretty big cock as well—and I give one helluva blow job." Because of the nudity and explicit language, the hour-long episodes, which aired at 10 on Sunday nights, carried a TV-MA rating to indicate the content was only suitable for mature viewers seventeen years of age or older.[3]

Slightly more than one million Showtime subscribers—who paid $40 a month beyond their basic cable charge—watched *Queer as Folk* during the five seasons that it was on the air, from 2000 to 2005. Most viewers were gay, but some straight women watched as well, apparently attracted to what critics dubbed, in a less-than-positive tone, the "soap opera" nature of the program.[4]

That wasn't the only criticism of the show. Poor writing was the most frequent complaint; the *New York Times* groused, "The characters handle their problems in a formulaic manner, seldom carrying the scars or the lessons from one episode to the next." A penchant for sensationalism was another concern; *USA Today* called the show "a voyeuristic tour of gay life." Weak acting was a problem, too; the *Washington Post* said the actors "convey emotions with all the subtlety of a circus parade."[5]

Queer as Folk focused on the hedonistic lives of five young men who resided in Pittsburgh. The two central characters were Michael, a boy-next-door type who was still in the closet when the series began, and his best friend Brian, who was featured in the anal sex scene in the premier episode. The other three main characters were the teenage Justin, the flamboyant Emmett, and the uptight Ted. A lesbian couple also appeared regularly, although the men dominated the plotlines. *Queer as Folk* was based on a similar series that had aired on British television, its title coming from the old English saying, "There's nowt so queer as folk," which means there's nothing so strange as people.[6]

At the same time that the program was telling provocative stories about its main characters, it was also sending messages about Gay America writ large. Heading the list was that the most important aspect of gay life is spelled S-E-X. A second pervasive statement was that many gay people isolate themselves, as much as possible, from straight people. Other statements involved topics that previous TV programs had largely ignored—gay bashing, HIV/AIDS, safe sex, and drug use.

"It's All about Sex"

Michael began *Queer as Folk*'s debut episode by telling the audience, "The first thing you have to know is: It's all about sex. They say men think about sex every twenty-eight seconds. Of course that's *straight* men. With gay men, it's every nine."[7]

Brian was the most promiscuous of the characters, typically having sex with several different men in each episode. In the premiere, he makes eye contact with a client during a business meeting and then leads the guy into the men's room for a quickie. Before the episode ends, Brian has also laid claim to Justin's virginity and has had sex with two other men in the backroom of his favorite bar, Babylon. "I don't believe in love," Brian says matter-of-factly. "I believe in fucking—get in and out with a maximum of pleasure and a minimum of bullshit."[8]

The other recurring characters were fans of casual sex, too. In the first segment, Michael rejects a guy who cruises him; when his friends point out that the pursuer has a bulging crotch, Michael takes the guy home for a one-night stand. In another episode, Justin applies to work as a go-go dancer, but the owner of the bar will only hire the teenage pretty boy if he agrees to have oral sex; so Justin drops his pants. Later in the series, Emmett takes a job as a maid for a gay couple he idolizes because they've been in a monogamous relationship for eleven years; within days, both men secretly seduce their new employee. Because Ted is less physically attractive than his friends, he has a harder time hooking up, so the accountant spends his workdays "interacting" with cumquik.com; his cyberspace sex life is disrupted when his boss discovers how Ted is spending his time—and promptly fires him.[9]

Queer as Folk's most intriguing sexual plotlines had to do with how two men who aren't monogamous can, nevertheless, have an emotionally committed relationship. The topic arises when Brian admits to Justin that he has feelings for the teenager and agrees that they can live together. "But don't get the idea we're some married couple," the promiscuous man warns his young lover, saying that he'll continue to have sex outside the relationship. "If I'm out late, just assume I'm doing what I want to do—I'm fucking. And when I come home, I'll also be doing exactly what I want to do—coming home to you." Justin accepts the rules but also sets some of his own. "You can fuck whoever you want to, as long as it's not twice—same for me," the teenager stipulates. He also insists that Brian limit himself to anonymous sexual encounters, never asking a man's name. The couple's other two rules are that they both will always get home by 3 a.m., and that neither will kiss another sex partner on the mouth.[10]

"A New Kind of Family"

Observers said the primary reason for *Will & Grace*'s success was that the sitcom balanced gay Will with straight Grace. In a vivid contrast to that strategic move by NBC, Showtime portrayed a world in which all the main characters were gay.

Numerous episodes showed the five gay men coming together to celebrate birthdays and holidays, while various plotlines illustrated the support they give each other. When Ted suffers a seizure that sends him into a life-threatening coma, for example, his gay friends take turns standing vigil beside his hospital bed. And after Ted introduces an acquaintance to his buddies, the newcomer says, "I love your friends. They're like family," prompting Ted to furrow his brow and say emphatically, "They *are* my family."[11]

Queer as Folk's gay family extended to the two lesbians. The premier episode revolved around Brian becoming a father, as he had provided the sperm that allowed his long-time friend Lindsay to become pregnant. A second gay-lesbian familial bond evolved later in the series when Melanie had a baby, with Michael filling the role of sperm donor this time.[12]

The only straight character with a recurring role was Michael's mother. It's no coincidence that the foul-mouthed, in-your-face woman consistently provided comic relief. For in the topsy-turvy world created by *Queer as Folk*, the overweight and over-the-top waitress with flaming red hair and a penchant for wearing T-shirts with goofy slogans— "I Love My Penis," "Foreplay is For Pussies"—takes the place of the stereotypically lisping and limp-wristed gay man who typically prompts snickers from the audience whenever he appears.[13]

News organizations felt compelled to reveal the sexual orientations of *Queer as Folk*'s cast members. Randy Harrison as Justin and Peter Paige as Emmett were the only actors in the original cast who were openly gay in real life, according to the stories. *Newsweek* took an additional step by reporting, soon after the show debuted, that one of the straight stars— he played Michael's boyfriend—was having a tough time kissing male cast members. The magazine quoted Chris Potter as saying: "What do you do? As soon as they say 'Cut'—you spit. You want to go to a strip bar or touch the makeup girls. You feel dirty." It surprised no one, after that statement was published, that Potter was not re-hired for season two. He was replaced by Robert Gant, who became the third openly gay member of the cast.[14]

The Realities of Gay Bashing

One of the chilling realities of gay life that *Queer as Folk* brought to American television is that homophobia sometimes leads to physical violence.

During the first season, the program's dramatic focus increasingly centered on Justin and his struggles at the private high school he was attending. One day, the teenager finds the words "Fags Die" painted on his locker. Another time, the school's star athlete calls Justin "queer" during class, and the teacher refuses to discipline the name caller.[15]

Viewers can feel the emotional pulse of the program pick up speed when Justin invites Brian to his senior prom and they steal the spotlight as the best dancers at the event. As the couple is in the parking lot preparing to leave, the boy who earlier had called Justin "queer" sneaks up behind him and slams a baseball bat into his skull. In classic soap-opera fashion, the season ends with viewers not knowing if the victim will live or die.[16]

The drama continued early in the second season, with Justin lying in a coma for two weeks and then going through intensive rehabilitation therapy for four more. After being released from the hospital, the previously self-assured young man is now plagued by fear and recurring nightmares. The gifted artist is also impaired physically, no longer able to draw for more than fifteen minutes at a time.[17]

Various news outlets reported on the storyline, including how *Queer as Folk* showed that the American judicial system often doesn't provide appropriately severe punishment for gay bashers. "In a sadly believable turn of events," the *Washington Post* reported, "the rich boy who assaulted Justin gets a mild slap on the wrist from the plainly evil presiding judge, who claims the bigot was 'unduly provoked' by the sight of two men dancing together." And so the straight attacker was convicted only of assault rather than attempted murder, and was required merely to complete a few hours of community service without spending a single day in jail.[18]

HIV/AIDS and Gay Life

Because protease inhibitors had been available for several years, many Americans of the early 2000s considered the AIDS epidemic to be either a relic of the past or a health crisis that existed in other parts of the world but not in the United States. For gay men, however, the fear of contracting HIV was still a very real concern. *Queer as Folk* reflected that reality.

Hundreds of references were made to the virus and the disease. HIV played a prominent role, for example, in episodes involving Hunter, a teenage hustler. Hunter had contracted the virus when his mother forced him, when he was only twelve years old, to earn money by having anal sex with gay men. In addition, Michael's gay uncle had full-blown AIDS; Vic suffers various ups and downs in his health and finances, ultimately dying from complications related to one of the drugs he was taking.[19]

The most compelling HIV plotline involved the relationship between a character who is positive and another who is negative. Soon after Ben, a college professor, meets Michael, he tells the younger man that he has the virus. Michael then seeks the counsel of his friends, who all tell him not to date the guy. "You're playing with fire," Brian says. "What happens if a condom breaks?" Brian shakes his head and says, "I wouldn't do it no matter how much I liked him."[20]

Despite the warnings, Michael can't shake his feelings for Ben, convinced that he's found the love of his life. The pair then begin talking, in earnest, about what it would take for a relationship between them to work. Michael assures Ben that he'll protect himself, while Ben insists that Michael must understand the realities of his health status, such as the fact that he takes fifty pills a day and that, for him, catching a cold could be fatal. While those details and warnings were meant to educate Michael, they served as a primer on HIV for *Queer as Folk* viewers as well.[21]

After a great deal of thought, the two men consummate their relationship, which evolves into a rich and nurturing one for both of them—as well as the first of its kind ever depicted on television. Indeed, Ben and Michael ultimately tie the matrimonial knot while traveling to Toronto, Canada, where same-sex marriage is legal.[22]

Gay Men as Safe-Sex Poster Boys

Along with emphasizing sex and HIV/AIDS, *Queer as Folk* also placed a great deal of attention on the importance of practicing safe sex. Indeed, the Showtime program focused more on this topic than any other television series before or since.

The show's campaign to encourage viewers to use condoms began early. The most widely discussed scene in the debut episode—the *New York Times*, *Washington Post*, and *Time* magazine all ran stories about it—involved Brian and Justin having sex, and was the first time that anal intercourse had been depicted on American television. Just as the sexually experienced Brian is about to insert his penis into Justin, the boy says, "Wait. In school we had this lecture about safe sex." Brian instantly produces a condom, smiles, and responds, "Now we're going to have a demonstration." He then gently continues, "Put it on me. Go ahead."[23]

Showtime's writers had, in short, placed a non-preachy lesson about safe sex smack dab in the middle of what soon became a classic media moment in the gay male culture. Legions of viewers either taped the segment off air or bought the DVD and then replayed it multiple times.

Queer as Folk repeatedly reinforced that potent public health message. When Justin wants to start a gay-straight alliance at his high school, he hands out free condoms to new members. And after Justin and Brian start living together, the safe-sex issue comes up again. The younger man points out that they've never had intercourse bareback style but says he'd like to try it. Brian refuses. "Never let anyone fuck you without a condom," he says sternly. "I want you safe. I want you around for a long time."[24]

Just because references to safe sex were sprinkled into the various episodes didn't mean that all the characters took precautions all the time. Brian doesn't protect the hundreds of men he indiscriminately has sex with, unless the guy mentions the topic, as Justin did.

Drug Use in the Gay Community

By the year 2000, half a century had passed since news organizations had ushered "perverts" onto the national radar screen. Since that time, a variety of news stories, movies, and TV programs had sent the American public any number of messages about gay people. One topic that had only been mentioned in passing, however, was drug use in the gay community. An article in 1950, for example, had described one homosexual as an "unshaven derelict who peddles dope." Then came *Queer as Folk*, which communicated that drugs play a major role in gay life.[25]

That message began when Ted meets a guy named Blake who agrees to have sex with the older and less-attractive accountant, *if* they use crystal meth. Ted is so smitten that he agrees, but he then overdoses on the drug and has to be hospitalized. And yet, even after that traumatic incident, he remains infatuated, persuading his friend Melanie to hire Blake as an assistant in her law firm. Only when the guy causes major problems for Melanie in the office is Ted forced to check Blake into a drug treatment center.[26]

Another drug storyline begins when Ted accepts an invitation to a party and arrives to find that the event is, in fact, a drug-powered orgy. After he joins the partygoers that first time, such all-night affairs soon grow to dominate his life. The big draw for Ted is that the men at the parties are so high they don't care that he's not particularly attractive, as long as he's willing to have sex. "I feel so hot, so sexy," Ted says. "Everybody wants me, and I want them. Fuck a room full of guys—and then fuck some more."[27]

But the new lifestyle takes its toll. After Ted had lost his job, Lindsay and Melanie asked him to manage their infant son's college savings account, hoping to make their friend feel useful. That plan goes awry when Ted's new acquaintances urge him to fly with them to a party in Palm Springs: "Tens of thousands of men who want to suck you and fuck you," one guy promises. With crystal meth and indiscriminate sex now ruling his life, Ted uses the baby's college fund to pay for his trip. After that incident, the members of Ted's gay/lesbian family conclude that he's an addict, though he denies it.[28]

Ted hits bottom when he goes to a party and sees a crowd of men laughing at a home video one of them had taped during a previous event. The image on the screen is of a line of men sticking their erect penises— one after another after another—into a drugged-out guy in a leather sling, so high he has no idea what's happening. When Ted gets closer, he sees that the man getting gang banged on the tape is him. Having no recollection of the degrading and highly dangerous session, he finally realizes that his life is out of control. He checks himself into the same drug rehabilitation center where he earlier had taken Blake.[29]

"Dealing with Heavy Issues"

Because *Queer as Folk* and *Will & Grace* were both television shows and many of their episodes aired during the same years, one way to identify final thoughts about the Showtime series is to re-visit some of the points that surfaced in the concluding assessment of its NBC counterpart. This process highlights some major differences between the two programs.

Will & Grace's signature characteristic was that it relied on straight characters to attract a broad audience. *Queer as Folk*, by contrast, was dominated by gay men, relegating straight people to only a few—and consistently negative—roles. The only recurring non-gay character was Michael's mother, whose outrageous appearance and personal style made her laughable. Likewise, memorable straights who appeared in one or two episodes included the boy who hit Justin with a baseball bat, the high school teacher who allowed that same boy to go unpunished after calling Justin "queer," the judge who ultimately failed to send the basher to jail, and the mother who forced her adolescent son to become a prostitute. The combination of having so few heterosexual characters and making many of them so reprehensible led to one of the myriad criticisms leveled at the program. "Nothing in 'Queer as Folk' bothers me more than how straight people are portrayed," a gay columnist wrote in the *New York Times*. "It seems so unnatural, so at odds with the issues of inclusiveness and commonality that concern the gay community right now."[30]

A second of *Will & Grace*'s important characteristics was its exceptional quality, with the NBC hit winning numerous Emmy Awards. The Showtime series, by contrast, was never nominated for an Emmy, and legions of critics offered plenty of reasons why it wasn't. Indeed, even members of the gay press condemned *Queer as Folk*. "The series isn't of the highest quality," wrote the *Washington Blade*, the weekly newspaper serving the gay community in the nation's capital, with the specific faults cited by the paper sounding much like those catalogued in the mainstream press—"blasé writing," "mediocre acting," "outlandish plots."[31]

For some observers who have compared *Will & Grace* and *Queer as Folk*, the biggest difference between them is how the shows approached the topic of physical contact between men. The *San Francisco Chronicle* criticized the network program for "playing it chaste" by not allowing Will to pucker up for a romantic kiss, while *Salon* magazine applauded the pay-cable show for "diving giddily and explicitly" into the sexual aspects of gay life. But several of *Queer as Folk*'s detractors said the program went too far. The *Los Angeles Times* dismissed the show as nothing but "an assembly line of orgasms," and *USA Today* lambasted it for communicating that gay men "have sex as often as they change their clothes," supporting the point by sending a reporter to the real-life Gay Pittsburgh and quoting a man there as saying, "I don't know any gay man who has that much sex."[32]

Some of the differences between *Will & Grace* and *Queer as Folk* evolve from the first show being a sitcom on a major network and the second being a drama on a pay-cable channel. *Queer as Folk*, as both the first gay-themed program on American television that wasn't a comedy and as the first that didn't have to be concerned about offending advertisers, had the opportunity to delve into subject areas that were off limits for its network predecessors such as *Soap* and *Ellen*. To its credit, the groundbreaking Showtime program took advantage of that opportunity. The *Chicago Sun-Times* praised *Queer as Folk*'s "bold style," and *Salon* applauded the series for "dealing with heavy issues" such as promiscuity and widespread drug use in the gay community. And so, reminiscent of how *Philadelphia* deserves praise as a landmark motion picture because it tackled the subject of AIDS, *Queer as Folk* should be credited for its effort to rise to that same stature in the world of television by portraying not only HIV/AIDS but also such topics as anti-gay violence and safe sex.[33]

Regrettably, the *Will & Grace/Queer as Folk* comparison illuminates two major shortcomings the programs shared. First, neither the comedy nor the drama gave gay women their due. While lesbians had some presence in the Showtime program, *Salon* was on solid ground when it called *Queer as Folk*'s depiction of gay women "superficial" because it consistently portrayed Lindsay and Melanie as "boring, scolding mommy figures" rather than multi-dimensional characters. Second, neither *Will & Grace* nor *Queer as Folk* reflected the racial diversity of the gay community, as no major gay character on either program was a person of color. After *Queer as Folk*'s first season, the *Los Angeles Times* asked, "Will the show begin to depict the gay community in all its diversity?" After the five seasons had ended in 2005, the answer to that question was a resounding "No."[34]

A final thought regarding *Queer as Folk* involves a comment that the *Washington Post* made about the series. The reason that conservative groups never attacked the show, the paper speculated, may have been that viewers had to subscribe to the cable channel on which it aired. "But it also may be," the *Post* continued, "because the show doesn't offer a very inviting picture of the gay world." While that final sentence is an accurate one, it alludes to what can, at the same time, be seen as one of the most *beneficial* aspects vis-à-vis gay, lesbian, and/or questioning young people. Even though many people familiar with gay life weren't happy with the "unvarnished treatment" *Queer as Folk* presented, anyone who has lived in that world has to admit that many of the plot points—drug use being a persistent problem, gay relationships being difficult to maintain, the judicial system treating gay people unfairly—are among the bewildering realities that a young person may encounter as he or she enters Gay and Lesbian America: Welcome to a whole new world.[35]

14 *Queer Eye for the Straight Guy*
The "Fab Five" as Gay Reality TV

Television viewers had their first glimpse of a homosexual in 1977 with the pioneering sitcom *Soap*. Two decades later, a new generation of Americans were given a somewhat broader look at gay men, beginning in 1998, through the two male characters featured on *Will & Grace*. Two years after that, pay-cable subscribers had the chance to meet several more men who lived and loved—or at least lusted—in the world created by *Queer as Folk*. Despite this continuum of groundbreaking shows, in 2003 a basic-cable channel crossed yet another threshold by exposing TV viewers to an entirely new category of gay men:

The real thing.

Indeed, the in-the-flesh quintet on *Queer Eye for the Straight Guy* displayed such a stunning mixture of charm, wit, and good taste that they created a whirlwind of public attention that turned the Bravo series into a media sensation. The *Los Angeles Times* praised the program for making "this year's biggest splash" in all of television, and an *Entertainment Weekly* cover headline screamed "Outrageous Breakout Hit!"[1]

Queer Eye was created by David Collins, an openly gay man, as part of the reality-TV phenomenon that exploded onto the cultural landscape in the early 2000s. Each hour-long episode aired on Tuesday at 10 p.m. and was repeated on other days at various times, day and night. The action swirled around five experts on fashion, grooming, home decorating, cuisine, and culture who descended on a straight man and, as the *New York Times* put it, "taught the hapless hetero the evils of matted back hair and dirty bath tubs." Everyone seemed to embrace the highly personable gay guys who, overnight, became known nationwide as the "Fab Five."[2]

The program, which was targeted primarily at gays and at young and middle-aged women, was soon attracting three million viewers—the largest in the twenty-five years that Bravo had been on the air. And it didn't take long for the Fab Five to expand their talents well beyond the TV show. Within six months after *Queer Eye* debuted, the five men released a CD containing music from the show, published the first of several books they ultimately would write, and appeared as Barbara

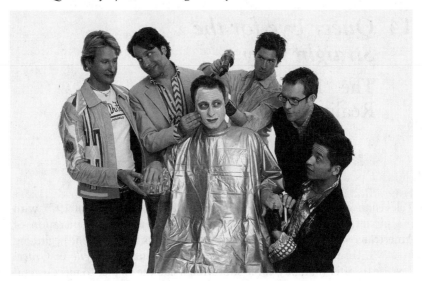

Figure 14.1 Queer Eye for the Straight Guy featured the "Fab Five" working their magic on one hapless hetero.
Courtesy of Bravo/Photofest.

Walters's guests on her annual special spotlighting "The Ten Most Fascinating People of the Year."[3]

As the *très gay* fellows cut their wide swath across the American culture, they garnered a mother lode of publicity. And the first question out of every reporter's mouth seemed to be the same: "Aren't you reinforcing stereotypes of gay men as swishy queens?" The responses varied only slightly with which Fab Fiver did the talking. Thom Filicia said, "I'm not playing the character of an interior designer. It's just me. How can we be stereotypes if we're being ourselves?" Kyan Douglas, the hunky grooming expert, said, "I'm all for guys being butch because I identify with that. But it's also perfectly OK with me for a gay guy to be effeminate. If somebody has a problem with that, they need to open up their mind."[4]

Criticism for reinforcing stereotypes wasn't the only controversy the show stirred up. The head of the Traditional Values Coalition condemned the program as part of Hollywood's "pro-homosexual agenda," and a station in Georgia refused to air segments during primetime, relegating them to 2 a.m. instead. The *New York Times* was among the journalistic voices that saw the opposition to *Queer Eye* as an anti-gay backlash in response to the Supreme Court ruling, a month before the program premiered, that anti-sodomy laws were unconstitutional.[5]

From the perspective of the evolution of the media's depiction of gay people, some of the messages sent during *Queer Eye*'s four seasons on the air are familiar, while others are strikingly new. At the top of the list are that gay men are endowed with impeccable taste and that these oh-so-gifted men are eager to share their talents to help the style challenged. Two more clear statements that *Queer Eye* sent are that gay men can be laugh-out-loud funny and that they're eager to build bridges with straight men.

Gay Men Have Impeccable Taste

Three members of the Fab Five arrived with impressive résumés inside the chic portfolios they carried to their auditions. Thom Filicia was on *House Beautiful* magazine's list of America's top 100 interior designers, Ted Allen wrote a food and wine column for *Esquire*, and Jai Rodriguez starred in the Broadway musical *Rent*. And by the end of the first segment, the trio had put their talent to good use. Filicia transformed Butch Schepel's non-descript apartment into a showplace—"You put a living room where a crack den used to be," Schepel gushed; Allen showed the burly carpenter how to create tasty *hors d'oeuvres*; and Rodriguez landed the aspiring artist a one-man show in a tony Manhattan gallery.[6]

One journalistic voice after another gave the Fab Five high marks for their work. The *Boston Globe* reported that every member of the group had proven that he was "armed with good taste," the *New York Times* described the five-member makeover team as "a league of superheroes, each gifted with a special power," and the *Chicago Sun-Times* gushed, "They're queer, they're here, but never fear. These stylish saviors want only to make you better, to pull you out of the abyss and into the light."[7]

Some news outlets expanded beyond the Fab Five to acknowledge the many contributions their gay forefathers had made to American fashion and grooming. "Gay men have been making over straight men at least as far back as the rise of the power suit," the *Washington Post* reported, going on to credit gay designers with a long list of style trends. "They popularized unconstructed blazers and square-toed loafers. They encouraged straight men to engage in monochromatic dressing in which their ties matched their shirts. They persuaded them to exchange their briefcases for messenger bags. And they've trained many a straight man to run a quarter-size dollop of gel through his hair before rushing out the door."[8]

Gay Men Are Helpful

Queer Eye didn't show merely that gay men are endowed with impeccable taste, as viewers also learned that men who love men are perfectly willing to employ their talent to help improve the lives of others.

Episodes typically began with the Fab Five arriving at the home of the style-deficient straight guy and promptly letting loose with a string of critical remarks. As fashion maven Carson Kressley, formerly a stylist for Ralph Lauren, looked through the items of clothing hanging in one man's closet, he turns to the guy and asks, "Were these alphabetized by ugly, uglier, and ugliest?" Kressley further dramatizes his point by refusing to touch any of the shirts and trousers in the closet with his bare hands, using a pair of salad tongs instead. As each segment unfolded, however, the *Queer Eye* stars stopped criticizing and started directing their expertise to the task at hand.[9]

One episode focused on an Army private who was being deployed to Iraq. Ray Steele had married his wife Maria in her native Colombia, and their daughter had been born a year later. None of Steele's relatives could afford to travel to South America for the wedding, though, and the couple couldn't afford to buy decent furniture for their apartment. Then the Fab Five sprang into action. First they created a dream-come-true marriage ceremony, the bride in a Vera Wang gown as she descended the stairs on a rooftop high above the Manhattan skyline. Next came the apartment, which the makeover artists decorated with vibrant colors to provide sensory stimulation for baby Sabrina. "You've made a miracle," Ray Steele told the men, adding that he was proud to fight for his country but had worried about leaving his wife and daughter. "Thanks to you, I know my family will be safe and secure in this beautiful home you've created."[10]

Especially touching in dealing with the Steeles was the thought the five men had put into their project. Thom Filicia chose a dining room table with rounded corners so Sabrina wouldn't hurt her head if she bumped into it. Carson Kressley bought enough clothes for the infant in progressively larger sizes so, as time passed, her mother could give the little girl new outfits while saying, over and over during the father's absence, "Your daddy bought this for you before he left." Before culture expert Jai Rodriguez gave Maria Steele a cashmere sweater, he sprayed it with her husband's favorite cologne so she'd be subtly reminded, every time she wore it, of her special soldier fighting on the other side of the world. "What you are doing for this country takes a lot of courage," a dewy-eyed Rodriguez told Ray Steele, "and we respect you for that."

Gay Men Are Funny

Critics and viewers could argue about which member of the Fab Five was the most gifted or the most helpful, but there's no debating which one was the funniest: Carson Kressley. The *New York Times* lauded "his hysterically campy quips," and the *Washington Post* praised him as "willing to go to any length to get a laugh."[11]

Much of the blond-haired fashionista's humor came from his non-stop witticisms. In one segment, he looked at the straight man's limp ponytail and said flatly, "I used to have hair just like yours." Then he paused for a moment before delivering the punch line: "Only my name was Louise, and I lived in Switzerland." Many of the zingers erupting from La Kressley relied on sexual innuendo. In one instance, he expressed his delight at the food being served at a baseball game, saying, "I love hot wieners and tight buns." Another time, the playful punster took a straight guy shopping at Saks Fifth Avenue, and when he rejoined his four gay buddies, he smiled seductively and boasted, "We had *Saks* together."[12]

Although "Hurricane Carson," as the *New York Times* called Kressley, got the most laughs, Jai Rodriguez managed to hold his own in the humor department as well. Many of Rodriguez's best lines came when he tried to teach new skills to his subjects. In one episode, he demonstrated how to make a proper bed by tucking in the sheets to create what he told his pupil were "hospital corners." When the straight man tried but failed to follow Rodriguez's example, the gay teacher quipped, "That's what I'd call a *mental-hospital* corner."[13]

Even though much of *Queer Eye*'s humor came at the expense of the straight men who appeared on the program, the heteros never showed any sign of feeling insulted. One of the men told the *New York Times*, "The great thing about the team is that even as your entire existence is being questioned, you're laughing along with everything they say."[14]

Gay Men Are Building Bridges to Straight Men

Some cynics argued that the straight men were so effusive in their praise of the Fab Five because the businesses that were highlighted on *Queer Eye* provided their products and services to the men free of charge. For those viewers who weren't so jaded, however, much of the sentiment that was expressed on the show—by the straight guys as well as the gay ones—appeared to come directly from the heart.[15]

Anyone looking for some old-fashioned romance would be hard pressed to find a more satisfying segment than the one built around John Bargeman. The earnest truck driver's major focus when the Fab Five entered the picture was his personal life, as he'd fallen in love with a woman who was earning a master's degree in business administration. They'd been dating for two years, and he wanted to ask Tina to marry him, but he was afraid she'd turn him down because he wasn't as sophisticated as she was. At the beginning of the episode, the five miracle workers articulated their goals. "We have to see if he can step up and become husband material," Ted Allen said. "Our mission is to get her to say, 'Yes,' to his perfect proposal."[16]

The most memorable moment in the episode came when the straight man followed his gay mentors through his redecorated apartment and into the backyard where he saw a beautiful Moroccan tent that Thom Filicia had created by draping fabric around sumptuous cushions, a mosaic table, and dozens of candles—the perfect place for a man to ask the love of his life to marry him. As Bargeman sits down, the Fab Five cluster around him. He starts to talk, intending to thank them for all they've done, but the words won't come. Too choked up by the emotions he's feeling, Bargeman can only hug the men, one after the other, as tears roll down his cheeks.

The straight men featured in other episodes were more successful in articulating their gratitude. A New York Jets fan said, "You guys are the greatest. Anybody that has you on their team—they're gonna win. I'll never forget you guys." A young father told them, "I appreciate everything you guys did, making our house a real home. I want to thank all of you, from the bottom of my heart." One straight man who clearly changed more than his grooming regimen during the segment was a Queens police officer who'd never met an openly gay man before he appeared on *Queer Eye*. Although his thank-you speech was not eloquent, it was brimming with affection:

> All that you guys done for me, man—I can't say enough about you. When I first heard about you guys, I was like, 'I don't know . . .' But after hangin' out with you, there's nobody better than you guys. I really appreciate what you done for me.[17]

"Dude, Maybe Someday that Could Be Me"

Queer Eye for the Straight Guy quickly became not only a cultural phenomenon but also a program recognized for its quality, winning an Emmy Award for best reality show. The fact that the Bravo hit joined *Will & Grace* in receiving one of the highly prized statuettes—while *Queer as Folk* didn't receive so much as a nomination—invites an assessment of *Queer Eye* to begin by re-visiting some of the observations related to those two shows.

One distinctive element of *Will & Grace* was the sitcom relying on straight characters to appeal to a broad audience; by contrast, all of *Queer as Folk*'s major characters were gay, with straight people relegated to minor, and largely negative, roles. *Queer Eye* clearly followed the first model. Although the five gay stars dominated every episode, the straight man of the hour was vital, as the action showed how the gay guys used their good taste and *joie de vivre* to improve his life. In fact, *Queer Eye* went further than *Will & Grace* when it came to gay/straight interaction in two fundamental ways. First, viewers knew the five stars weren't merely actors filling the roles of gay characters but were bona fide gay men. Second, the straight man on each segment wasn't just interacting with the gay men but was devoting a good deal of time and effort to *emulating* them. In the words of the *New York Times*:

All across America, straight guys are watching the show from their stained, sagging couches where they sit in their boxer shorts drinking Budweiser from a can. They see people's lives being transformed by queerness, and they're thinking, 'Dude, maybe someday that could be me.'[18]

Another major difference between *Will & Grace* and *Queer as Folk* involved physical contact: the NBC series was skittish about showing so much as a kiss between two men, while the Showtime series routinely aired images of men engaging in oral and anal sex. On this topic, *Queer Eye* was positioned squarely between the other two shows. The Fab Five playfully touched each other—here, there, and pretty much everywhere— while occasionally exchanging a quick kiss as a casual greeting. These public displays of affection didn't include sex acts, however, as the show's carnal content was limited to zippy one-liners about loving "hot wieners" and "having *Saks* together." At the same time, though, *Queer Eye*'s physical contact and sexual innuendo crossed an entirely new threshold, as the Fab Five didn't confine either their touching or their verbal comments to themselves but often included the straight men as well. Indeed, the program frequently showed one of the five gay men stroking a partially undressed straight guy in such intimate spaces as bedrooms, bathrooms, and fitting rooms. In a typical scene, Carson Kressley is lecturing the Queens police officer about how proper clothing can increase a guy's self-esteem. The fashion expert lets loose with a series of questions: "Are we clear?" Pause. "Are we excited?" Pause. "Do you want to kiss me?" Kressley is clearly being silly rather than serious, as he then throws himself into the man's arms and the officer laughs heartily without flinching. The message: Gay men are sexual, but in a fun way— they're *not* sexual predators.[19]

On providing role models for young people who are exploring their sexual identity, *Queer Eye* clearly was more aligned with *Will & Grace* than *Queer as Folk*, as the Fab Five didn't live in a world defined by drugs and promiscuity. One gay man spoke for many others when he wrote appreciatively of the Bravo program in an article for the *Philadelphia Inquirer*: "Part of growing up gay is imagining queer versions of *American Bandstand* in the 1960s or *Friends* in the 1990s, from which we were excluded. Thanks to shows like *Queer Eye*, we don't have to do that anymore." The Bravo program, like *Will & Grace*, showed gay teenagers that men who love men come in more than one variety. From a segment featuring the Dallas Cowboys Cheerleaders during which Carson Kressley unashamedly joined the girls as they ran laps, passed balls, and waved their pompoms, to another one in which Kyan Douglas showed a beefy cop some weight-loss exercises so he could fit into his uniform again, the Fab Five represented a range of positions on the nellie-to-butch continuum. At the same time, all members of the style-savvy quintet shared several characteristics that every gay youth should aspire to, such as excelling in his career, being eager to help other people, having a robust sense of humor, and—perhaps most important of all—being, in the words of the *Village Voice*, "genuinely comfortable in their gay skin."[20]

One intriguing by-product of *Queer Eye* and its unapologetically gay stars was a linguistic shift that occurred as the program became popular. "Thanks to 'Queer Eye,'" the *Washington Post* reported, "the word 'queer' has gone from a detested epithet to a term embraced by gay groups, thus claiming the word while taking away its sting." Other journalistic voices made the same point. "The increasing use of 'queer,' as in the prime-time TV show 'Queer Eye for the Straight Guy,'" the Associated Press reported, "is changing the word's image." The word "queer" previously had been synonymous with "pansy," "sissy," and "pervert," the news service pointed out, but it was now "sneaking into the mainstream and taking on a hipster edge." Such a dramatic linguistic change is no small matter, as it meant that the members of a stigmatized minority group were becoming culturally empowered.[21]

An assessment of the reality show's performance in the area of diversity is mixed. With regard to race, the fact that Jai Rodriguez was of Puerto Rican heritage was a huge plus, as he made history as the first gay person of color to be featured in a prominent role on a television program. With regard to gender, the record was more complicated. After *Queer Eye for the Straight Guy* succeeded in attracting substantial numbers of viewers during its first two years on the air, Bravo introduced *Queer Eye for the Straight Girl*. Along with the three gay male makeover artists on the program was, in the words of the *Los Angeles Times*, "an attractive lesbian equally at home wearing a tool belt or getting a treatment for her posterior." Regrettably, however, the *Times* continued, "'Straight Girl' has none of the warmth or wit of the original." After four months on the air, the show was canceled.[22]

Another contribution that *Queer Eye* made is related to the process of coming out—or, more accurately, "post" coming out. Beginning in 1977 when *Soap* ushered homosexuality onto the small screen and continuing through *Ellen* twenty years later, gay TV had been fixated on a person struggling to become comfortable with his or her sexuality. That tendency continued, though it lessened in intensity, during the 1990s when a number of *Will & Grace* and *Queer as Folk* episodes focused on gay men acknowledging their sexuality to themselves and others. From the moment the Fab Five exploded onto the cultural landscape, however, there was no question that they were gay, gay, gay—and proudly so. To an unprecedented degree, then, *Queer Eye* told the American public that there's a lot more to being gay than just coming out of the closet.

Members of the Fab Five spending much of their lives buying expensive home furnishings and grooming products prompted the nation's journalists to write another spate of news stories about gay buying power. "Research indicates gays have substantial disposable incomes," the *Boston Globe* reported, while a *USA Today* story about *Queer Eye* described Gay America's spending power as "awesome" and a piece in the *New York Times* opted for the adjective "immense."[23]

The conservative *Wall Street Journal* stressed a different angle of the story, pointing out that all those high disposable incomes were creating a challenge for gay rights activists. "Marketers stress the buying power of gay Americans," the *Journal* reported, "but civil-rights advocates worry that an image of economic comfort and success hurts their battles for protection from discrimination." Despite this reality, other news organizations continued to report on the ever-growing size of gay spending power. By the time *Queer Eye* ended its final season in 2007, *Daily Variety* estimated that the figure had risen to $660 billion a year.[24]

15 Notes on Gay Visibility vs. Lesbian Visibility

On the eve of the year 2000, gay men had been on the media's radar screen for fifty years. They had entered the news arena in 1950 with the "Perverts on the Potomac" scandal, and then had also become the subject of major films and network television shows, including a blockbuster sitcom that introduced a pair of highly likeable gay men to millions of Americans.

Lesbians had, by contrast, received relatively little media attention. A few of them had been mentioned in the news coverage of the Stonewall Rebellion and the debate over gays in the military, and a few more had made fleeting appearances in the early 1990s and then as part of the *Ellen* phenomenon. There's no question, however, that gay women had been much less prominent than gay men.

Some media scholars have made passing reference to the relative invisibility of lesbians. Suzanna Danuta Walters observed, in her book *All the Rage: The Story of Gay Visibility in America*, that "the relationship of lesbians to the media has always been complex and more deeply coded by invisibility than that of gay men." Likewise, Larry Gross and James D. Woods noted, in *The Columbia Reader on Lesbians and Gay Men in Media, Society, and Politics*, that the second half of the twentieth century saw an "increase in gay (and less often lesbian) visibility."[1]

While these and other authors have pointed out that gay men have had a larger media presence than lesbians, none of them has moved to the next logical level of analysis by attempting to answer the question: Why?

That reluctance evolves partly from these scholars having concentrated their efforts on the important step of breaking new ground by documenting the slow emergence of gay people of either gender. In addition, the authors may have recognized that answering this particular "Why?" is no simple task. Indeed, the number of factors that help explain the increasing media visibility of gay men compared to the paucity of depictions of lesbians is formidable.

One powerful concept that's played a role in this phenomenon is stereotyping. When the word "lesbians" is mentioned, a critical mass of

Americans immediately think of conventionally unattractive creatures with mannish mannerisms, coarse facial features, close-cropped hair, and unshaven legs and armpits—hardly the kind of women that the media like to showcase. Conventional wisdom also defines gay women as being overweight and poorly dressed, covering their hefty bodies with flannel shirts, baggy trousers, and work boots—again, totally at odds with the highly attractive and stylishly dressed women that Hollywood typically embraces. By contrast, the term "gay men" brings to mind good-looking guys who have an innate sense of how to dress and groom themselves —think Rupert Everett in *My Best Friend's Wedding* or Will on *Will & Grace*. With this factor, the exception proves the rule; when lesbians finally stepped onto the big and small screen in the 1990s, they were the media-defined beauties such as Sharon Stone in *Basic Instinct* and Mariel Hemingway on *Roseanne*.[2]

A second stereotype that contributes to the relative invisibility of lesbians is that they're perceived as being humorless harpies. During the 1960s and 1970s, gay women were seen by many Americans as the angry, man-hating "dykes" who were portrayed as being among the leaders of the Women's Liberation Movement. Filmmakers and television executives, therefore, were reluctant to bring such unpleasant people to either the large or the small screen. Gay men are more likely to be embraced by the media, by contrast, because they're often perceived as charming, witty, and fun-loving guys who know how to have a good time—and make sure the people around them do as well. Again, the exception proves the rule; the first gay woman to have a recurring presence on a TV program was Ellen DeGeneres, a comedian who had earlier been crowned the funniest person in America.[3]

Another reason for gay men having more prominence in the media than lesbians is related to the economic factor behind the overall shift, since the mid 1990s, toward positive messages being sent about gay people generally. That is, while various news organizations have reported that many gay people have higher-than-average expendable incomes, they also have said, more specifically, that gay men have higher incomes than lesbians. A *New York Times* story on the topic, for example, stated that the average lesbian household earns only 78 percent of what the average gay male household earns.[4]

Another reason gay men have been propelled into media prominence, relative to gay women, is bedrock sexism. Throughout most of this country's history, women didn't play a major role in public life. Even after they were finally granted the right to vote in 1920, they continued to be treated as second-class citizens, as they were generally excluded from such influential spheres as law and business. In the context of this long-held tradition of gender-based discrimination, it's not surprising that the various media genres ignored gay women for so long.[5]

Sheer numbers also may play a role. Dr. Alfred C. Kinsey's two groundbreaking studies—*Sexual Behavior in the Human Male* in 1948 and *Sexual Behavior in the Human Female* in 1953—provided the first statistics on the sexual behavior of Americans. The Indiana University researcher classified 10 percent of adult men as homosexual, while he found the comparable figure for adult women to be only 5 percent. It's logical that the larger of the two demographic groups would receive more attention in the media.[6]

One of the more complex dynamics related to this topic involves sexual acts. Most media consumers are more accepting of physical affection between two women than between two men. Indeed, the idea of one man inserting his erect penis into the mouth or the anus of another man still causes discomfort or disgust—in some instances, *rage*—in a large number of Americans. Because the thought of two men having sex with each other creates such a strong negative reaction in so many readers and viewers, it can provide the element of conflict—sometimes referred to as the "edge"—that the worlds of journalism, film, and television all recognize as part of the formula that can lead to a compelling media product.[7]

A final factor relevant to visibility involves the Gay Mafia issue that was raised as a partial explanation for *Will & Grace*'s blockbuster success. When the *Los Angeles Times* reported that a large number of gays working in the entertainment industry were going out of their way to see that gay media content was both substantial in size and positive in tone, the paper listed a number of gay people who were in positions of power in Hollywood. Every single name on the *Times*'s list was that of a man—not a woman among them. What's more, after *Queer Eye for the Straight Guy* became a hit, the name of yet another gay man, the program's creator David Collins, joined the Gay Mafia boys' club.[8]

16 *The L Word*
Lesbians Move into the Spotlight

After the media depictions of gay men had steadily increased between 1950 and the early 1990s, a handful of fleeting images of lesbians had surfaced when a few women were shown killing in *Basic Instinct,* kissing on *Roseanne,* and looking chic in the pages of several national magazines. Later in the 1990s, the hoopla surrounding *Ellen* had propelled another gay woman into the glare of public attention, although the role proved to be short-lived because the show was canceled soon after Ellen Morgan/ Ellen DeGeneres came out. Next, a pair of Sapphic women appeared in *Queer as Folk,* but they were overshadowed by all the boys. And so, as the gays-in-the-media phenomenon moved into the new millennium, lesbians were still hard to find.

Gay women finally found a place in the spotlight in January 2004 when Showtime, after airing *Queer as Folk* for four seasons, introduced *The L Word.* Many of the country's leading news organizations took note of the program's arrival.

The *Los Angeles Times* pointed out that the pay-cable channel's decision to air the series was propelled by the hope that a large number of lesbians would subscribe to Showtime specifically to see this one program. The strategy worked, as almost one million viewers—most of them lesbians—were soon tuning in.[1]

The two most prominent statements that *The L Word* communicates are that lesbians can be stunningly beautiful and that they also can be obsessively sexual. Additional messages include that the lesbian community is racially diverse, that not everyone fits into the gay/straight dichotomy, and that women who love women have great difficulty remaining monogamous.

Lesbians Living Large

The twenty- and thirty-something denizens of *The L Word* are upscale women who chat on their cell phones as they pilot their Saab convertibles, at break-neck speed, either to Pilates class or to the trendiest of restaurants. Regardless of where they're headed, these ladies wouldn't dream

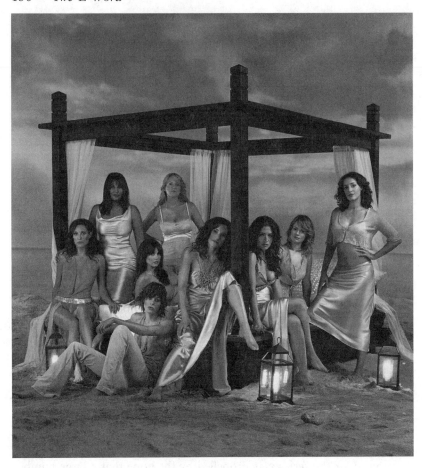

Figure 16.1 In 2004, Showtime introduced pay-cable viewers to a bevy of
beautiful and highly sexual women starring in *The L Word.*

Courtesy of Showtime/Photofest.

of leaving the house until they're coiffed to perfection, styled to within
an inch of their lives, and outfitted in the latest fashion—Jimmy Choo
stilettos, Marc Jacobs miniskirts, vintage Courrèges jackets. In the words
of *USA Today*, the program presents a "highly lip-glossed-and-polished
slice of lesbian life."[2]

At center stage is the aloof, ambitious, and short-tempered workaholic
Bette, a mover and shaker in the world of avant-garde art. The Yale-
educated overachiever is portrayed as being the product of a biracial
marriage between a white mother and a black father.[3]

Another major character is Bette's on-again/off-again partner Tina, a
development executive who temporarily put her career on hold to devote

fulltime to having a baby. Among the couple's closest friends are Shane, an androgynous hairstylist-to-the-stars who dresses and grooms herself like a glam rock star, and Dana, a professional tennis player who achieves celebrity status when she signs a contract to appear in Subaru ads. The newest addition to the group is Jenny, a pouty fiction writer who sells her autobiographical novel to a major publisher.[4]

News organizations reported that the only openly lesbian actress in the cast is Leisha Hailey, who plays a fun-loving bisexual magazine writer named Alice. "I feel like I'm part of something really big," the pixie-like Hailey said after she landed her part in the trailblazing series. "I love the thought of some confused girl in Nebraska or somewhere watching me on the show and realizing that she's not the only one who has certain feelings after all."[5]

Lesbians Can Be Stunningly Beautiful

Because *The L Word* is the first program of its kind, the country's major newspapers published reviews when it debuted. Regardless of which journalistic voice was speaking, one topic that was covered in every piece was how physically attractive the characters are.

The *New York Times* set the pace by telling its readers, "All the women are beautiful." Other publications quickly followed suit, the *Boston Globe* observing, "It is nice to see beautiful women portraying lesbians," and the online magazine *Slate* weighing in with "*The L Word* is eye candy, a glossy production on which everyone is luminous."[6]

While the various publications were of a single mind with regard to the women on the show being gorgeous, they disagreed about which is the fairest of them all.

Bette deserves the title, according to the *Los Angeles Times*. Jennifer Beals's long dark hair accents her dark complexion, the paper wrote, while her expressive eyes make her "exotically beautiful." But the most striking aspect of the biracial character's appearance, the *Times* continued, is how her body language and her "pinstripe power suits with Prada, Pringle and Paul Smith men's dress shirts tailored to fit her" communicate that she's not only on top in the looks department but also an in-charge professional who insists on being taken seriously.[7]

Tina is the "easiest on the eyes," argued the country's most widely respected gay and lesbian newspaper, the *Washington Blade*. The blond bombshell, played by Laurel Holloman, is appealing because she's alluringly vulnerable, the *Blade* wrote. And when the character becomes pregnant and begins to swell with child—Va-va-voom! Tina is so appealing with her enormous breasts and protruding stomach, the paper said, that neither women nor men could possibly see her as anything other than "feminine perfection."[8]

Jenny ranks as the most attractive woman in the cast, the *New York Times* argued. "Mia Kirshner is just stunning," the paper wrote. "She has a riveting beauty that is unlike anyone else's." The *Times* was particularly complimentary of how Jenny's voluptuous body suggests her character's femininity and passivity while "her pondlike green eyes" framed by her black hair communicate that she is, at the same time, a woman of substantial emotional depth who can write intense and brooding prose.[9]

Lesbians Can Be Obsessively Sexual

Beginning in 1950 when news stories portrayed homosexual men as predators who coerced underage boys into having sex with them and continuing through the early 2000s when *Queer as Folk* began its portrayal of gay life with the statement "It's all about sex," the media had been relentless in communicating that gay men place enormous value on sex. *The L Word* sends the message that this preoccupation crosses the gay gender line.

"The women on this program are obsessed with sex," *New York* magazine reported. "Scene after scene in the series fully qualifies as soft-core pornography." Other publications agreed. The *Washington Post*, for example, said the hour-long program, which airs at 10 p.m. Sundays, fully deserves its mature-audience-only rating because of its "sexual frankness."[10]

The various publications pointed to Shane as the most promiscuous of the characters. Anyone who watched the debut episode understood the choice, as an early scene showed the wafer-thin hairstylist stripping off her jeans and T-shirt to provide viewers with a glimpse of the full-frontal nudity that recurs periodically on the series. After getting naked, the shaggy-haired Lothario lures a nubile blonde into a swimming pool and makes love to her. That memorable image prompted *USA Today* to dub Shane "a sexual animal on the prowl."[11]

Love-'em-and-leave-'em Shane maintained her reputation after the premiere, with viewers later learning that she's slept with upwards of 1,000 women. Despite the character's promiscuity, her chiseled facial features and smoky voice are so appealing to female viewers that the *Los Angeles Times* reported that one fan used the Internet to sell thousands of T-shirts that read "I'd Go Gay for Shane."[12]

Casual sex on *The L Word* is not, however, confined to the androgynous girl-magnet. Indeed, Alice finds it so difficult to keep track of all the sexual interplay among her friends that she creates an elaborate wall chart with crisscrossing lines indicating who's hooked up with whom. The line between Jenny and the owner of a local bar is a blazing red, as many of their lustful meetings—including one inside a bathroom stall—

are as erotic as anything in a XXX video; regrettably for the two women, those sessions come to an abrupt end after Jenny's fiancé, Tim, comes home unexpectedly one day and finds the bar owner's face buried in the crotch of the woman he's about to marry.[13]

The Lesbian Community Is Racially Diverse

As the number of gays in the media had gradually increased during the second half of the twentieth century, the persons of color among them had been minuscule—Bernard in *The Boys in the Band*, Miguel in *Philadelphia*, and Jai Rodriguez in *Queer Eye*. In the early 2000s, *The L Word* has become the first high-profile media product to reflect that the gay—or at least the lesbian—community is racially diverse.

Bette is the most prominent non-white woman in the series, with her biracial background being placed front and center in one of the earliest storylines. Much of the debut episode was built around her and Tina's search for a man to supply the sperm they need so Tina can become pregnant. After several failed attempts, Bette tells Tina she's found the perfect donor. The successful artist is leaving the country the next afternoon, however, so Bette arranges for him and Tina to go to the sperm bank the next morning. Tina's somewhat piqued that Bette has chosen the father of their baby before she's even met the guy, and her frustration escalates into downright rage when she comes face to face with him for the first time and sees that he's black. Tina is furious partly because her partner hadn't said anything in advance about the guy's race and partly because, in her words, "Look at me, Bette," referring to her blond hair and pale skin, "I don't feel qualified to be the mother of an African-American baby." Bette is angry as well, interpreting Tina's discomfort with having a mixed-race child as a rejection of her partner being biracial.[14]

Later in the series, race again emerges as a major factor when Shane becomes romantically involved with a Mexican beauty. As the relationship progresses, Carmen wants to take her new girlfriend home to meet her family, but she first has to admit to Shane that she hasn't told her relatives that she's a lesbian, pointing out that her culture vehemently opposes homosexuality. "The whole coming out to your parents," Carmen says, "in a Mexican family, it doesn't really play." Shane agrees to go along with the charade, and a mutual affection gradually develops between the tomboy and the ultra-traditional Mexican family. The situation goes sour, however, when the relatives try to fix Shane up with a man, propelling Carmen to explode and impulsively announce that she and Shane are lovers. "We live in the same house," she says defiantly, "and we sleep in the *same bed*." That statement, in turn, angers Carmen's mother. "Get out," she says firmly. "Both of you, get out of my house.

Get out!" But this particular racial storyline has a happy ending because the family, after a cooling-off period of several weeks, embraces Carmen as well as Shane.[15]

Another woman of color who appears in every episode is Kit, the only straight character with a recurring role in the series. Kit is Bette's half sister, but she's African American rather than biracial because her mother was black. The major issues in the sexy singer's life don't have to do with race, however, but with her dual addictions to alcohol and to ne'er-do-well men.[16]

Several lesser characters who've appeared in a varying number of episodes also have been non-white. They include the Tahitian bar owner who has an affair with Jenny, a Latina carpenter who has an affair with Bette, and an African-American soldier named Tasha, just back from duty in Iraq, who becomes romantically involved with Alice.[17]

In its third season, *The L Word* moved diversity in a whole new direction when Academy Award winner Marlee Matlin, who is deaf, joined the cast and began a relationship with Bette.[18]

Venturing into New Sexual Territory

While the media had showcased only a handful of gay people of color between 1950 and the early 2000s, they'd offered even fewer images of individuals whose sexual orientation veered beyond the gay/straight dichotomy. *The L Word* is doing its part to fill this gap.

In the debut episode, Alice identifies herself as a bisexual, saying, "I'm looking for certain qualities in a person, and it doesn't matter if I find them in a man or a woman." As the series unfolds, Alice remains true to her word, with the number of men ending up in her bed pretty much equaling the number of women. At one point, the magazine writer seems to give up on women altogether, lamenting that "I've had enough lesbian drama," but then, a few segments later, when she fears she's pregnant, she decides to swear off men instead. Like many real-life bisexuals, Alice has trouble convincing other people that she's not in transition from one sexual orientation to another; in one segment, a friend asks, "When are you going to decide between dick and pussy?"[19]

Jenny emerges as a second prominent bisexual. Although she was engaged to a man early in the series, her fiancé finding her having sex with a woman leads to the end of the relationship. After that, she careens back and forth between the two categories of lovers, often causing considerable pain to the man or woman she's left behind. Several news organizations have condemned this particular character's oscillation from one lover to the next. The *Boston Globe* described her as "chewing up people and spitting them out," and the *New York Times* called her "a very despicable character who is selfish and indulgent."[20]

By the end of the third season, Tina also could be accurately described as a bisexual. After she and Bette work their way through the complexities of having a biracial child and then resume life as a couple, their relationship is still troubled. The difficulties escalate when Tina is so attracted to a divorced father that she begins a sexual relationship with him, the couple eventually moving in together.[21]

The major transgender character in the series initially appeared as a butch lesbian who becomes sexually involved with Jenny. But Moira soon announces that she has, since childhood, considered the possibility of becoming a man. "I've never felt comfortable in a girl's body," she says. "I want the outside of me to match the inside of me." Moira then starts taking hormone shots and insists on being called Max. Jenny and Max continue to have a sexual relationship during this period, although Max sometimes has sex with men as well. The storyline illuminates both the joys and the sorrows that transgender people face. Max is elated, for example, the first time he appears in public dressed as a man and everyone tells him how handsome he looks. Max is devastated, however, when he becomes romantically involved with a woman but then, when he tells her that he used to be a woman, she screams, "You're a freak. I don't date freaks. You're a fucking freak!"[22]

Struggling with the "M" Word

During the debut episode of *The L Word*, a gay man refers to the reputation that lesbians have for rushing into romantic relationships. The guy asks, "What do lesbians bring on the second date?" and then immediately responds, "A U-Haul." That light-hearted question and answer introduce a decidedly serious subject of numerous storylines, as the program repeatedly communicates that gay women have a tough time remaining monogamous.[23]

At the beginning of the series, Bette and Tina appeared to be a stable couple, with one friend telling them, "You guys have the best relationship of anybody I know, gay or straight," but, as the first season unfolds, the two women grow more and more distant from each other. Infidelity first enters the picture when Bette has an affair, prompting Tina to end the relationship. After a period of separation during which both women have brief affairs, they give their romantic partnership another try. Within a few months, however, another act of infidelity—this time by Tina—leads to the couple splitting up once again.[24]

Shane and Carmen's relationship is also plagued by the inability to remain faithful. After Shane has a fling with one of her former lovers, an irate Carmen pulls out a dictionary and reads the entry for "monogamy"— "It is a noun, and it is the condition of having a single mate. Does that mean anything to you, Shane?" Carmen eventually agrees to resume the relationship, but not until she has an affair of her own. Soon after the two women reconcile, Shane asks Carmen to marry her, propelling the couple's friends and Carmen's relatives to work together to plan an elaborate wedding ceremony. Carmen arrives at the altar in a full-length wedding gown and a billowing veil—only to discover that Shane has backed out, communicating through a friend that she can't be monogamous.[25]

Dana is yet another gay woman who's portrayed as being incapable of committing to a long-term relationship. The professional tennis player and Lara meet and begin dating early in the series. Dana soon ends the relationship, though, and quickly takes up with Tonya. This relationship moves along so fast—they begin living together two days after they meet—that the two women are soon planning to exchange vows in a high-profile wedding. But the plans come to a screeching halt when Dana becomes sexually involved with Alice. That pairing ends, too, when Dana reconnects with Lara. All seems well with that relationship until Dana is diagnosed with breast cancer and becomes so severely depressed that she pushes her partner away. By the time the disease takes Dana's life, she is alone.[26]

"L" Is for Landmark

There's no question that *The L Word* is a groundbreaking television series. After more than fifty years of men dominating the gays-in-the-media phenomenon, lesbians are finally being depicted on a program that attracts a sufficiently large audience that it has stayed on the air for multiple seasons. Nor is there any doubt that the series is sending some significant messages by depicting a group of Sapphic women who are stunningly beautiful and obsessively sexual, while also communicating that Lesbian America is a racially diverse community, that not everyone fits into the gay/straight dichotomy, and that lesbians have a tough time being sexually faithful.

With regard to the program's overall quality, the reviews have been mixed. The *New York Times* pronounced it "a well-written, entertaining show," *People* magazine dubbed it "engrossing," and the *Philadelphia Inquirer* headlined its review "Kudos to The L Word" before going on to crown the series "glistening" and "addicting." But the *Village Voice* sniped that "the writing isn't quite sharp enough," and *USA Today* panned the show, saying that "the L stands for 'lackluster' because the series is nothing more than a repetitive soap opera that is too often satisfied to do no more than shock and titillate."[27]

During *The L Word*'s first two seasons, the critics' most frequent complaint was that the series excluded a particular category of gay women. "The whole butch side of the lesbian community is not shown," the *Boston Globe* wrote, "which means the program is not an accurate portrayal of the culture." The *Los Angeles Times* made the same point. "What's missing from 'The L Word,'" the paper grumbled, "is the

'B word.' With nary a butch lesbian or Birkenstock or buzz cut in sight, the program's feminized image of lesbians has left some wondering: Where are the dykes?"[28]

Lesbian journalists were quick to defend the series. "These characters are not every lesbian," one woman wrote in the gay magazine *The Advocate*. "They're a very real depiction of one particular group of L.A. lesbians." The editor of AfterEllen.com, a Web site that tracks lesbian images in the media, said:

> From a marketing perspective, there is no way 'The L Word' could be accurate and be a success. They have to appeal to a wide audience, which means they have to pick the most conventionally attractive characters. This show is subject to the same conventions as all of television.

Another Sapphic journalist, this one writing in the lesbian magazine *Curve*, took a humorous tack in her defense of the show's emphasis on slender, glamorous women: "I for one am glad these lesbians are on television. If I want to see an overweight dyke with no fashion sense, I'll look in the mirror."[29]

The where-are-the-dykes? criticism subsided by season three when Moira arrived. Although thin and with model-like facial features, the character's wardrobe, grooming, and mannerisms were masculine— *People* wrote, "Moira could be mistaken for male"—long before she began the hormone shots and changed her name to Max. Then again, some viewers undoubtedly agreed with the concern Kit expressed to Max as he began his transition into manhood:

> It saddens me to see so many strong, butch girls giving up their womanhood to be a man. We're losing our warriors—our greatest women—and I don't want to lose you. Why can't you just be the butchest butch in the world and keep your body?[30]

With regard to how *The L Word* fits into the media's changing depiction of lesbians, the series reinforces many of the messages that previous news stories, films, and TV shows sent.

At the top of the list is that gay women can be promiscuous. This statement first appeared in the flurry of newspaper and magazine articles that appeared after 1969's Stonewall Rebellion, with the *San Francisco Chronicle* reporting, "In lesbian bars, there is a lot of cruising" and "a fair amount of one-night stands." The message was repeated during the fleeting-images-of-lesbians phenomenon in the early 1990s, with the Sharon Stone character in *Basic Instinct*, for example, sharing her bed with dozens of different partners. *The L Word* makes the same point so vehemently that numerous publications that have written about the program have placed this particular message at the top of their reviews and feature stories, such as the *New York Times* commenting, "Everyone on the program has sex constantly."[31]

Number two on the list of messages about lesbians that the Showtime program reinforces is that lesbians can be beautiful. Sharon Stone's highly alluring on-screen persona in *Basic Instinct* was a memorable example of how this statement had been made in the early 1990s, as was Mariel Hemingway in the much-ballyhooed "lesbian kiss" episode of *Roseanne*. Numerous of the actresses who appeared on *Ellen*—Cindy Crawford, Helen Hunt, Demi Moore—repeated the point in the late 1990s. In the beginning of the new millennium, it's now *The L Word*'s turn to provide television viewers with a lineup of stunningly beautiful gay women.

Third on the list of messages that *The L Word* reinforces is that many women are fluid with regard to their sexuality. Several of the magazines that promoted the lesbian chic concept in the early 1990s made this point, with *Mademoiselle*, for example, stating, "One of the hottest issues among lesbians of any age is bisexuality." Showtime's pioneering series moves sexual fluidity onto the TV screen by including bisexuals Alice, Jenny, and Tina as central players and also featuring Moira/Max in a recurring role. Indeed, the number of lesbians on the show had shrunk so dramatically by the fourth season—of the seven major characters in the original cast, the number of lesbians had dwindled to only two, Bette and Shane—that *The Advocate* asked: "Where have all the lesbians gone? It is called *The L Word*, after all."[32]

Another question that could be asked is: Where have all the committed relationships gone? When the series began, Bette and Tina were portrayed as a model of stability, and other pairs of women also have loaded up their U-hauls at various points. But those relationships encountered hard times as the women's highly active libidos have repeatedly prevented them from remaining sexually—or, for that matter, emotionally—committed to their partners. Because *Queer as Folk* aired on the same channel and included plenty of promiscuity, it's logical to compare the two shows with regard to romantic relationships. Michael and Ben's marriage comes first to mind, followed by Brian and Justin's non-traditional—yet ultimately successful—relationship based on emotional commitment while allowing sexual freedom. In short, *Queer as Folk* provided viewers with two models of gay male pairings that succeeded, but *The L Word* offers up a long list of gay female pairings that have failed.

17 Same-Sex Marriage
A Journalistic Love Fest

Neither Kay Ryan nor Carol Adair had any chance of being cast as one of the beauties on *The L Word*. Ryan had too many extra pounds around her middle, and Adair had too many of the wrinkles that appear on the faces of people in their fifties. Despite these physical imperfections, CBS chose to place the two women front and center in its coverage of one of the biggest news stories of 2004. And yet, at the same time, that decision clearly had been driven as much by what the lesbian couple looked like as by how they put words together, which was extremely well.

When the *60 Minutes* correspondent pointed out to the two women that the majority of Americans oppose same-sex marriage and then asked how that situation could be changed, Ryan responded:

> Simply more exposure to faces like ours—ordinary lives like ours, seeing this on television and seeing that we just flat out don't look scary—will make the difference.

Next came Adair's answer to the reporter's question, as she shrugged her shoulders slightly and said, more concisely but no less poignantly than her partner: "I would just invite them to our house for dinner."[1]

Kay Ryan and Carol Adair were two in a long parade of ordinary-looking lesbians and gay men who trooped across the TV screen and the front pages of the country's newspapers during the early 2000s when same-sex marriage exploded into the national spotlight.

Unambiguous statements on the editorial pages of the nation's leading liberal news voices made it crystal clear that the publications supported the initiative. "The arguments are strong for allowing committed gay and lesbian couples to enjoy the benefits and obligations that accrue to marriage," proclaimed the *Washington Post*, while the *Boston Globe* stated that permitting same-sex couples to unite in civil unions but not to marry would "create an odious 'separate but equal' version of partnership under the law." The nation's most prestigious news organization joined the chorus as well, with the *New York Times* saying, "Denying gays the benefits of marriage deprives them of equal protection."[2]

Even more telling was how the titans of journalism treated the issue in their news columns, as several observers argued that the coverage provided a stunning example of a tendency on the part of the Fourth Estate to promote an initiative by consistently portraying it in a positive light. The *Washington Post*'s ombudsman stated point-blank, "The coverage of same-sex marriage could use more balance," while his counterpart at the *Boston Globe* said she personally supported same-sex marriage, "But, as a journalist, I'm not sure the *Globe* is giving sufficient coverage to the opponents as it should be." The harshest critique came from an editor at the *New York Times* who wrote that "the gay marriage issue provides a perfect example" of his newspaper's liberal bias. "On a topic that has produced one of the defining debates of our time," he continued, "*Times* editors have failed to provide the three-dimensional perspective that balanced journalism requires."[3]

Indeed, examining the overwhelmingly supportive coverage of same-sex marriage reveals that news organizations sent manifestly positive messages about both the issue itself and the legion of couples who appeared in the stories. First on the list of admirable traits was that gay couples have stable relationships, with the women and men featured in the news coverage consistently having been together for many years. Gay people also were depicted as being highly productive members of society, as being relentlessly happy, and as being loving and responsible parents. A final positive message was that gay couples are monogamous women and men who value love much more than sex.

Gay Marriage Moves onto the Radar Screen

A long list of developments during the early years of the new millennium propelled the issue of gay marriage onto the national agenda, with three events in particular standing out as the most significant:

- In April 2000, Vermont became the first state to give legal recognition to same-sex civil unions. Among the 300 benefits that couples received were the right for one partner to transfer property to the other without a tax penalty and the right for a partner to have the same hospital visitation privileges as a married spouse.[4]
- In May 2004, Massachusetts became the first state to allow a woman to marry another woman or a man to marry another man. The law was enacted after the state's highest court ruled, in response to a lawsuit, that it was unconstitutional to ban gay people from marrying.[5]
- In June 2008, California became the second state to legalize same-sex marriage. Among the brides who soon tied the knot was Ellen DeGeneres, who was hosting a highly successful daytime talk show and who married actress Portia de Rossi.

News organizations across the country devoted huge quantities of coverage to these developments, with the stories frequently being placed on the front page or at the top of the newscast. On the day the first couples exchanged vows in Massachusetts, for example, *USA Today* marked the occasion by publishing seven separate pieces, including a cover story on its front page and a feature article about same-sex marriages "sending thousands of wedding planners into a swoon at the prospect of tapping into the huge new market, which is estimated at $16.8 billion a year."[6]

One important factual detail that soon emerged from the avalanche of stories was that lesbians were more likely to tie the nuptial knot than were gay men. During the first wave of marriages in Massachusetts, the *Washington Post* reported, fully two-thirds of the couples were of the Sapphic variety.[7]

News organizations also sent plenty of other messages about the gay people being profiled in their stories.

Same-Sex Couples Are Stable

Philadelphia had been the first major media product to showcase a gay couple involved in a long-term relationship, with the 1993 film depicting the Tom Hanks and Antonio Banderas characters as having been together for nine years. When the parade of real-life lesbian and gay couples began marching down the aisle a decade later, many of them were able to boast of having been together at least that long—often much longer.

On the day that same-sex marriage became legal in California, among the women who exchanged vows were Tracy Weddell and Sylvia Simms, who had been together for twenty-six years. The *Los Angeles Times* quoted Simms as saying, "It's been the longest engagement ever."[8]

Many of the Massachusetts brides and grooms headed for Provincetown, a popular destination among gay vacationers, with Gloria Bailey and Linda Davies securing a spot at the front of the line. "When Bailey and Davies first pledged their commitment to each other," *USA Today* reported, "their love and union were a secret." The paper went on to quote Bailey as saying, "We had a private ceremony, just the two of us, 33 years ago." Her legal marriage to Davies in 2004, Bailey told the *Washington Post*, was "the culmination of a lifelong dream."[9]

State officials did not release statistics on the average length of time that gay and lesbian couples had been together before they legalized their relationships, so the *San Francisco Chronicle* took it upon itself to come up with such a figure. After interviewing 400 sets of brides and grooms, the paper reported that they had been together an average of twelve years. In the story announcing the finding, the *Chronicle* wrote, "Gay couples can and do stick together—and legalizing same-sex marriage will result in still more stable relationships."[10]

Gay People Are Productive Members of Society

When *Queer Eye for the Straight Guy* pranced onto the American cultural landscape in 2003, some observers criticized the Fab Five as reinforcing stereotypes of gay men being hairdressers and interior decorators. No such concerns were raised when same-sex marriage moved into the national spotlight, however, as the couples represented a broad range of occupations and brought along some impressive credentials.

Julie and Hillary Goodridge received an enormous amount of media attention because they were the lead plaintiffs in the lawsuit that led to same-sex marriage being legalized in Massachusetts. The *New York Times* was among the publications that provided details on the educational and professional backgrounds of the two women, who had begun using the same surname eight years earlier when their daughter Annie had arrived. Julie Goodridge had earned a master's from Harvard and now owned her own investment firm in Boston; Hillary Goodridge had picked up her college degree from Dartmouth before becoming director of the grant-making arm of the Universalist Church. The women didn't spend all their time succeeding in the financial world, though, as they'd met twenty years earlier at a seminar focused on ending apartheid in South Africa.[11]

The most frequent route that newly minted brides and grooms had followed on their way to becoming productive members of society was by working as educators. CBS reported, for example, that Carol Adair was an English professor and Kay Ryan was a high school teacher as well as a poet—in 2008, she would be named the nation's poet laureate. The *Oregonian* in Portland introduced its readers to another pair of educators, Diane Groff and Elizabeth Cahill, who both taught at a high school in rural Oregon. In other cases, only one of the individuals exchanging vows was earning a livelihood by preparing lesson plans and grading exams. The *Boston Globe* published a story about Diana Eck, a professor of comparative religion at Harvard, marrying Dorothy Austin, an Episcopal priest.[12]

Other women and men who marched down the aisle earned their livelihoods in other fields. Manhattanite Bill Atmore was an anesthesiologist and his partner Jamie McConnell was a corporate litigator at a prestigious law firm. Massachusetts newlyweds Shane Brooks and Martin Pearce were a doctor and a public relations executive. Rosie O'Donnell was an actress who had just ended a stint as the host of a daytime talk show on national television, and Kelli Carpenter was a former executive at the Nickelodeon cable network.[13]

Still other lesbians and gay men were depicted as laudable members of society not because of their professional accomplishments but because of their commitments to their families. The *Boston Globe*'s coverage of the civil union story included a piece about two Louisiana men who, after thirty years together, had driven all the way to Vermont so they could be among the first couples to exchange vows. Chuck Turner and Bill Miller were the primary caregivers for their aged mothers, though, and were reluctant to leave the women alone at home. "So they arrived in a trailer," the *Globe* reported, "bringing along their white-haired mothers, both named Mildred."[14]

Gay People Are Happy

Billy Crystal had been the first good-humored homosexual to enter the nation's living rooms, thanks to *Soap* in the late 1970s, and Ellen DeGeneres had followed twenty years later as a high-profile lesbian with an equally genial nature. And then, in the early 2000s, media consumers learned that being happy extended well beyond this pair of gay comedians, as the news coverage of same-sex marriage—particularly on television—featured lots of affable folks entering into committed relationships.

On the first day that Massachusetts began allowing couples to marry, that event was the lead story on *ABC World News Tonight*. As the reporter gave the details, the screen was filled with an image of an elated Julie Goodridge. The camera was positioned so it looked directly at her, standing tall and elegant in her white Armani pantsuit, with only the back of Hillary Goodridge's head in the picture. But then, as the minister gave the couple his official blessing, Hillary's entire body began bouncing up and down with such an abundance of excitement that, when the man finally said "legally married," the one bride exploded into the other bride's arms, Hillary planting a kiss firmly on Julie's highly receptive lips.[15]

CNN opted to put a male couple at the center of its coverage on that momentous day. "David Wilson and Robert Compton, together for nine years and with eight children and grandchildren from previous marriages, wept as they exchanged vows," the reporter said, leading into a clip that clearly showed the tears to be ones of happiness. "Rob, I commit to love you," Wilson said, the camera focusing on Compton's smiling face as he listened to the heartfelt words that came haltingly from his partner's mouth, "until death do us part." Then followed the nuptial kiss while hundreds of onlookers cheered and applauded.[16]

Other couples who appeared in the various TV stories on the historic day in May 2004 were not identified by name, but every one of them grinned broadly—just like the newlyweds they were. During the *CBS Evening News* segment, two men in their fifties, one African American and the other white, mugged for the camera while holding up matching T-shirts emblazoned with the words "I do." Among the two dozen couples who appeared on screen during *NBC Nightly News* coverage was a pair of giddy women cutting a three-tiered wedding cake, another Sapphic twosome dancing merrily during the reception that followed their ceremony, and a blond woman in a saucy beret who surprised her partner by suddenly lifting her off the ground and carrying her as if they were crossing a threshold. The coverage on Fox, the most conservative of the network news operations, included images of several couples smiling as they held hands, although none of them was shown kissing.[17]

Gay People Make Excellent Parents

American media consumers were first exposed to gay people being parents in the late 1970s when Billy Crystal's character on *Soap* fathered a child. Later media products had provided more glimpses of gay parents—the Robin Williams character in *The Birdcage* comes to mind. But it wasn't until the issue of same-sex marriage moved onto the national radar screen that the topic was explored with any real depth.

When CBS correspondent Bob Simon interviewed Kay Ryan and Carol Adair, he asked about their daughter, Peggy, who by the time of the interview in 2004 was a grown woman with three children of her own. Adair was fully prepared for the question, as her response was articulate as well as thoughtful. "I think people who are raised in homes that are slightly non-traditional are more flexible," she said. "And flexible people are strong, while rigid people are weak. People who can bend and look and think—they have a better time finding their own ethical center."[18]

Other news organizations also sent positive messages about gay people being parents. A front-page story in the *St. Louis Post-Dispatch* quoted a sociology professor as saying that children with two parents of the same sex "are every bit as likely to be well-adjusted and psychologically stable as their classmates" who have one father and one mother. The paper also reported that a significant number of gay couples nationwide had children—33 percent of the women, 22 percent of the men.[19]

The most compelling direct quotes in the *Post-Dispatch* story came from a forty-one-year-old mother. "The concept of being a parent is so huge that it completely overshadows being a lesbian," Lisa Mandel said. "It doesn't matter what I am or how much money I make or what religion I am or what sexual orientation I am—the fact is, I'm a parent first."[20]

How the *New York Times* covered the subject of gay parents provided some of the most persuasive evidence that the country's major news organizations allowed their support of same-sex marriage to influence their reporting on the subject. One story was headlined "For Children of Gays, Marriage Brings Joy," and another—this one on the front page—was headlined "Two Fathers, With One Happy to Stay at Home."[21]

The first of the *Times* pieces included quotes from several children talking about how happy they were that their parents were finally being allowed to marry. Thirteen-year-old Gabriel Damast had served as the ringbearer in his mothers' wedding; the *Times* quoted him as saying,

"It was so cool. I felt thick inside with happiness—just thick." Twenty-one-year-old Parke Humphrey-Keever spoke from the perspective of an adult who had spent his entire life with lesbian parents; the college junior said, "I've had a really stable household. I've had two excellent role models with a strong work ethic. I've seen two people who loved each other."[22]

The second *New York Times* story reported that many gay male couples with children had worked so hard to become parents—which generally required either adopting a child or finding a surrogate mother—that one member of the couple had given up his career to become a stay-at-home dad. One of the most memorable quotations in the page-one piece was from Bernie Cummings, who left his job as a public relations executive when he and his partner had a baby girl through a surrogate mother. "If I were working," Cummings said, "I'd miss that moment when Caelan was just getting up from her nap, grabbing and holding on to me." By the time the story was published, Cummings and Ernie Johnston, a marketing executive at Warner Brothers, had added twins to their family, also through surrogacy.[23]

Gay Couples Are Monogamous

Most of the media products that ranked as milestones in the evolution of how gay men and lesbians had been depicted—such as *The Boys in the Band* and news coverage of the AIDS epidemic and the TV shows *Queer as Folk* and *The L Word*—had portrayed sexual promiscuity as part of the DNA of gay people. News stories about same-sex marriage, by contrast, often made a point of portraying lesbians and gay men as steadfastly monogamous.

A front-page article in the *New York Times* reported that Dolores Trzcinski and Marie Auger, who had been together for twenty-five years, "represent an often-overlooked slice of gay America: the monogamous homebodies more likely to have met their mates at Bible study than at a bar." The piece, headlined "Gay Couples Seek Unions in God's Eyes," also included information about two gay men who were sexually faithful. "Jeffrey Manley found Jusak Bernhard five years ago after posting a note in an online chat room for a Roman Catholic man looking to share his life with another Christian man," the *Times* reported. The story quoted Bernhard as saying, "Our relationship is faith-based. We do our prayers and our Bible readings together, and we depend a lot on our faith to carry us through difficult times." Another telling detail included in the piece was that both men, aged thirty-nine and forty-five, had asked each other's parents for permission before they married.[24]

When the *Washington Post* published a page-one profile of a San Francisco couple who became wife and wife, the paper emphasized that the women had been monogamous throughout their relationship of fifty-one years—Yes, that's right, *fifty-one years!* "Fidelity Was Their Path" read one of the subheads in the story about long-time activists Phyllis Lyon and Del Martin. "We were too busy to run around and have affairs," the seventy-nine-year-old Lyon told the *Post*. "We just stayed the course." Eighty-three-year-old Martin then added her perspective on how they'd been able to remain faithful to each other for half a century. "We love each other," Martin said. "That's all it takes."[25]

Broadcast outlets also made a point of communicating that the gay couples in their stories were not promiscuous. National Public Radio's coverage of the first civil unions in Vermont included a lengthy interview with a pair of teachers, Paul Mayoni and Tom Kidd. "We love each other," Mayoni said. "There's nobody else. There's not going to be anybody else." CNN sent the same message in a segment that focused on a gay male couple from New Hampshire. "Our relationship is not about sex," Declan Buckley said. "It's about two people being together and loving each other and having a partnership over our lifetimes." His partner Kevin Gato then said, "I've always wanted the same thing that my parents have, but I wanted it with a man—and now I'm getting it." The CNN reporter ended the piece by smiling into the camera and saying, "Kevin Gato's parents have been married fifty-nine years."[26]

Downplaying the Downside

During the early 2000s when news organizations were portraying same-sex marriage as becoming commonplace in American society, other developments suggested that marriage would continue to be an institution largely restricted to heterosexuals. Among those realities were several major developments that news outlets tended either to ignore or not give prominent placement:

- The benefits that Vermont granted to couples who joined together in civil unions were generally not recognized beyond the borders of that single state.
- In February 2004, President George W. Bush publicly endorsed amending the U.S. Constitution to prohibit marriages between members of the same sex.
- Although the brides and grooms who exchanged vows in Massachusetts and California were legally married, their rights as couples generally did not extend beyond the state line and did not include federal benefits, such as the right to receive a deceased partner's Social Security payments as male-female marriages allow.
- According to a 2008 Gallup poll, a majority of American voters—55 percent—opposed same-sex marriage.[27]
- By 2008, forty-three states had passed either laws or constitutional amendments that defined marriage as an institution between one man and one woman.[28]

Fifty Years, 180 Degrees

Same-sex marriage was not only a major news story but also a momentous milestone in the changing depiction of gay people. The enormity of this particular media product's importance comes into sharp focus when the fact is noted that the major messages that the coverage sent were the *exact opposite* of those that had been sent in the coverage of the "Perverts on the Potomac" scandal some fifty years earlier.

In 1950, homosexuals had been portrayed as a threat to the nation's well-being because they were emotionally unstable and morally corrupt; in the early 2000s, gay people were portrayed as emotionally stable individuals who were in long-term relationships of many years and were highly productive members of society who worked as teachers, lawyers, and doctors. In 1950, homosexuals had been described as being pathetically sad people who were afflicted with a "nauseating disease"; in the early 2000s, lesbians and gay men were shown to be relentlessly happy people who were constantly smiling and laughing. In 1950, homosexuals were depicted as being obsessed with sex and as representing a grave danger to young boys; in the early 2000s, gay people were depicted as *not* being promiscuous and as being loving and responsible parents.

This 180-degree turn was so dramatic that the *Washington Post* made note of it. In an editorial piece labeled "Gay Chic," *Post* writer Richard Harwood observed:

> The media, once vigilantes in the anti-homosexual campaigns, have conspicuously switched sides during the past decade or so. News organizations now root out and expose homophobes, crusade for tolerance and gay-rights laws and recruit gay journalists. The television networks routinely depict gays in a sympathetic light in prime-time sitcoms.[29]

Another noteworthy change that had occurred with the passage of half a century had to do with the degree to which individuals were stigmatized because of having sexual desires for persons of the same sex. Although the "Perverts on the Potomac" scandal spawned a flood of news stories in a wide variety of newspapers and magazines, homosexuality was considered so reprehensible that not a single name of a gay person was mentioned in any of the stories. Coverage of the initiative to legalize same-sex relationships was overflowing with names of women and men—from Julie and Hillary Goodridge to David Wilson and Robert Compton to Gloria Bailey and Linda Davies—who were downright *eager* to have their names and photos on the front pages of the nation's newspapers and in the stories at the top of the network newscasts.

Significant as well was the fact that more than a few of those names had a feminine ring to them. During the second half of the twentieth century, several topics involving gay people had become major news—beginning with the "perverts" scandal and continuing with the Stonewall Rebellion in 1969, the AIDS crisis in the 1980s, and the gays-in-the-military debate in the 1990s. But all of these stories had focused primarily on gay men, while lesbians were rarely mentioned. That situation changed dramatically with coverage of same-sex marriage. Whether the specific topic was civil unions in Vermont or marriages in Massachusetts or California, the Sapphic presence was central, reflecting the fact that the number of brides who were tying the nuptial knot far surpassed the number of grooms doing the same.

Kay Ryan and Carol Adair are among the many women who illustrate still another way in which news coverage of same-sex marriage differed from the vast majority of the media milestones that had come before it. From *The Boys in the Band* and *Soap* in the 1970s, through *My Best Friend's Wedding* and *Ellen* in the 1990s, and all the way to *Queer Eye for the Straight Guy* and *The L Word* in the early 2000s, media products with gay content had consistently focused on men and women who were young and physically attractive. That tendency ended when the TV cameras captured the images of couples walking down the aisle to exchange their vows, however, as many of the women and men were like Kay Ryan, with her extra pounds around the middle, and Carol Adair, with wrinkles on her face. For as the various news organizations went out of their way to put a positive spin on their stories, gay people being pretty or being young took a backseat to couples who sent the message: Gay Americans are mature, stable, and highly responsible citizens who are involved in long-term, committed relationships and who fully deserve—without question—the right to marry.

The *New York Times*'s supportive stance on same-sex marriage was so dramatic that it prompted several news organizations to report on one of the factors that observers had previously identified as driving the media's shift toward portraying gay people and gay issues in a positive light. Specifically, these journalistic voices—including the *Washington Times*, *Los Angeles Times*, and *New York Daily News*—reported that the Gay Mafia wasn't limited to gay artists in Hollywood working to place admirable gay characters in films and on television, but that it also extended to gay reporters at the *Times* working to make the paper's coverage of same-sex marriage consistently favorable. The *Village Voice* was among the news outlets that framed the discussion as an indictment of mainstream journalism and its claim of fairness. "The larger story is about the hypocrisy that drives media reporting," the *Voice* wrote. "It's a dirty little secret that few editors expect reporters to remain neutral on any topic."[30]

18 *Brokeback Mountain*
"A Breakthrough Gay Romance"

Between 1970 and the late 1990s, American moviegoers had been offered depictions of a wide variety of gay men—from a group of bitchy friends in *The Boys in the Band*, to a heroic AIDS patient in *Philadelphia*, to a dapper high school teacher in *In & Out*. It wasn't until 2005, though, that Hollywood provided the media-consuming public with a film that focused specifically on how a same-sex couple experienced the joys and the sorrows of being in love across a span of many years.

"'Brokeback Mountain' is the mainstream gay romance that many people have been waiting for," announced the *Chicago Sun-Times*, while *Entertainment Weekly* called the movie "a kind of *Romeo and Romeo* on horseback."[1]

But publications made it clear, at the same time, that the film wasn't merely a run-of-the-mill "chick flick" in which the boy/girl pairing had been changed to boy/boy.

The *Boston Globe*, for example, heralded the film as "a cultural milestone," and *New Yorker* magazine dubbed it "an elegy for tamped-down lives." Some publications argued that labeling *Brokeback Mountain* a "gay" movie was too limiting, the *Washington Post* stating, "It's a Hollywood romance with broad, universal themes."[2]

Regardless of precisely how the movie was classified, critics loved it. The film received unwavering praise not because of its gay content but because it was a quality cinematic production on several counts, winning Academy Awards for best director, best adapted screenplay, and best musical score.[3]

Most reviewers didn't find the sexual content of the R-rated film to be in the least bit offensive. "'Brokeback Mountain' is ultimately not about sex, and there is very little of it in the film," reported the *New York Times*, pointing out that no male genitalia is visible in any of the sex scenes. Indeed, the *San Francisco Chronicle* complained, "There is more man-on-woman sex than man-on-man sex," referring to the fact that the film includes scenes in which two beautiful young actresses bare their breasts.[4]

When the movie is examined for messages that it sends about gay people, heading the list is that not all men fit the commonly held stereotypes. Another of the film's prominent statements is that gay men who hide their sexuality bring misery both to themselves and to others. *Brokeback Mountain* also communicates that gay men face the very real possibility of becoming victims of anti-gay violence, and, finally, the film makes a dramatic plea for American society to put an end to homophobia.

Finding an Unexpected Love

The movie begins in 1963 in the big-sky country of Wyoming, the opening scene showing two dirt-poor ranch hands—Ennis is played by Heath Ledger, Jack by Jake Gyllenhaal—applying for jobs on Brokeback Mountain. After they're hired to keep a herd of sheep safe from coyotes, the two nineteen-year-old men gradually come to enjoy each other's company.

And then one night when they're both overpowered by cheap whiskey, raging hormones, and a desire that neither of them saw coming, they unbuckle their belts and, in the words of *New York* magazine, "commence an act of sex that manages to be both rough and tender,

Figure 18.1 Handsome young actors Jake Gyllenhaal, left, and Heath Ledger starred as the gay ranch hands in the 2005 film *Brokeback Mountain*.

Courtesy of Focus Features/Photofest.

romantically intimate and lustily intense." The next day, Ennis says, "You know I ain't queer," and Jack responds, "Me neither." And yet, that first sexual encounter is followed by numerous others during the next several weeks.[5]

When the two men leave the mountain at the end of the summer, Ennis utters a simple, "I'll see you around," appearing to be more upset about having forgotten a shirt up on the mountain than about having to say goodbye to Jack. Four years then pass before Ennis, who stays in Wyoming, receives a postcard from Jack, now living in Texas, saying he'll be passing through the area soon and would like to stop by for a visit. The moment the two men set eyes on each other, they kiss passionately and race off to a motel room—even though they are both now husbands and fathers.

So begins a sporadic and tortured love affair in which the men get together once or twice a year under the guise of going on fishing trips. Jack suggests they end their marriages and set up a ranch together, but Ennis won't even consider such an idea. And so, for the next twenty years, they endure their separate existences, waiting for the brief interludes when they can steal away a few days to be with each other. The relationship ends when Jack dies.

Brokeback Mountain is a film very much of its time, beginning in the era before the Stonewall Rebellion when the vast majority of Americans saw homosexuality as a sickness. Although two decades pass as the action in the film progresses, it's doubtful that either Ennis or Jack, who are geographically and culturally separated from cities such as New York and San Francisco, ever so much as utter the word "gay."

Belying the Stereotypes

By the time *Brokeback Mountain* was released, the media had presented the public with two categories of stereotypically gay man. The first was a composite of the friends who gathered for the birthday party in *The Boys in the Band*—effeminate, narcissistic, promiscuous, and emotionally weak. The second came by way of *Will & Grace* and the parade of men who appeared in the high-profile gay films of the 1990s—handsome, charming, successful, and blessed with impeccable taste.

The men in *Brokeback* fit neither profile.

In the 1997 *New Yorker* short story that first brought Ennis and Jack to life, the author described the main characters as "high school dropout country boys with no prospects, brought up to hard work and privation, both rough-mannered, rough-spoken, inured to the stoic life." When reviewers talked about the movie, they also sketched two men who belied the common gay stereotypes. The *Los Angeles Times* characterized them, for example, as "men who would mightily resist an avowedly gay lifestyle or the label homosexual."[6]

As the film unfolds, viewers learn that Ennis's aspirations are no higher than a vague idea that he might someday own a small ranch. When reviewers talked about the Ennis character, they focused mostly on his refusal to acknowledge that he had any emotions whatsoever. "His voice is a mumble and a rumble," wrote *The New Yorker*, "because he hopes that by swallowing his words, he can swallow his feelings, too."[7]

Jack also lacks the traits commonly associated with the stereotypically gay man. A *Los Angeles Times* review of the film described him as "laconic and wedded to the cowboy life," having dropped out of high school to join the rodeo circuit. Jack's mediocre performance at bull riding contributed significantly to his gradual alienation from the people around him.[8]

Bringing Misery to Themselves and Others

More than any of the major gay media products that came before it, *Brokeback Mountain* is a study of two men attempting to repress their homosexuality. When Ennis and Jack first connect with each other physically, they try to stifle their desires and live according to the dictates of heterosexual society.

After his summer of tending sheep, Ennis marries his sweet-faced girlfriend, played by Michelle Williams, and he and Alma have two daughters. Jack's personal life follows a similar path when he meets and quickly marries a high-spirited Texas beauty named Lureen, played by Anne Hathaway, who then gives birth to a son.

The first victims of the two men's efforts to suppress their sexual desires are the lovers themselves. One wrenching moment in the film comes immediately after the two ranch hands separate at the end of their summer idyll on the mountain. As Jack drives off in his dilapidated pickup truck, Ennis turns his back and starts to walk away. But he's so overcome with emotional pain and the yearning for what he's leaving behind that he stumbles into an alleyway, falls to his knees, and heaves up the contents of his stomach. Conflicted and angry at himself for what's happened, Ennis slams his fist against the wall, bloodying his knuckles.

During the years that follow, Ennis is miserable during the long expanses of time he's away from Jack. The *Boston Globe* said, "Ennis hunches over and pulls his emotions under his canvas coat; he doesn't age so much as he slowly caves in."[9]

Jack suffers a similar fate. After he enters into his marriage of convenience with Lureen, he finds himself with a wife and son to support but is unable to earn a living on the rodeo circuit. So he starts selling farm equipment in the company owned by his wife's overbearing father—"who hates my guts," he tells Ennis. In addition, Jack finds it impossible to limit his homosexual activities to the occasional times he and Ennis are together. By the early 1970s, he begins having trysts with other married men and with male prostitutes.

The misery soon spreads beyond Ennis and Jack. After the two men leave Brokeback Mountain and are separated from each other for four years, Ennis is so eager to reconnect that he impulsively kisses Jack in broad daylight, not noticing that his wife is watching from a window. Alma is stunned but doesn't confront her husband, allowing the feelings of rejection to eat away at her until, several years later, she finally divorces him. Ennis's children are also part of what *Newsweek* called the "collateral damage" of the two men trying to conceal their sexuality; the secret that Ennis keeps from his two daughters prevents them from getting close to him.[10]

Jack's wife also pays a high price for her husband living a lie. Although it's not clear if Lureen knows about Jack's homosexual desires, she definitely suffers the pain that inevitably destroys a loveless marriage. In the words of the *New York Times*, "Lureen slowly calcifies into a clenched robotic shell of her peppery younger self."[11]

Being Threatened by Anti-Gay Violence

Queer as Folk had introduced gay bashing to cable-television viewers in 2001, but *Brokeback Mountain* dramatized the topic for a much larger audience four years later.

Anti-gay violence first surfaces when Jack raises the idea of the two men buying a little ranch together. Ennis responds, "It ain't gonna be that way," followed by his description of a childhood memory:

> There was these two old guys ranched together down home. They was a joke in town, even though they were pretty tough old birds. Anyway, they found Earl dead in a irrigation ditch. They took a tire iron to him, spurred him up, drug him around by his dick 'til it pulled off.

While Ennis recounts the story, the movie screen shows a father leading two little boys to the edge of a ditch. As the young Ennis sees the body, his eyes widen and a look of horror engulfs his face. "My daddy, he made sure me and my brother seen it," Ennis says. He then pauses for a moment, shakes his head, and concludes, "Two guys livin' together? No way."

The second reference to anti-gay violence is also brief but memorable. In 1982, Ennis is shown walking out of a post office when he abruptly stops because he sees that the postcard he sent to Jack has been returned with a single word stamped across it: "Deceased."

Ennis rushes to a payphone and dials Jack's number in Texas. Lureen answers, and Ennis tells her he's an old friend of Jack's. "I'm callin' to see what happened."

Lureen says Jack was killed in a freak accident. He was changing a flat tire, she says, when somehow the tire blew up and the rim struck his face, knocking him unconscious. "By the time somebody came along, he had drowned in his own blood," she says in a cold, direct tone. "He was only thirty-nine years old."

The images on the movie screen, however, tell a dramatically different story. The action comes in a flash and lasts for only a matter of seconds, but the harsh reality of what happened is crystal clear. Jack is shown being shoved to the ground by three men who then savagely kick and beat him, one of them smashing a tire iron into his face and killing him.

Pleading for an End to Homophobia

Many reviewers found the final scenes of *Brokeback Mountain* to be the most poignant, as they provide a dramatic plea for American society to put an end to hatred of gay people.[12]

After Lureen tells Ennis about the circumstances of Jack's death, he asks her where the body was buried. She says he was cremated, with half of his ashes buried in Texas and the rest sent to his parents in Wyoming. "He used to say he wanted his ashes scattered on Brokeback Mountain, but I wasn't sure where that was," she says. "I thought it might be around where he grew up." Ennis then says, "No, ma'am, we was herdin' sheep up on Brokeback one summer." And Lureen adds, "Well, he said it was his favorite place."

The next scene shows Ennis stopping his pickup truck in front of a wind-beaten house. He goes inside and meets Jack's parents. "I feel awful bad about Jack," he begins, then pauses. "I come by to say that if you want me to take his ashes up there on Brokeback like his wife said he wanted, I'd be proud to." The mother wants to accept Ennis's offer, but the father says sternly, "We got a family plot, and he's goin' in it."

Jack's mother, who seems to have some sense of the relationship that her son had with the visitor, then says that she's kept Jack's room exactly the way he left it and tells Ennis he can go upstairs by himself to see it. "I'd like that," he says.

Once Ennis is in the room, he studies its contents to remind himself of his lost love, eventually noticing a hidden space at the back of Jack's closet. Inside, Ennis finds a shirt on a wire hanger. When he looks closer, he sees there are actually two shirts, one inside the other. The outer one is made of denim and has blood on the sleeve, Ennis's own blood from the last day they were together on Brokeback two decades earlier, when Jack accidentally hit Ennis in the nose while the men were wrestling playfully. The second shirt is the one Ennis had worn that long-ago summer, its sleeves now carefully worked down inside the sleeves of the denim shirt Jack had worn. The shirts are like two skins, one inside the other, that are joined together to create a symbol of the love Jack had felt for Ennis, though neither man had ever put his feelings into spoken words.

The film's final scene shows those two shirts hanging from a nail that Ennis has tacked onto the door of the closet in the rickety house trailer where he now lives. Next to the shirts, he's positioned a picture postcard of Brokeback Mountain. Ennis looks at the shirts and the postcard through a few stinging tears and gently closes the door to the closet.

When the *New York Times* reviewed the film, it began with a detailed description of the shirts and their role in that final scene, ending with the statement:

> In a country that makes not just a virtue but a fetish of rugged individualism—and set against the big-sky backdrop most identified with that virtue—'Brokeback Mountain' strikes a deep and haunting chord. It's the story of people who, for no good reason, are not allowed to live their lives as they would like.[13]

Entertainment Weekly was another publication that interpreted the final scene as a plea for an end to homophobia, writing: "*Brokeback Mountain* is far from being a message movie, yet if you tear up in the magnificent final scene, with its hauntingly slow waltz of comfort and regret, it's worth noting what, exactly, you're reacting to: a love that has been made to knuckle under to society's design."[14]

"It's a Story America Is Ready to Hear"

Brokeback Mountain was clearly a landmark cinematic work because it broke new ground by bringing a same-sex love story to the big screen and because it set a new high-water mark for the number of Academy Awards presented to a motion picture with substantial gay content.

Another reason the film deserves to be classified as a milestone involves the messages that it sends. For example, while some earlier media products had highlighted individuals who belied the commonly held gay stereotypes, none of them did so as unequivocally as did this film about a pair of rough-mannered, long-suffering ranch hands who lived in the American West. A second of the movie's messages is that gay men who hide their sexuality cause great misery to themselves and to others, a point that no major media product before it had addressed. And, finally, another pair of statements the movie makes—that gay men can be victims of hate crimes and that homophobia must end—were treated with such a high level of artistry that many observers believed the film had the potential to change the thinking of anyone who saw it.

On that last point, after the film was released and began to attract sizable audiences, a story on the front page of the *Los Angeles Times* asked: "Can 'Brokeback Mountain' Move the Heartland?" That question had an unusual resonance among the nation's journalists, with several newspapers responding directly to the question. "It will win hearts all across America," said the *Detroit News*, and "'Brokeback Mountain' sneaks into your heart," agreed the *Miami Herald*. The nation's pre-eminent news voice, the *New York Times*, weighed in on the question as well, saying the answer was "a resounding yes" and then adding, "The culture is seeking out this movie not just because it is a powerful, four-hankie account of a doomed love affair but also because the film delivers a story previously untold. It's a story America is ready to hear."[15]

Box office receipts support that assertion. *Brokeback* cost a modest $13 million to make; within six months after its release, it had grossed more than $140 million in revenue.[16]

Many of the reviewers who wrote about the film reported that the public had only recently reached the point that it was ready to embrace a depiction of same-sex romance. Soon after the original short story about Ennis and Jack had appeared in *The New Yorker* in 1997, a Pulitzer Prize-winning author and his writing partner turned the piece into a moving screenplay that they tried to sell to one of Hollywood's major studios, but none of those studios would take on the project. "Ten years ago, the film's placement in mainstream movie theaters seemed unthinkable," the *Sacramento Bee* wrote in early 2006. "But the success of TV shows such as 'Will & Grace' and 'Queer Eye for the Straight Guy' have made Americans more comfortable with gay content."[17]

More evidence of the public being ready to accept a gay love story unfolded after social conservatives were so outraged by the film that they demanded that Wal-Mart not sell the *Brokeback Mountain* DVD. The country's largest retailer ignored those demands, however, with a Wal-Mart spokeswoman saying, "The fact that we are stocking the movie is not an endorsement of the content of the movie or any specific belief. We simply stock the titles that consumers want."[18]

Another indication that capitalism was instrumental in the *Brokeback* success story is the fact that the only widely held gay stereotype the two leading characters in the film exhibited was that they were physically attractive. In other words, the motion picture industry was willing to forego the stereotypes of gay men being effeminate and narcissistic or as being professionally successful and blessed with impeccable taste, but The Powers That Be knew they'd attract more viewers if they cast two actors who sent moviegoers just one of the stereotypical messages about gay men: They are handsome.

When placing *Brokeback* into the larger context of the media's changing depiction of gay people, several of its characteristics are consistent with those of earlier media products. The fact that no lesbians are portrayed in the movie, for example, reinforces a point that was made by the content of numerous films, TV shows, and news stories of various eras: Gay men are far more visible in the media than are gay women. That not all gay people fit the commonly held stereotypes and that the threat of hate crimes is a reality in the lives of gay men are two more familiar messages, as both of those statements had been made by other media products before *Brokeback*.

The new message sent by the landmark film is challenging to assess with regard to whether it is a positive or a negative statement about gay men. The complicating factor is that the film was released in 2005, but the time period it portrays is the 1960s through the early 1980s. While there's no question that creating *Brokeback Mountain* was an effort by Hollywood to lead the American public toward a more supportive attitude toward gay rights, the new message casts gay men—at least those who try to suppress their homosexual feelings—in a decidedly negative light. Specifically, the two ranch hands depicted in the film are portrayed as bringing misery both to themselves and to those around them. And so, if viewed from the vantage point of 2005, it may seem that *Brokeback* was supporting gay rights but condemning the two particular gay men whose portraits it painted so vividly and so memorably. The more fair-minded standpoint from which to consider their actions, however, is within the framework of the time period, the geographic location, and the social mores that defined the two men's lives. When those factors are considered, the decisions that the young men made are understandable, and the villainous force that caused the misery was neither Ennis nor Jack, but homophobia.

With regard to factors that have contributed to the media creating positive depictions of gay people in recent years, *Brokeback Mountain* is an example of a film in which several of the artists involved in creating the work were committed to doing their part to advance gay rights. Lead actor Heath Ledger, who was nominated for an Academy Award for his role as Ennis, spoke to this dynamic. Ledger said in 2005:

> The story of the destructive power of homophobia is one that needed to be told, and it was a real honor for me to be part of that telling. Many members of the public still have highly negative feelings toward gay people, and there's no question that films can play a part in reducing that hatred. *Brokeback* is a film that made a difference, and if my being in the film brought more people into the theaters to see it, that's something I'm very proud of.[19]

Anne Hathaway's strongest statement regarding her decision to appear in the film came after an interviewer asked her why she'd been willing to accept the supporting role of Lureen after she'd previously been cast in leading roles in such films as *Princess Diaries*, *Princess Diaries 2*, and *The Devil Wears Prada*. Hathaway said:

It's very rare in Hollywood today to find a motion picture that tells a story that's never been told before. *Brokeback Mountain* was not only such a movie, but it also was an incredibly poignant one that changed the thinking of many of the people who saw it. If me appearing in such a profoundly important film meant that more people would come to movie theaters to see it, then playing a supporting role instead of a leading one was a small price for me to pay.[20]

Social conservatives have cited such statements by Ledger and Hathaway—as well as earlier ones by Robin Williams about starring in *The Birdcage* and Jerry Zucker about producing *My Best Friend's Wedding*—when lambasting the entertainment industry as promoting gay rights. One front-page article in the *Washington Times*, for example, stated, "Hollywood's pro-homosexual agenda is in keeping with the fact that most actors and studio bosses champion left-wing political and cultural causes."[21]

Among the Hollywood luminaries who have responded to those comments is Ang Lee, who won the best director Academy Award for his work on *Brokeback Mountain*. Lee told one interviewer:

I believe it is part of the motion picture industry's responsibility to reflect the lives and the issues facing all members of society, and that includes persons of color, women, and gay people. It is curious to me that we often hear accusations about Hollywood promoting a pro-gay agenda, but we never hear accusations that Hollywood promotes a pro-woman agenda or a pro-African-American agenda, even though there are many, many films today that portray women and African Americans in positive ways.[22]

Conclusion: From "Perverts" to "Fab Five"

Progress in Three Stages . . . and Waiting for a Fourth

I ended the first chapter of this book with an observation that brought a broader perspective to the relentlessly negative depiction of homosexual men that appeared in American newspapers and magazines in 1950. Specifically, I quoted nineteenth century women's rights leader Lucretia Mott as saying that the publications of her era had consistently "ridiculed and slandered us" but that this treatment was not surprising because the press typically goes "through three stages in regard to reforms; they first ridicule them, then report them with comment, and at last openly advocate them." She then added, "We seem to be still in the first stage." In other words, Mott was pointing out that the media initially oppose most reform efforts. But as time passes, and if a particular idea has merit, the various communication outlets begin reporting on or otherwise portraying the topic in a neutral manner. And after still more time goes by, the media ultimately endorse at least some of the reform initiatives that they had earlier condemned.[1]

Mott's observation offers a useful framework for looking at how the media's depiction of gay people evolved between the midpoint of the twentieth century and the early years of the twenty-first. For when the case studies illuminated in the previous chapters are examined with her comment in mind, a three-stage progression comes into focus.

News stories about homosexual men that appeared in 1950 repeatedly referred to them as "perverts," thereby creating a resolutely negative depiction. News coverage of 1969's Stonewall Rebellion was unremittingly negative as well, with such terms as "queens" and "fags" reflecting the contempt that pervaded the stories about the historic event. When *The Boys in the Band* moved homosexuals onto the motion picture screen in 1970, the pejorative depiction continued, with the film's most memorable line—"Show me a happy homosexual, and I'll show you a gay corpse"—communicating that all gay men, without exception, were sad and pathetic creatures.

The second stage began in 1977. The vehicle for that shift to neutral treatment was TV's first series to feature a recurring gay character. *Soap*, unlike its predecessors in the realms of news and film, provided media consumers with a mixture of some negative and some positive messages about what it means to be gay.

In the early 1980s, the progression to a neutral depiction suffered a severe setback because of the advent of AIDS. Coverage of gay men became persistently negative again, as their obsession with sex was portrayed as leading them to spread the deadly "gay plague."

Late 1980s news coverage of AIDS moved back into the second stage because the stories included—as had *Soap*—some positive messages and some negative ones. Depictions then remained in the second stage in news coverage of the gays-in-the-military debate as well as with the fleeting images of lesbians that appeared in the early 1990s.

The third stage began in 1993. *Philadelphia* was the media product that signaled this important step forward, as all of the film's major messages were positive. The gay man portrayed by Tom Hanks was courageous, professionally accomplished, and well liked by everyone who knew him—except for the despicable homophobes in his law firm.

Most of the major media products of the late 1990s and early 2000s stayed in the third stage. *Ellen* showed TV viewers that lesbians could be physically attractive as well as laugh-out-loud funny, while *The Birdcage*, *In & Out*, and *My Best Friend's Wedding* defined a new set of highly positive gay male stereotypes. *Will & Grace* and *Queer Eye for the Straight Guy* also sent numerous positive messages about gay men, and *Brokeback Mountain* portrayed two handsome ranch hands from an earlier era whose love for each other was thwarted by the evils of homophobia. News coverage of same-sex marriage communicated that lesbians and gay men are stable in their personal relationships, productive in their professional lives, and exceptionally responsible in their roles as parents.

At the same time that this long list of relatively recent media products sent positive messages about gay people, however, two TV shows were making some positive and some negative statements, thereby placing them in the second stage rather than the third. *Queer as Folk* painted a portrait of a segment of Gay America that was a model for practicing safe sex, but the Showtime series also portrayed gay men as living hedonistic lives defined by sex and drugs. *The L Word* communicates that women who love women can be stunningly beautiful, but the show also depicts lesbians as being so obsessed with sex that they're incapable of sustaining monogamous relationships.

And so, while the media's depiction of gay people has improved enormously over time, the progress is by no means unqualified.

Is the Glass Half Full?

When the three-stage evolution of how gay people have been depicted is viewed from a glass-is-half-full perspective, one point that must be made is that the media have changed their treatment relatively quickly. The negative characterization that defined 1950 news coverage was replaced with a manifestly positive portrayal that was clearly evident in 1993's *Philadelphia* and has generally continued since that time. For the media to transform their views of a stigmatized subgroup of American society so dramatically in a mere forty years is remarkable, particularly when compared to the much slower progression in the depiction of, for example, African Americans or people of Arab descent. The media's embrace of gay men and lesbians also stands in stark contrast to how other powerful institutions have treated them; the U.S. Congress, for example, still hasn't seen fit to pass federal legislation to prevent gay people from being fired from their jobs or otherwise discriminated against because of their sexual orientation.

Another observation that belongs in a glass-is-half-full discussion has to do with a question that students and scholars of communication often debate: Should the media *reflect* the attitudes and values of their audience or should they seek to *change* those attitudes and values? This book provides a case study of a subject on which the media have gone the latter route, as they clearly have been, at least in recent years, attempting to lead American society toward a more enlightened view of homosexuality. When the messages sent by films such as *Philadelphia, The Birdcage,* and *Brokeback Mountain,* TV shows such as *Ellen, Will & Grace,* and *Queer Eye,* and news coverage of the same-sex marriage initiative are looked at as a whole, there's no question that a critical mass of media products have, in the last decade and a half, been committing their power and influence to convincing the public that gays should be accepted and supported as first-class citizens.

Is the Glass Half Empty?

When the three-stage evolution is viewed from a glass-is-half-empty perspective, it first must be pointed out that the media's positive portrayals of gay people have been largely limited to individuals who possess specific characteristics. If contemporary Americans were asked to name the most visible lesbian and gay man in the media today, the most frequent names mentioned would probably be Ellen DeGeneres and Carson Kressley— or, perhaps, "that nellie guy who was on *Queer Eye.*" While it's certainly laudable that any gay people whatsoever are widely known and that DeGeneres and Kressley are both viewed in a positive light, the reality is that they represent a strikingly narrow range of humanity: They're both white, physically attractive, and financially secure, and they also both make their livelihoods as comedians. If the individuals being surveyed were asked to name an openly gay person of color who is prominent in the media, either female or male, most of them would draw a blank. Those same respondents would again be stumped if asked to name a gay person in the media who is *not* physically attractive . . . or is older than fifty . . . or is known for something other than his or her ability to make people laugh.

The narrow range of gay people the media has chosen to place in the spotlight also has led to few bisexuals having a presence in this book. Bisexuals didn't appear until the chapter that focused on the handful of fleeting images of lesbians that erupted during the early 1990s; the three major female characters in *Basic Instinct* were bisexual, and several magazines that were part of the "lesbian chic" phenomenon also made reference to women who had sex with men and women both. The only media product to keep bisexuality front and center for a sustained period of time is *The L Word*, with Alice declaring her attraction for both sexes in the premier episode and other characters later exhibiting that same orientation.

Transgender people also have only a limited presence in this book—and in the media. Stories about the 1969 Stonewall Rebellion reported that drag queens played a significant role in the event, though the references were demeaning, such as the *New York Daily News* stating that men dressed in women's clothing "stood bra strap to bra strap against" the police. *Soap's* portrayal of the Billy Crystal character planning to have a sex change was not much better, as it gave TV viewers misleading information about why a man might consider making such a decision. Indeed, it wasn't until the early 2000s that *The L Word* finally introduced an accurately depicted transgender character in the form of Moira/Max.[2]

Another point that emerges from a glass-is-half-empty perspective is that the media's increased attention to gay people has been motivated not primarily by a commitment to portraying members of a minority group fairly and accurately but by a desire to profit financially. It's not coincidental that the first unequivocally positive portrayal of gay men occurred with *Philadelphia* in 1993, at the same moment that market researchers began reporting that gays had unusually high disposable incomes. In a capitalist society, every genre of the media is a business, and by the final decade of the twentieth century, The Powers That Be in the various genres had come to recognize that rose-colored gay content would produce profits because of the prosperous gay consumers and the straight allies who are eager to see that content.

A Fragile Commitment

That there's been a sea change in the depiction of gay people between 1950 and the early 2000s doesn't mean that all contemporary media representations are laudable. Far from it.

An example of the kind of shockingly offensive story that still pops up, from time to time, is one that appeared in the *New York Times* in late 2005. Prominently displayed on the front page of the local news section, the story relied on anonymous sources to report that closeted gay men were having furtive sexual encounters near a parking lot in suburban Queens. The piece was illustrated with a three-column photo of an overweight and unidentified man, shot from the waist down, walking away from his car and toward a wooded area. The article contained any number of statements that sounded like they'd been written by a hate group determined to cast gays in the most negative light possible. "The parking lot serves the lonely as well as the lusty," the story said. It then went on:

> Many regulars say they make arrangements to go home together or to a motel since a strong police presence makes sex in the car or the woods too risky. They add, however, that for certain men this risk only increases the excitement and allure of on-site sex.

The reporter described the men as "trolling the remote parking lot" and flashing their car headlights "as mating calls." Many of the statements sounded like dialogue from 1970's *The Boys in the Band*, such as the sentence: "There's so much loneliness among gay men."[3]

Such disappointing portrayals aren't limited to the news media, as they periodically occur in films and on television as well. The 2007 Adam Sandler film *I Now Pronounce You Chuck and Larry* revolved around two Brooklyn firemen who pretended to be gay so they could get domestic partnership benefits. Not only was the movie bursting with anti-gay slurs, but it also gave viewers the impression that the nation's fire departments provide benefits to same-sex couples, which most do not. A year earlier, a prissy gay man named Marc appeared in the cast of the television comedy series *Ugly Betty*. It wasn't a concern when the fashionista was over the top both in his flamboyance and bitchiness, as he was merely a fictional version of *Queer Eye*'s Carson Kressley. Observers of how gay people are portrayed in the media were outraged, however, when one episode showed Marc dressing up in women's clothes. With only a handful of gay characters—no more than half a dozen—appearing on network television, was ABC playing fair when it put one of them in an evening gown, pearls, and opera gloves?[4]

Answering the Big Questions

At the beginning of this book, I listed four broad questions that I promised would be answered in the pages that were to follow. I believe I've already fulfilled that commitment, but I also think it may be worthwhile for me to summarize and highlight those answers here as well.

What factors caused the media's depiction of gay men to be transformed so radically in a mere fifty years?

In a word: Money.

As I mentioned earlier in this chapter, first on the list of reasons why media decision-makers started sending positive messages about gay people in the early 1990s was their recognition that gay buying power was too big to ignore. "It's the market of the decade," the *Chicago Sun-Times* announced. "America's gay population is now in the limelight among an increasing number of forward-thinking businesses that want to appeal to well-heeled consumers." Among those businesses were the nation's motion picture studios and television networks, which came to realize that major financial benefits could result if appealing gay content was communicated to gay people and their straight allies.[5]

The second factor on the list is the eagerness of many people in Hollywood to support gay rights by portraying gay characters in a positive light. Billy Crystal was a pioneer in this phenomenon, as he committed his natural charm and comic talent, beginning in 1977, to making sure that TV's first recurring gay character was a man to be admired. Crystal said in 2004:

> It was a risky role for me to take, but I took it because it gave me the chance to do something very important for gay people. I worked very hard to make my character a regular guy-next-door kind of man who just happened to be gay. It was during a time when most people in this country thought a homosexual was weird and scary. Seeing my character on the TV screen helped them realize that being gay wasn't really strange at all. That was a huge step forward, and I'm very proud that I played a role in making it happen.

Tom Hanks and Robin Williams are among the Academy Award-winning actors who've followed in Crystal's footsteps, using their celebrity status to draw huge numbers of Americans into movie theaters to see positive gay content.[6]

A third factor that caused the media's depiction of gay men to be transformed is the phenomenon known as the Gay Mafia. Dating back at least to 1998 when Max Mutchnick not only created *Will & Grace* but also pushed hard to get the program on the air, an abundance of gay artists in Hollywood have committed their talent and energy to seeing that positive portrayals of gay people reach audiences watching both the large and the small screen. The *Los Angeles Times* had it right when it stated, "Unlike Latinos, blacks and Asian Americans, gay people are fully integrated into the Hollywood power structure," going on to say that these talented and tenacious artists use their positions to raise gay visibility. During the news media's same-sex marriage love fest in the early 2000s, the *Village Voice* and other journalistic voices reported that the Gay Mafia was having an impact not only in Hollywood films and TV shows but also at the venerable *New York Times*.[7]

What impact did that seismic shift have on the nation's collective attitude toward people who are attracted to members of their own sex?

Although it's impossible to prove a direct cause-and-effect relationship between the content of the media and the degree to which the public has come to accept gay people, a combination of polling data and observations by members of the news media suggest that the positive depictions have been an enormous influence on the public's changing attitude toward this once-reviled segment of society.

In 1982, during an era when the media were sending a mixture of some negative and some positive messages about gays, the Gallup Organization asked a sampling of Americans, for the first time: "Do you feel that homosexuality should be considered an acceptable alternative lifestyle?" Of the individuals responding to the poll, only 34 percent said yes.[8]

By 1996, after millions of moviegoers had seen *Philadelphia* and reviewers had published comments such as *Time* magazine calling Tom Hanks's gay on-screen persona "a wonderful fellow: chipper, supremely competent, lavishing genial respect on colleagues high and low," and the *Washington Post* calling the character "a noble gay hero," that figure had jumped to 44 percent.[9]

By 1999, after Hollywood had spotlighted—through *The Birdcage, In & Out,* and *My Best Friend's Wedding*—a group of gay men who were, without exception, not only highly personable but also so physically attractive, so blessed with excellent taste, and so accomplished in their professional lives that *Newsweek* dubbed the composite of the men "a new homosexual role model," the figure had risen to 50 percent.[10]

By 2007, after the network TV blockbuster *Will & Grace* had provided eight years of what the *Philadelphia Inquirer* called "gay sensitivity training" that had succeeded in "moving the center of public opinion," the cable hit *Queer Eye for the Straight Guy* had given viewers four seasons of what the *New York Times* labeled "a league of superheroes," and the country's leading news organizations had turned coverage of same-sex marriage into a journalistic love fest, the figure had shot up to 57 percent.[11]

Did the portrayal of lesbians follow the same route as that of gay men or did the media treat gay women differently? If there was a difference, why?

Various chapters of this book have documented that gay men have consistently, since 1950, been more prominent in the various genres of the media than gay women have been. A few lesbians were mentioned in news stories about the Stonewall Rebellion and the debate about gays in the military, and other women made brief appearances in the early 1990s and then as part of the *Ellen* phenomenon. But it wasn't until the early 2000s when *The L Word* began airing on Showtime and the same-sex marriage story moved onto the national radar screen that gay women achieved a sustained visibility in the media.

As for why women have lagged behind their gay brothers, my analysis of the reasons is summarized in chapter 15, Gay Visibility vs. Lesbian Visibility. At the top of the list is that unflattering stereotypes of gay women as being unattractive and humorless compelled the media to keep lesbians out of the spotlight. The powerful role that these persistent stereotypes played, for many decades, in the sidelining of women who love women is shown by the fact that the first lesbians the media finally highlighted for any sustained length of time—on *The L Word* beginning in 2004—were stunningly beautiful and without a humorless bone in their shapely bodies.

Finally, which genre of the media—journalism, film, or TV—has been the most effective in changing the public perception of gay people?

If I had to choose one genre, it would be television. My decision is driven partly by the pivotal importance of the groundbreaking shows *Soap* in the 1970s and *Will & Grace* in the 1990s but mainly by the nature of the three forms of media. If someone isn't inclined to support same-sex marriage, that person can easily skip over the news stories about the topic that are published in a newspaper or on a Web site. Likewise, if an individual isn't interested in seeing a movie about a gay man with AIDS or a pair of gay ranch hands, there are plenty of action films or chick flicks to go see instead. But if someone is chilling out in the living room and watching whatever happens to come on the TV, there's the very real possibility that the viewer might, without really making a choice, run into that sitcom about those two gay dudes with that hot redhead named Grace and that crazy brunette named Karen and, hey, they're all pretty funny so why not see what they're all up to this time around. And the gay sensitivity training begins.

Then again, I feel a need to say that I give the Most Effective Medium Award only to *network* television. For the eight years that NBC was creating new episodes of *Will & Grace*—with viewership soaring to an unprecedented 19 million at its peak—and since then as reruns have continued to air, all Americans with one or more television in their home have been exposed to the series. Significantly fewer television viewers, by contrast, saw *Queer as Folk* when it was on the air or now see *The L Word*, as only those of us subscribing to Showtime have the chance to tune into those shows.

Waiting for the Fourth Stage

The final topic that begs to be discussed as part of this conclusion is the one that consistently played a central role in the various milestones that have charted the media's changing depiction of gay people: S-E-X.

From 1950 when the *Washington Times-Herald* reported that every homosexual man is so obsessed with sex that he "will go to any limit to attain his abnormal purposes" to early AIDS coverage highlighting a study that found, "the median number of lifetime partners for infected homo-sexual men was 1,160" to the first episode of *Queer as Folk*'s unvarnished look at gay life beginning with "The first thing you have to know is: It's all about sex," carnal activities have been a staple element in how the media have portrayed gay people.[12]

Indeed, sex played such a prominent role in so many of the media products described in this book that it was noteworthy when one of them did *not* depict gay men being sexual. Numerous reviews of *Philadelphia*, for example, criticized the movie for not showing the central couple in bed together. Two men living in the same apartment but not getting frisky?—couldn't happen.

Over time, it became crystal clear what was happening: The Powers That Be had decided to take the *sex* out of homo*sex*ual.

That executives in the motion picture industry were the first to conclude that media products could attract a larger audience if they featured gay men as eunuchs was shown by all the leading characters in the three Hollywood hits of the second half of the 1990s being depicted as having abandoned their libidinous ways. The Robin Williams and Nathan Lane characters were unwaveringly faithful to each other in *The Birdcage*, and the big-screen personas of Kevin Kline and Tom Selleck in *In & Out* and Rupert Everett in *My Best Friend's Wedding* were all chaste. *Brokeback Mountain* at least acknowledged that gay men have sex, although the film's downplaying of the topic prompted the *San Francisco Chronicle* to complain that the movie featured "more man-on-woman sex than man-on-man sex."[13]

TV executives learned the benefits of creating de-sexed gays through the *Ellen* phenomenon. After the Ellen DeGeneres character came out as a Sapphic woman on her ABC sitcom and then had the audacity to become romantically involved with another woman, she was *tout suite* pronounced "too gay." So executives at NBC decided to build a sitcom around a handsome gay lawyer who was virtually sexless, not shown even kissing a beau—much less "doin' the nasty." When *Will & Grace* triumphed in the ratings like no gay-oriented series before it, Bravo followed in the show's footsteps and offered viewers *Queer Eye* and its whole quintet of charming eunuchs.

There's evidence that the journalistic arm of the media was also learning the no-gay-sex-sells lesson during the same era. The biggest gay news story of the early 2000s was same-sex marriage. Although news organizations committed massive amounts of coverage to the topic, they steered clear of the sexual aspects of the story. The *New York Times* was among the leaders of what appeared to be a concerted effort by the titans of journalism to portray the parade of same-sex couples marching down the aisle as *not* being promiscuous. One front-page story in the *Times*—headlined "Gay Couples Seek Unions in God's Eyes"—focused on a lesbian couple who had been together for twenty-five years and "represent an often-overlooked slice of gay America: the monogamous homebodies more likely to have met their mates at Bible study than at a bar."[14]

When the most recent milestones in the media's progression from "perverts" to "fab five" are considered as a whole, the only products to show their subjects having active sex lives are the pair of programs on Showtime. Yes, viewers who were willing to pay $40 a month to subscribe to the premium channel could, for five years, catch glimpses of the gay lads of *Queer as Folk* with their pants down in the backroom of Babylon, and they can still see the lasses of *The L Word* writhing between their 600-count-per-inch designer cotton sheets. But for all those millions of TV viewers who depend on the major networks and basic cable, Gay and Lesbian America is pretty much defined by reruns of gay masters of repartee spending a lot of time making jokes about sex—but not actually having any.

Will it ever happen? Will the media at some point move into what might be called a fourth stage during which the major networks will show two men or two women having sex during primetime?

There's reason for hope. Observers have credited the randy sexual content of HBO's *Sex and the City* with pushing ABC to create such steamy shows as *Desperate Housewives* and *Grey's Anatomy*. And so, anyone tracking the media's gay content is justified in wondering if the relative success of *Queer as Folk* and *The L Word* on Showtime just might propel one of the major networks to showcase gay men and/or lesbians with their libidos intact.[15]

I ended the introduction of this book by talking about how the rise of gay content in the media has coincided with the evolution of my own life. And so, as a final thought in this book, I've chosen to say that I'm keeping my fingers crossed that, at some point before the end of my lifetime, the double standard that keeps gay characters from engaging in the same sexual activities as straight characters will finally end. That progress could play out by a TV network showing a hunky actor such as Jamie Foxx boinking another hottie such as Ashton Kutcher for all to see. If it happens, I promise to tune in.

Notes

Introduction

1 *New York Times*, "Perverts Called Government Peril," 10 April 1950, A25; "Federal Vigilance on Perverts Asked," December 16, 1950, A3.

2 For the "campy quips" quote, see John Bartlett, "Straight Eye for the Queer Guy," *New York Times*, September 21, 2003, F86; for the "league of super-heroes" quote, see John Sellers, "Queen for a Day: My Gay Makeover," *New York Times*, July 13, 2003, B1.

3 Dick Polman, "Gays' Wins Met by Line in the Sand," *Philadelphia Inquirer*, August 10, 2003, A14.

4 Greg Braxton, "Nice Gays Finish First," *Los Angeles Times*, December 21, 2003, E40; Robin Wallace, "Does Spending Power Buy Cultural Acceptance?," Fox News Channel, September 16, 2003.

5 Deborah Sharp, "Cities Come Out About Wooing Gays—and Their Dollars," *USA Today*, December 8, 2003, A3.

6 "Judging Books by Covers" aired February 9, 1971, on CBS and featured a gay man who was a retired professional football player. *An Early Frost* aired on NBC and featured a gay man who was forced out of the closet when he told his family that he had AIDS.

1 "Perverts" on the Potomac: Homosexuals Enter the News Arena

1 Willard Edwards, "Didn't Mean to Condone Hiss, Acheson Says," *Washington Times-Herald*, March 1, 1950, A1; "Senators Hear Acheson Deny Condoning Hiss," *Los Angeles Times*, March 1, 1950, A1; William S. White, "Never Condoned Disloyalty, Says Acheson of Hiss Stand," *New York Times*, March 1, 1950, A1.

2 On coverage of the subcommittee session prompting outrage among congressmen and readers, see David K. Johnson, *The Lavender Scare: The Cold War Persecution of Gays and Lesbians in the Federal Government* (Chicago: University of Chicago Press, 2004), 2. For examples of the few scholars who have discussed the significance of these pioneering news articles about homosexuals, see John D'Emilio, *Sexual Politics, Sexual Communities: The Making of the Homosexual Minority, 1940–1970* (Chicago: University of Chicago Press, 1983), 41–43; Johnson, *Lavender Scare*, 5; Rodger Streitmatter, *Unspeakable: The Rise of the Gay and Lesbian Press in America* (Boston: Faber and Faber, 1995), 17. For the initial reference to use of the phrase "Perverts on the Potomac," see Max Lerner, "The Washington Sex Story: Panic on the Potomac," *New York Post*, July 10, 1950, A4.

3 For the first story about McCarthy's accusations, see Frank Desmond, "M'Carthy Charges Reds Hold U.S. Jobs," *The Intelligencer*, Wheeling, WV, 10 February 1950, 1. On McCarthy's anti-communist campaign, see, for example, Edwin R. Bayley, *Joe McCarthy and the Press* (New York: Pantheon, 1981).

4 White, "Never Condoned Disloyalty," A1.

5 White, "Never Condoned Disloyalty," A1; "Senators Hear Acheson," A1; Edwards, "Didn't Mean to Condone Hiss," A1. For previous examples of stories about homosexuals, see, for example, *New York Times*, "Police Department," July 26, 1929, 44; "Curran Criticizes Justice's Charges," December 28, 1944, 34.

6 "New Shocker," *Newsweek*, 29 May 1950, 18; Max Lerner, "Blick of the Vice Squad," *New York Post*, July 18, 1950, A2.

7 "New Stripes," *Time*, July 24, 1950, 18; Richard H. Rovere, "Letter from Washington," *The New Yorker*, April 22, 1950, 103–10; Lloyd Wendt, "The Vilest of the Rackets," *Esquire*, April 1950, 53, 140–42; Ralph H. Major Jr., "New Moral Menace to Our Youth," *Coronet*, September 1950, 101–08; Joseph and Stewart Alsop, "Why Has Washington Gone Crazy?," *Saturday Evening Post*, July 29, 1950, 20–21.

8 "U.S. Urged to Screen Employees," *Miami Herald*, December 16, 1950, A4; "Probers Ask Tossing Out of Perverts," *Dallas Morning News*, December 16, 1950, A2; Willard Edwards, "Probers Assail U.S. Hiring of Sex Perverts," *Chicago Tribune*, December 16, 1950, A2; "Senators Demand U.S. Bar Hiring of Sex Perverts," *Cleveland Plain Dealer*, December 16, 1950, A4; "Sex Perverts Called Risks to Security," *San Francisco Chronicle*, December 16, 1950, A9; "Senators Hit Perversion in Capital," *Detroit Free Press*, December 16, 1950, A19; Edwards, "Probers Assail U.S. Hiring," A2; "Senators Demand Perverts Be Kept Off U.S. Payroll," *Boston Globe*, December 16, 1950, A2.

9 *New York Times*, "Perverts Called Government Peril," 10 April 1950, A25; "Federal Vigilance on Perverts Asked," December 16, 1950, A3.

10 For examples of the term "perverts" being used in the *New York Times*, see "More Confusion Over McCarthy Case," April 30, 1950, D1; "Perverts Called Government Peril," A25; William S. White, "Inquiry by Senate on Perverts Asked," May 20, 1950, A8; William S. White, "M'Carthy Asserts Budenz Named Red in Acheson Office," April 26, 1950, A3. For examples of the term "homos" being used in the *New York Times*, see "More Confusion over McCarthy Case," D1. For examples of the term "deviates" being used in the *New York Times*, see "Federal Vigilance on Perverts Asked," A3; White, "Inquiry by Senate on Perverts Asked," A8.

11 "Senators Demand U.S. Bar Hiring," A4; Edwards, "Probers Assail U.S. Hiring," A2; "Sex Perverts Called Risks," A9.

12 "U.S. Urged to Screen Employees," A4; "Senators Demand Perverts Be Kept Off U.S. Payroll," *Boston Globe*, December 16, 1950, A2; "Probers Ask Tossing Out of Perverts," A2; Wendt, "Vilest of the Rackets," 53, 140–42; "Bergen Tells Charlie" (editorial cartoon), *Washington Times-Herald*, March 31, 1950, A14; Robert C. Ruark, "Abnormal Humans," *New York World-Telegram*, March 23, 1950, B1; Major, "New Moral Menace," 102.

13 "Senators Hear Acheson," A1.

14 For examples of articles describing the blackmail scenario, see Edwards, "Probers Assail U.S. Hiring," A2; Ferdinand Kuhn, "Denounces Disloyalty in Testimony to Senators," *Washington Post*, March 1, 1950, A2; John O'Donnell, "Capitol Stuff," *New York Daily News*, March 24, 1950, 4; Bert

Wissman, "Inquiry May Touch on Red Blackmailing," *Washington Times-Herald*, March 24, 1950, A1.

15 Lerner, "Washington Sex Story," July 10, 1950, A4.

16 Westbrook Pegler, "Fair Enough," *Washington Times-Herald*, March 31, 1950, A14; Robert C. Ruark, "Hierarchy of Misfits," *New York World-Telegram*, March 24, 1950, C1.

17 Ruark, "Abnormal Humans," B1.

18 "To Close Sex Law Loopholes," *Washington Evening Star*, December 16, 1950, A4.

19 Max Lerner, "'Scandal' in the State Department," *New York Post*, July 16, 1950, A2; "Bergen Tells Charlie"; Peter Edson, "How Sen. McCarthy Spilled the Beans," *Washington Daily News*, March 9, 1950, 5.

20 Major, "New Moral Menace," 103, 104.

21 Wendt, "Vilest of the Rackets," 140.

22 Lerner, "'Scandal' in the State Department," July 11, 1950, A5. On homosexuality not being a genetic trait, see also Major, "New Moral Menace," 106. On overly protective mothers causing their sons to become homosexual, see also Major, "New Moral Menace," 106.

23 Alfred C. Kinsey, *Sexual Behavior in the Human Male* (Philadelphia: W. B. Saunders, 1948), 651; Lerner, "'Scandal' in the State Department," July 12, 1950, A5, A34. On the percentage of homosexuals among the American male population, see also Major, "New Moral Menace," 102. Kinsey defined adult males as those between the ages of sixteen and fifty-five.

24 "The Abnormal," *Time*, April 17, 1950, 86.

25 Lerner, "'Scandal' in the State Department," July 16, 1950, A2; "Move to Bar Perverts from ECA Beaten," *Washington Times-Herald*, April 1, 1950, A2.

26 Louis Chunovic, *One Foot on the Floor: The Curious Evolution of Sex on Television from* I Love Lucy *to* South Park (New York: TV Books, 2000), 34.

27 Lerner, "'Scandal' in the State Department," July 21, 1950, A2; Lerner, "'Scandal' in the State Department," July 16, 1950, A2; Major, "New Moral Menace," 102.

28 Lerner, "'Scandal' in the State Department," July 18, 1950, A2.

29 "Move to Bar Perverts from ECA Beaten," A2.

30 Ruark, "Abnormal Humans," B1; Lerner, "'Scandal' in the State Department," July 11, 1950, A5.

31 Major, "New Moral Menace," 102.

32 Major, "New Moral Menace," 102–03.

33 Major, "New Moral Menace," 104.

34 Major, "New Moral Menace," 104.

35 "The Woman's Rights Convention—The Last Act of the Drama," *New York Herald*, September 12, 1852, 2; Miriam Gurko, *The Ladies of Seneca Falls: The Birth of the Woman's Rights Movement* (New York: Macmillan, 1974), 104; Lucretia Mott, "National Convention at Cincinnati, Ohio," in Elizabeth Cady Stanton, Susan B. Anthony, and Matilda Joslyn Gage, eds., *History of Woman Suffrage* (New York: Fowler & Wells, 1881), 164.

2 Stonewall Rebellion: Reporting on an Epic Event

1 On the Stonewall Rebellion being compared to the Boston Tea Party, see Steven V. Roberts, "Homosexuals in Revolt," *New York Times*, August 24, 1970, A28. On conditions at the Stonewall Inn, see Martin Duberman,

Stonewall (New York: Dutton, 1993), especially 181–90; Paul Berman, "Democracy and Homosexuality," *New Republic*, December 20, 1993, 22, 25–26.

2 "Judy Garland: A Star Dies," *Los Angeles Times*, June 29, 1969, G5.

3 On specific details about the Stonewall Rebellion, see Edward Alwood, *Straight News: Gays, Lesbians, and the News Media* (New York: Columbia University Press, 1996), 82–83; Berman, "Democracy and Homosexuality," 22, 25–26; Charles Kaiser, *The Gay Metropolis: 1940–1996* (New York: Houghton Mifflin, 1997), 197–202; Dick Leitsch, "Police Raid on N.Y. Club Sets Off First Gay Riot," *Los Angeles Advocate*, September 1969, 3; Jerry Lisker, "Homo Nest Raided, Queen Bees Are Stinging Mad," *New York Daily News*, July 6, 1969, B1; Howard Smith, "Full Moon Over the Stonewall," *Village Voice*, July 3, 1969, 1, 25, 29; Lucian Truscott IV, "Gay Power Comes to Sheridan Square," *Village Voice*, July 3, 1969, 1, 18.

4 "4 Policemen Hurt in Village Raid," *New York Times*, June 29, 1969, A33; "Police Again Rout Village Youths," *New York Times*, June 30, 1969, A22; "Hostile Crowd Dispersed Near Sheridan Square," *New York Times*, July 3, 1969, A19; Dennis Eskow, "3 Cops Hurt as Bar Raid Riles Crowd," *New York Daily News*, June 29, 1969, 30; Lisker, "Homo Nest Raided," B1; Jay Levin, "The Gay Anger Behind the Riots," *New York Post*, July 8, 1969, 36; Smith, "Full Moon Over the Stonewall," 1, 25, 29; Truscott, "Gay Power Comes to Sheridan Square," 1, 18.

5 "N.Y. Homosexuals Protest Raids," *Washington Post*, July 1, 1969, E2; "Gays Go Radical," *Christianity Today*, December 4, 1970, 40–41; Leo Skir, "A Look at Gay Power," *Mademoiselle*, September 1970, 150–51, 195–96, 198. See also Richard Foster, "They're Organized, They're Angry, They're Fighting for Their Rights," *Chicago Sun-Times Magazine*, December 14, 1969, 40–41.

6 Lisker, "Homo Nest Raided," B1; Levin, "Gay Anger Behind the Riots," 36; Truscott, "Gay Power Comes to Sheridan Square," 1, 18.

7 Lisker, "Homo Nest Raided," B1.

8 "Policing the Third Sex," *Newsweek*, October 27, 1969, 76; "The Homosexual: Newly Visible, Newly Understood," *Time*, October 31, 1969, 61.

9 Smith, "Full Moon Over the Stonewall," 1, 25, 29.

10 Roberts, "Homosexuals in Revolt," A1, A28; "Police Again Rout Village Youths," A22.

11 "The Homosexual: Newly Visible," 56; "Policing the Third Sex," 76.

12 Richard Foster, "Three Speak Out on Harassment, Parents, Analysts and Girls," *Chicago Sun-Times Magazine*, December 14, 1969, 45; Joseph Epstein, "Homo/Hetero: The Struggle for Sexual Identity," *Harper's*, September 1970, 49; Tom Burke, "The New Homosexuality," *Esquire*, December 1969, 316.

13 Enid Nemy, "The Woman Homosexual: More Assertive, Less Willing to Hide," *New York Times*, November 17, 1969, A62; "The Homosexual: Newly Visible," 65.

14 Roberts, "Homosexuals in Revolt," A28.

15 "The Homosexual: Newly Visible," 66.

16 Burke, "New Homosexuality," 304.

17 Epstein, "Homo/Hetero," 37, 51.

18 Truscott, "Gay Power Comes to Sheridan Square," 1, 18.

19 "The Homosexual: Newly Visible," 61; "The Tenderloin—A Gay Sub-culture," *San Francisco Chronicle*, July 1, 1969, A17.

20 Julie Smith, "How Does Girl Meet Girl?," *San Francisco Chronicle*, July 1, 1969, A17; "Four Lives in the Gay World," *Time*, October 31, 1969, 62.
21 Nemy, "The Woman Homosexual," A62. On lesbians being mentally ill, see also Gerald Caplan, "A Psychiatrist's Casebook," *McCall's*, November 1969, 65.
22 Lisker, "Homo Nest Raided," B6.
23 Lisker, "Homo Nest Raided," B6.
24 Alwood, *Straight News*, 88.
25 On lesbians having a significant presence in the Stonewall Rebellion, see Duberman, *Stonewall*, especially 196; Kaiser, *Gay Metropolis*, 197–198; John Loughery, *The Other Side of Silence: Men's Lives and Gay Identities: A Twentieth-Century History* (New York: Henry Holt, 1998), 316.
26 Lisker, "Homo Nest Raided," B6. On drag queens being leaders in the Stonewall Rebellion, see Duberman, *Stonewall*, especially 196–204; Kaiser, *Gay Metropolis*, 197, 200; Loughery, *Other Side of Silence*, 316.

3   *The Boys in the Band*: Homosexuality Comes to the Big Screen

 1 On praise for the acting, see John Gruen, "The Boys in the Band, 'Explosive,'" *Vogue*, May 1970, 152, and on praise for the script, see "Eight Desperate Men," *Newsweek*, March 30, 1970, 91; "Shades of Lavender," *Time*, March 30, 1970, 100. On the overall tone being too melodramatic, see Gary Arnold, "Solid Hit," *Washington Post*, March 19, 1970, C13, and on the camerawork being amateurish, see Vincent Canby, "Screen: 'Boys in the Band,'" *New York Times*, March 18, 1970, 36; Pauline Kael, "The Boys in the Band," *The New Yorker*, March 21, 1970, 167; Moira Walsh, "The Boys in the Band," *America*, April 11, 1970, 398. For other positive reviews, see Leo Lerman, "Catch Up With Love," *Mademoiselle*, May 1970, 120, 203; Jack Star, "The Faces of the Boys in the Band," *Look*, December 2, 1969, 63–64, 67. For other negative reviews, see Hollis Alpert, "Harold's Birthday," *Saturday Review*, April 4, 1970, 24; Stanley Kauffman, "The Boys in the Band," *The New Republic*, April 18, 1970, 20.
 2 "The Faces of the Boys in the Band," *Look*, December 2, 1969, 63; "Shades of Lavender," 100; Gruen, "Boys in the Band," 152.
 3 On reviews that quoted the line, see George N. Boyd, "Purgatory and Downward," *Christian Century*, 5 August 1970, 944; "Shades of Lavender," 97; Walsh, "Boys in the Band," 398.
 4 *The Boys in the Band* was released by National General and rated R. It was directed by William Friedken and written by Mart Crowley from his own play. For articles about the play, see Clive Barnes, "Theater: 'Boys in the Band' Opens Off Broadway," *New York Times*, April 15, 1968, 48; Clive Barnes, "'The Boys in the Band' Is Still a Sad Gay Romp," *New York Times*, February 18, 1969, 36; Clive Barnes, "Stage: Birthday for 'Boys in the Band,'" *New York Times*, April 18, 1970, 34.
 5 Harold was played by Leonard Frey.
 6 Michael was played by Kenneth Nelson.
 7 Bernard was played by Reuben Greene.
 8 Tex was played by Robert La Tourneaux.
 9 Donald was played by Frederick Combs.
10 Larry was played by Keith Prentice, and Hank was played by Larry Luckinbill.
11 Emory was played by Cliff Gorman.
12 "Shades of Lavender," 100.

13 Westbrook Pegler, "Fair Enough," *Washington Times-Herald*, March 31, 1950, A14.

14 Kael, "Boys in the Band," 167.

15 Alan was played by Peter White.

16 Emory is an interior decorator, and Larry is a fashion photographer; Hank is a math teacher, and Bernard is a clerk in a Doubleday bookstore.

17 See David Ansen, "Gay Films Are a Drag," *Newsweek*, March 18, 1996, 71; Richard Barrios, *Screened Out: Playing Gay in Hollywood from Edison to Stonewall* (New York: Routledge, 2003), 355–63; Richard Dyer, ed., *Gays and Film* (London: British Film Institute, 1977), 32–33, 37, 48; Larry Gross, *Up from Invisibility: Lesbians, Gay Men, and the Media in America* (New York: Columbia University Press, 2001), 62–63; Larry Gross and James D. Woods, "Up From Invisibility: Film and Television," in Larry Gross and James D. Woods, eds., *The Columbia Reader on Lesbians and Gay Men in Media, Society, and Politics* (New York: Columbia University Press, 1999), 292–93; Charles Kaiser, *The Gay Metropolis, 1940–1996* (New York: Houghton Mifflin, 1997), 185–92; John Loughery, *The Other Side of Silence: Men's Lives and Gay Identities: A Twentieth-Century History* (New York: Henry Holt, 1998), 293–302; Gene D. Phillips, "The Boys on the Bandwagon: Homosexuality in the Movies," in Thomas R. Atkins, ed., *Sexuality in the Movies* (Bloomington: Indiana University Press, 1975), 157–71; William Scroggie, "Producing Identity: From *The Boys in the Band* to Gay Liberation," in Patricia Juliana Smith, ed., *The Queer Sixties* (New York: Routledge, 1999), 237–54; Vito Russo, *The Celluloid Closet: Homosexuality in the Movies* (New York: Harper & Row, 1981), 175, 177; Suzanna Danuta Walters, *All the Rage: The Story of Gay Visibility in America* (Chicago: University of Chicago Press, 2001), 134–35; Thomas Waugh, *The Fruit Machine: Twenty Years of Writings on Queer Cinema* (Durham, North Carolina: Duke University Press, 1995), 18–19, 60.

18 Russo, *Celluloid Closet*, 175, 177; Walters, *All the Rage*, 134; Gross, *Up from Invisibility*, 62.

19 Judy Klemesrud, "You Don't Have to Be One to Play One," *New York Times*, September 29, 1968, D1, D2.

4   *Soap*: A Gay Man Comes to TV Land

1 *Soap*, ABC Television, 1977, episode 1.

2 On criticism of *Soap*, see, for example, Larry Gross, *Up from Invisibility: Lesbians, Gay Men, and the Media in America* (New York: Columbia University Press, 2001), 84; Stephen Tropiano, *The Prime Time Closet: A History of Gays and Lesbians on TV* (New York: Applause Theatre & Cinema, 2002), 242. On praise for *Soap*, see, for example, Steven Capsuto, *Alternate Channels: The Uncensored Story of Gay and Lesbian Images on Radio and Television* (New York: Ballantine, 2000), 142; Suzanna Danuta Walters, *All the Rage: The Story of Gay Visibility in America* (Chicago: University of Chicago Press, 2001), 61.

3 Judy Klemesrud, "From Rah-Rah Cheerleader, to 'Soap's' Creator," *New York Times*, June 17, 1978, 10. In 1972 ABC had introduced a comedy titled *The Corner Bar* set in a New York City saloon and featuring a gay theater set designer named Peter Panama. The program did not draw a large audience and was not renewed for a second season.

4 Sander Vanocur, " 'Soap' in ABC's Eye," *Washington Post*, November 3, 1976, D1, D6.

5 Harry F. Waters, "99 and 44/100% *Im*pure," *Newsweek*, June 13, 1977, 92; John J. O'Connor, "TV: Stir Over 'Soap' Continues," *New York Times*, July 12, 1977, 59.

6 Les Brown, "TV: 4 Church Units Plan to Fight 'Soap,'" *New York Times*, August 31, 1977, C20 (The minister was the Rev. Everett C. Parker, director of the office of communication of the United Church of Christ.); "Is Prime Time Ready for Sex?," *Time*, July 11, 1977, 75.

7 Les Brown, "'Soap,' ABC's Explicit Comedy, Has Critics in Lather," *New York Times*, June 27, 1977, 53.

8 David E. Anderson, "Soap Watching, Reacting Urged," *Los Angeles Times*, September 5, 1977, D10; Les Brown, "TV: 4 Church Units Plan," C20; "Local Rabbis Decry ABC's 'Soap' Series," *Los Angeles Times*, August 6, 1977, A25; Molly Selvin, "Somebody Is Being Manipulated in the Big TV Flap Over 'Soap,'" *San Diego Union*, August 28, 1977, C4. The Rev. Donald Wildmon, a Methodist minister, founded the National Federation of Decency in early 1977; the organization was later renamed the American Family Association.

9 Klemesrud, "From Rah-Rah Cheerleader," 10.

10 Episodes 1; 21; 2; 6; 13; 28; 19.

11 Episodes 10; 19; 21.

12 Episode 1.

13 Episode 28.

14 Episode 24.

15 Episode 34.

16 "How to Launder a TV Show: A Secret Memo," *New York Daily News*, July 10, 1977, TV1.

17 Episodes 22; 29; 50; 53.

18 Carole-Anne Tyler, "Transsexualism," in George E. Haggerty, ed., *Gay Histories and Cultures: An Encyclopedia* (Garland: New York, 2000), 891.

19 Frank Swertlow, "The Lather Over Soap," *Los Angeles Times*, July 13, 1977, D16; Selvin, "Somebody Is Being Manipulated," C1; Frank Rich, "Viewpoint: "Soap, Betty & Rafferty," *Time*, September 12, 1977, 74.

20 Episodes 2; 4.

21 Episode 2.

22 Episode 3.

23 Episode 8.

24 Gross, *Up from Invisibility*, 84; Tropiano, *Prime Time Closet*, 242.

25 Walters, *All the Rage*, 61; Capsuto, *Alternate Channels*, 142. On praise for *Soap*, see also Gross, *Up from Invisibility*, 84; Tropiano, *Prime Time Closet*, 240–43.

26 Klemesrud, "From Rah-Rah Cheerleader," 10.

27 Billy Crystal's career has also included playing leading roles in the films *City Slickers II* and *Analyze That*, and hosting the televised Grammy Awards three times and the Academy Awards eight times.

28 *The Nat King Cole Show* aired on NBC from 1956 to 1957, and *The Mary Tyler Moore Show* aired on CBS from 1970 to 1977.

29 Jack Nichols, "Billy Crystal: Interview with A Gay Icon," *Gay Today*, January 26, 2004.

5 AIDS Enters the News: Reporting on the "Gay Plague"

1 Lenny Giteck, "The Gay Pursuit of Muscle," *The Advocate*, June 11, 1981, 27.

2 Harry Nelson, "Outbreaks of Pneumonia Among Gay Males Studied," *Los Angeles Times*, June 5, 1981, A3; David Perlman, "A Pneumonia that Strikes Gay Men," *San Francisco Chronicle*, June 6, 1981, A4; Lawrence K. Altman, "Rare Cancer Seen in 41 Homosexuals," *New York Times*, July 3, 1981, A20.

3 *Morbidity and Mortality Weekly Report*, June 5, 1981, 2.

4 Nelson, "Outbreaks of Pneumonia," A3, A25; Perlman, "A Pneumonia that Strikes Gay Men," A4.

5 On early news coverage of AIDS suggesting that it was strictly a gay disease, see Larry Gross, *Up from Invisibility: Lesbians, Gay Men, and the Media in America* (New York: Columbia University Press, 2001), 97.

6 Harry Nelson, "Started with Gays—Mysterious Fever Now an Epidemic," *Los Angeles Times*, May 31, 1982, A1, A3, A20.

7 Jean Seligman, "The AIDS Epidemic: The Search for a Cure," *Newsweek*, April 18, 1983, cover, 74–79. The *Newsweek* reporter was Vincent Coppola.

8 "Family Contact Studied in Transmitting AIDS," *New York Times*, May 6, 1983, A21; James Kinsella, *Covering the Plague: AIDS and the American Media* (New Brunswick, NJ: Rutgers University Press, 1989), 56–57; 263. The study was based on the fact that a larger number of babies were diagnosed with the disease and one pediatrician speculated that they must have contracted it in their homes. Medical experts pointed out that it was more likely the infants had become infected while inside their mothers' wombs.

9 Cristine Russell, "Research Indicates AIDS Is Connected to a Cancer Virus," *Washington Post*, April 17, 1984, A1, A4.

10 On stories about Rock Hudson being ill with AIDS marking a turning point in the coverage, see Edward Alwood, *Straight News: Gays, Lesbians, and the News Media* (New York: Columbia University Press, 1996), 234–35; Gross, *Up from Invisibility*, 98–99; Kinsella, *Covering the Plague*, 144–45; David Shaw, "Hudson Brought AIDS Coverage Out of the Closet," *Los Angeles Times*, December 21, 1987, A1, A28–A31.

11 Jerry Bishop, "Mysterious Ailment Plagues Drug Users, Homosexual Males," *Wall Street Journal*, December 10, 1981, 41.

12 Alwood, *Straight News*, 216.

13 Kinsella, *Covering the Plague*, 1; Gross, *Up from Invisibility*, 95, 99; David Shaw, "Coverage of AIDS Story: A Slow Start," *Los Angeles Times*, December 20, 1987, A36; David Shaw, "Why They Wouldn't Talk about AIDS," *Los Angeles Times*, April 8, 1990, book review section, 5.

14 Robert Pear, "Health Chief Calls AIDS Battle 'No. 1 Priority,'" *New York Times*, May 25, 1983, A1.

15 Lawrence Mass, "Disease Rumors Largely Unfounded," *New York Native*, May 18, 1981, 7.

16 Randy Shilts, *And the Band Played On: Politics, People, and the AIDS Epidemic* (New York: St. Martin's, 1987), 191.

17 Kinsella, *Covering the Plague*, 128. The CBS executive was Ernest Leiser.

18 Edward Alwood, "Journalism," in George E. Haggerty, ed., *Gay Histories and Cultures: An Encyclopedia* (New York: Garland, 2000), 503; Shaw, "Coverage of AIDS Story," A40; Kinsella, *Covering the Plague*, 128.

19 The NBC story aired on June 17, 1982. On Tom Brokaw's wording, see Gross, *Up from Invisibility*, 97; Kinsella, *Covering the Plague*, 127. Television news continued to give scant coverage to AIDS. By June 1983, the evening news program on NBC had broadcast thirteen stories, ABC had broadcast eight, and CBS had broadcast six.

20 On news coverage of AIDS communicating that gay men are promiscuous, see John Nguyet Erni, "AIDS in the U.S. Media," in Haggerty, *Gay Histories and Cultures*, 29.

21 Lawrence K. Altman, *New York Times*, "Rare Cancer Seen in 41 Homosexuals," July 3, 1981, A20; "New Homosexual Disorder Worries Health Officials," May 11, 1982, C6.

22 Seligman, "The AIDS Epidemic," 75; Michael Daly, "AIDS Anxiety," *New York*, June 20, 1983, 26; David Black, "The Plague Years," *Rolling Stone*, March 28, 1985, 52.

23 John Leo, "The Real Epidemic: Fear and Despair," *Time*, July 4, 1983, 58, 57.

24 Dudley Clendinen, "AIDS Spreads Fear Among Ill and Healthy Alike," *New York Times*, June 17, 1983, B4; Michael Daly, "AIDS Anxiety," *New York*, June 20, 1983, 25, 28; Leo, "The Real Epidemic," 56.

6 AIDS Becomes Major News: "Now No One Is Safe"

1 Ted Thackery Jr., "Rock Hudson Dies at 59 after Fighting AIDS," *Los Angeles Times*, October 3, 1985, A1.

2 Kim Painter, "A Checkered History of Tragedy, Despair and Hope," *USA Today*, June 4, 1991, 4.

3 "Hudson Has AIDS, Spokesman Says," *New York Times*, July 26, 1985, C3.

4 "Final Battle Became His Legacy," *USA Today*, October 3, 1985, A1.

5 Carla Hall, "Double Lives and Damaged Careers," *Washington Post*, August 15, 1985, B1, B2.

6 David Shaw, "Hudson Brought AIDS Coverage Out of the Closet," *Los Angeles Times*, December 21, 1987, A1. See also, Larry Gross, *Up from Invisibility: Lesbians, Gay Men, and the Media in America* (New York: Columbia University Press, 2001), 101; Randy Shilts, *And the Band Played On: Politics, People, and the AIDS Epidemic* (New York: Penguin, 1987), xxi.

7 David Shaw, "Why They Wouldn't Talk about AIDS," *Los Angeles Times*, April 8, 1990, book review section, 5; "AIDS and the Press," *Time*, August 22, 1994, 15. The *Time* study looked at coverage in six major newspapers (*Boston Globe, Chicago Tribune, Los Angeles Times, New York Times, San Francisco Chronicle*, and *Washington Post*) and the three major news magazines (*Newsweek, Time*, and *U.S. News & World Report*).

8 David Shaw, "Coverage of AIDS Story: A Slow Start," *Los Angeles Times*, December 20, 1987, A40.

9 Jane E. Brody, "Personal Health," *New York Times*, February 12, 1986, C6; Lawrence K. Altman, "Fact, Theory and Myth on the Spread of AIDS," *New York Times*, February 15, 1987, A1. For other examples of the use of explicit terms in the *New York Times*, see William F. Buckley Jr., "Identify All the Carriers," March 18, 1986, A27 ("anal sex"); Jane Gross, "Homosexuals Stepping Up AIDS Education," September 22, 1985 ("anal intercourse"); Joyce Purnick, "City Closes Bar Frequented by Homosexuals," November 8, 1985 ("anal intercourse").

10 Larry Thompson, "Safe Sex in the Era of AIDS," *Washington Post*, March 31, 1987, Z10; Harry Nelson, "AIDS Study to Test Condoms," *Los Angeles Times*, January 16, 1987, A3; Richard A. Knox, "Row Grows over AIDS Pamphlets Too Graphic, Critics Charge," *Boston Globe*, November 20, 1987.

11 James Kinsella, *Covering the Plague: AIDS and the American Media* (New Brunswick, NJ: Rutgers University Press, 1989), 135, 136.

12 Suzanna Danuta Walters, *All the Rage: The Story of Gay Visibility in America* (Chicago: University of Chicago Press, 2001), 61.

13 Kinsella, *Covering the Plague*, 210.

14 "AIDS: A National Inquiry" aired the week of March 27, 1986; Julie Morris, "Infected Individuals Scrutinized in Ga., Texas," *USA Today*, October 3, 1985, A7; "Police Trail AIDS Victim Who Vows to Have Sex," *Chicago Tribune*, October 3, 1985, A4; "Defiant AIDS Victim Checks into Hospital," *Los Angeles Times*, October 3, 1985, A2; Howard Rosenberg, "'Frontline' AIDS Controversy," *Los Angeles Times*, March 27, 1986, A1.

15 Kinsella, *Covering the Plague*, 102, 149, 265; Shaw, "Hudson Brought AIDS Coverage," A30; Shilts, *And the Band Played On*, 568; "Now No One Is Safe from AIDS," *Life*, July 1985, cover, 12–19.

16 "Now No One Is Safe," 12.

17 "Now No One Is Safe," 15.

18 John Leo, "The Real Epidemic: Fear and Despair," *Time*, July 4, 1983, 58; Robin Marantz Henig, "AIDS: A New Disease's Deadly Odyssey," *New York Times Magazine*, February 6, 1983, 38, 42.

19 *Honolulu Star-Bulletin*, Bill Cox, "A Journalist with AIDS," September 1, 1986, A8; "Journalist Bill Cox Dies After Long AIDS Battle," May 20, 1988, 1.

20 Margaret Engel, "AIDS and Prejudice," *Washington Post*, December 1, 1987, Z10; Robert Reinhold, "AIDS Book Brings Fame to a Gay San Franciscan," *New York Times*, October 31, 1987, A7.

21 Gross, "Homosexuals Stepping Up," A1, A2; Lawrence K. Altman, "Who's Stricken and How: AIDS Pattern Is Shifting," *New York Times*, February 5, 1989, A1, A2.

22 On the statistics, see Kim Painter, "A Checkered History of Tragedy, Despair and Hope," *USA Today*, June 4, 1991, 4.

23 Walters, *All the Rage*, 50.

24 David Jefferson, "How AIDS Changed America," *Newsweek*, May 15, 2006, 36.

25 On the news coverage of AIDS not leading to increased attention to gay women, see, for example, Gross, *Up from Invisibility*, 103.

26 Clarence Page, "Acute Info Deficiency Syndrome," *Chicago Tribune*, October 27, 1985, B13.

27 Max Lerner, "'Scandal' in the State Department," *New York Post*, July 11, 1950, A5; Enid Nemy, "The Woman Homosexual: More Assertive, Less Willing to Hide," *New York Times*, November 17, 1969, A62; "The Homosexual: Newly Visible, Newly Understood," *Time*, October 31, 1969, 65.

28 Lacey Fosburgh, "Thousands of Homosexuals Hold a Protest Rally in Central Park," *New York Times*, June 29, 1970, A1.

7   Gays in the Military: The Debate over Lifting the Ban

1 Eleanor Clift, "How the Candidates Play to Gays," *Newsweek*, September 14, 1992, 40; David Maraniss, "Clinton Finds New Voice of Emotion," *Washington Post*, May 20, 1992, A1; J. Jennings Moss, "Politics: Bill Clinton," *The Advocate*, June 25, 1996.

2 "Clinton Acts to End Ban on Gays," *San Francisco Examiner*, January 29, 1993, A1, A16; "Gays in the Military," *Austin American Statesman*, January 31, 1993, H1.

3 Kenneth J. Cooper, "House Backs Senate on Gays in the Military," *Washington Post*, September 29, 1993, A8; John Lancaster, "Final Rules on

Gays Set," *Washington Post*, December 23, 1993, A1; Jeffrey H. Birnbaum, "Clinton Adopts Policy to Ease Military Gay Ban," *Wall Street Journal*, July 20, 1993, A2.

4 Max Lerner, "'Scandal' in the State Department," *New York Post*, July 16, 1950, 2; "Move to Bar Perverts from ECA Beaten," *Washington Times-Herald*, April 1, 1950, A2.

5 "A Battle for the Military's Soul," *Chicago Tribune*, January 2, 1993, A21.

6 Catherine S. Manegold, "The Odd Place of Homosexuality in the Military," *New York Times*, April 18, 1993, E1; Howard Rosenberg, "Coverage of Hearings Suggests a Gay Hunt," *Los Angeles Times*, May 17, 1993, F9.

7 "Battle for the Military's Soul," A21.

8 *Chicago Tribune*, David Evans, "Clinton's Promise on Gays Could Cloud the Military's Future," October 23, 1992, A25; Timothy J. McNulty, "Gay Debate Goes to Core of Military Ethos," January 31, 1993, D1.

9 "Keep the Military's Homosexual Ban," *Wall Street Journal*, February 1, 1993, A10.

10 "Lifting Gay Military Ban Hits Emotional Chord," *Los Angeles Times*, November 19, 1992, A5.

11 *NBC Nightly News*, May 10, 1993 (the newscast was anchored by Tom Brokaw; the segment was reported by Lisa Myers); *ABC World News Tonight*, January 27, 1993 (the newscast was anchored by Peter Jennings; the segment was reported by Mike von Fremd); *CBS Evening News*, November 24, 1992 (the newscast was anchored by Dan Rather; the segment was reported by Jim Stewart).

12 "The High Cost of Military Prejudice," *New York Times*, June 2, 1992, A20.

13 *New York Times*, Anna Quindlen, "With Extreme Prejudice," June 24, 1992, A21; Anthony Lewis, "The Issue Is Bigotry," January 29, 1993, A27.

14 "A Need for Some Uniform Rules," *Los Angeles Times*, June 13, 1992, B7; Barry Goldwater, "The Gay Ban: Just Plain Un-American," *Washington Post*, June 10, 1993, A23; "Clinton Is Right to End Ban on Gays in the Military," *USA Today*, January 27, 1993, A10.

15 *NBC Nightly News*, January 26, 1993 (the newscast was anchored by Tom Brokaw).

16 Bettina Boxall, "A Different Battlefront," *Los Angeles Times*, August 9, 1992, A3.

17 Lynne Duke, "Military's Last Social Taboo," *Washington Post*, August 19, 1991, A1; Timothy Egan, "Dismissed from Army as Lesbian, Colonel Will Fight Homosexual Ban," *New York Times*, May 31, 1992, A18.

18 "The High Cost of Military Prejudice," *New York Times*, June 2, 1992, A20; Deeann Glamser, "Lesbian Nurse Fights Ouster from Military," *USA Today*, June 11, 1992, A2; Bettina Boxall, "A Different Battlefront," *Los Angeles Times*, August 9, 1992, A3; "A Need for Some Uniform Rules," *Los Angeles Times*, June 13, 1992, B7.

19 Debbie Howlett, "Lesbians in Line of Fire," *USA Today*, July 15, 1993, 7A.

20 See, for example, Joseph Epstein, "Homo/Hetero: The Struggle for Sexual Identity," *Harper's*, September 1970, 37, 51.

21 Jeffrey Schmalz, "Difficult First Step," *New York Times*, November 15, 1992, A22; Frank Rich, "Public Stages; Men in Uniform," *New York Times Magazine*, April 11, 1993, 54.

8   Fleeting Images of Lesbians: Killing, Kissing, Being Chic

1 *Basic Instinct*, which was rated R, was written by Joe Eszterhas, directed by Paul Verhoeven, and released by TriStar Pictures.
2 Bernard Weinraub, "Violent Melodrama of a Sizzling Movie Brings Ratings Battle," *New York Times*, January 30, 1992, C15.
3 Lewis Beale, "Gays vs. Hollywood," *Chicago Tribune*, March 29, 1992, K10.
4 Janice Simpson, "Out of the Celluloid Closet," *Time*, April 6, 1992, 65; "Censors on the Street," *Time*, May 13, 1991, 70; David J. Fox, "Activists 'Dis-Invited' to 'Basic' Screening," *Los Angeles Times*, March 11, 1992, F3; Matthew Gilbert, "Beyond Villains & Buffoons," *Boston Globe*, March 22, 1992, B25; Carla Hall, "'Instinct' Battle Plan," *Washington Post*, March 19, 1992, C1; Scott Harris and Miles Corwin, "Opposition to Film 'Basic Instinct' Rises," *Los Angeles Times*, March 21, 1992, B3; Julie Lew, "Gay Groups Protest a Film Script," *New York Times*, May 4, 1991, A11; Weinraub, "Violent Melodrama," C15.
5 Diane White, "This 'Instinct' Isn't Basic, Just Base," *Boston Globe*, March 25, 1992, 69; David Ansen, "Kiss Kiss Slash Slash," *Newsweek*, March 23, 1992, 54.
6 David J. Fox, "'Instinct' Sizzles at the Box Office," *Los Angeles Times*, March 23, 1992, F1, F6; Gilbert, "Beyond Villains & Buffoons," B25; Brian D. Johnson, "Killer Movies," *Maclean's*, March 30, 1992, 48; John Weir, "Gay-Bashing, Villainy and the Oscars," *New York Times*, March 29, 1992, A1.
7 Karen Freifeld, "Not Just a Kiss," *Newsday*, February 7, 1994.
8 "'Roseanne' and ABC Clash over a Kiss," *New York Times*, February 9, 1994, C19; "Roseanne's Notorious Kiss Will Air," *Boston Globe*, February 18, 1994, 68.
9 John Carmody, "The TV Column," *Washington Post*, February 18, 1994, G6; David Zurawik, "ABC a Little Too Brazen in Promoting Its Prime-Time Lesbian Kiss," *Baltimore Sun*, March 1, 1994, D1.
10 "A Kiss Is Still a Kiss," *USA Today*, February 18, 1994, D1. Mariel Hemingway had appeared as a lesbian in the 1982 film *Personal Best*.
11 "'Roseanne' Will Show Star Kissing Mariel Hemingway," *Orlando Sentinel*, February 19, 1994, A2; Greg Braxton, "ABC's Response to 'Roseanne' Episode," *Los Angeles Times*, March 1, 1994, F1.
12 Zurawik, "ABC a Little Too Brazen," D1; "Roseanne's Kiss Works Ratings Magic," *Los Angeles Times*, March 9, 1994, F14.
13 Elise Harris, "Women in Love," *Mademoiselle*, February 1993, 180–183, 208.
14 Alexis Jetter, "Goodbye to the Last Taboo," *Vogue*, July 1993, 86, 88.
15 Catherine Eaton, "A Matter of Pride: Being a Gay Woman in the Nineties," *Cosmopolitan*, November 1993, 226, 227.
16 Louise Sloan, "Do Ask, Do Tell," *Glamour*, May 1994, 293.
17 Jeanie Russell Kasindorf, "Lesbian Chic: The Bold, Brave New World of Gay Women," *New York*, May 10, 1993, 33.
18 Barbara Kantrowitz, "A Town Like No Other," *Newsweek*, June 21, 1993, 56–57.
19 Kasindorf, "Lesbian Chic," 30.
20 Harris, "Women in Love," 182. The professor who was quoted in the article was Eve Kosofsky Sedgwick.
21 Eaton, "A Matter of Pride," , 228.
22 Kara Swisher, "We Love Lesbians!," *Washington Post*, July 18, 1993, C1.

23 Booth Moore, "Dressed-up Diversity," *Los Angeles Times*, February 8, 2004, E4.

24 Internet Movie Database (http://printable.pro.imdb.com/title/tt0103772/box office)

25 Scholars of pornography date the appearance of girl-on-girl sex scenes to the 1960s; see, for example, Deborah Swedberg, "What Do We See When We See Woman/Woman Sex in Pornographic Movies," *National Women's Studies Association Journal*, vol. 1, no. 4 (Summer 1989), 604.

26 "The Tenderloin—A Gay Subculture," *San Francisco Chronicle*, July 1, 1969, A17.

27 "Four Lives in the Gay World," *Time*, October 31, 1969, 62.

28 "The Homosexual: Newly Visible, Newly Understood," *Time*, October 31, 1969, 61.

29 Enid Nemy, "The Woman Homosexual: More Assertive, Less Willing to Hide," *New York Times*, November 17, 1969, A62.

9   *Philadelphia*: "A Quantum Leap for Gays on Film"

1 Matthew Gilbert, "Beyond Villains & Buffoons," *Boston Globe*, March 22, 1992, B25.

2 David J. Fox, " 'Instinct' Sizzles at the Box Office," *Los Angeles Times*, March 23, 1992, F6.

3 Internet Movie Database (http://printable.pro.imdb.com/title/tt0107818/box office). The low-budget independent film *Longtime Companion*, released in 1990, also dealt with AIDS; it received strong reviews as well as an Oscar nomination for actor Bruce Davidson, but it performed poorly at the box office.

4 Ann Oldenburg, "Philadelphia, A Quantum Leap for Gays on Film," *USA Today*, December 3, 1993, D7.

5 "Tidings of Job," *Time*, December 27, 1993, 70. Jonathan Demme, who won an Oscar in 1992 for *Silence of the Lambs*, directed the PG-13 film for TriStar Pictures.

6 Leah Rozen, "Philadelphia," *People Weekly*, December 20, 1993, 17; "Playing the Part," *Newsweek*, February 14, 1994, 46.

7 Jesse Green, "The 'Philadelphia' Experiment," *Premiere*, January 1994, 57. Clarence B. Cain won a $157,000 judgment in April 1990.

8 Rozen, "Philadelphia," 17; "Tidings of Job," 70.

9 Hal Hinson, "Our Hate-Love Relationship," *Washington Post*, December 26, 1993, G8; Jennel Conant, "Tom Hanks Wipes That Grin off His Face," *Esquire*, December 1993, 82.

10 "Tidings of Job," 71; Julie Salamon, "Film: the Road to Dull Is Paved with Good Intentions," *Wall Street Journal*, 23 December 1993, A9; Larry Kramer, "Lying About the Gay '90s," *Washington Post*, January 9, 1994, G1.

11 Green, " 'Philadelphia' Experiment," 58.

12 Green, " 'Philadelphia' Experiment," 60.

13 Charla Krupp, "The Movie of the Year," *Glamour*, February 1994, 111.

14 The brother was played by John Bedford Lloyd.

15 Sarah Beckett was played by Joanne Woodward, and Bud Beckett was played by Robert Castle.

16 The sister was played by Ann Dowd.

17 Michael Cunningham, "Breaking the Silence," *Vogue*, January 1994, 58. The friends were played by David Drake, Peter Jacobs, and Ford Wheeler.

18 David Denby, "Emotional Rescue," *New York*, January 3, 1994, 52.

19 Joe Miller's wife, Lisa, was played by Lisa Summerour.
20 Kenneth Turan, "Bittersweet 'Philadelphia' Actors Deliver Strong Perform-ances in Socially Conscious Film," *Los Angeles Times*, December 22, 1993.
21 Conant, "Tom Hanks Wipes That Grin off His Face," 80.
22 David Ansen, "'Tis Not a Jolly Season," *Newsweek*, December 27, 1993, 46; Anthony Lane, "Against the Law," *The New Yorker*, December 27, 1993–January 3, 1994, 149.
23 Krupp, "Movie of the Year," 111. On reviews and articles commenting on the lack of physical contact between the Hanks and Banderas characters, see Ansen, "'Tis Not a Jolly Season," 46; Conant, "Tom Hanks Wipes That Grin Off His Face," 77; Richard Corliss, "The Final Frontier," *Time*, March 11, 1996, 66; Cunningham, "Breaking the Silence," 59; Green, "'Phila-delphia' Experiment," 61; Michele Ingrassia, "Playing the Part," *Newsweek*, February 14, 1994, 46; Kramer, "Lying About the Gay '90s," G1; Oldenburg, "Philadelphia, a Quantum Leap," D7; Andrew Sullivan, "Washington Diarist," *The New Republic*, February 21, 1994, 42; Michael Wilmington, "Hollywood's First AIDS Movie Reveals Society's Lack of Brotherly Love," *Chicago Tribune*, January 14, 1994.
24 Janice C. Simpson, "Out of the Celluloid Closet," *Time*, April 6, 1992, 65. The speaker was Joel Schumacher, who had directed *Flatliners* and *Dying Young*.
25 Jane Applegate, "Gay Households," *Chicago Sun-Times*, April 28, 1993, Financial 54.
26 Janet Beighle French, "Catalog Supports Gay Businesses," *Cleveland Plain Dealer*, July 10, 1993, F2.

10 A New Gay Man in Town: Hollywood Shifts to Positive Stereotypes

1 Robin Williams won an Academy Award for best supporting actor in the 1997 film *Good Will Hunting*, and Kevin Kline won an Academy Award for best supporting actor in the 1988 film *A Fish Called Wanda*. On Nathan Lane being gay, see Alex Witchel, "'This Is It—as Happy as I Get, Baby': Nathan Lane," *New York Times Magazine*, September 2, 2001, 22.
2 *The Birdcage* was directed by Mike Nichols and rated R.
3 *In & Out* was directed by Frank Oz and rated PG-13.
4 *My Best Friend's Wedding* was directed by P.J. Hogan and rated PG-13.
5 Rita Kempley, "'Affection': Two Men and a Barbie," *Washington Post*, April 17, 1998, B4. On the gross profits for the three films, see Internet Movie Database. *My Best Friend's Wedding* grossed $287 million (http://printable. pro.imdb.com/title/tt0119738/boxoffice), *The Birdcage* grossed $185 million (http://printable.pro.imdb.com/title/tt0115685/boxoffice), and *In & Out* grossed $83 million (http://printable.pro.imdb.com/title/tt0119360/box office).
6 Richard Corliss, "The Final Frontier," *Time*, March 11, 1996, 66. Gene Hackman won an Academy Award for best actor in the 1971 film *French Connection*.
7 Tom Gliatto, "In & Out," *People Weekly*, September 22, 1997, 23.
8 Patrick Goldstein, "How One Actor Changed a Movie Before It Even Came Out," *Los Angeles Times*, June 23, 1997, F1; David Ansen, "Always the Bridesmaid," *Newsweek*, June 23, 1997, 76. On Everett's performance being the best part of the film, see also Kevin Gray, "Everett May Be a Movie's 'Best Friend'," *USA Today*, June 24, 1997, D1; Janet Maslin, "Someone

Borrowed and Blue," *New York Times*, June 20, 1997; Mark Peyser, "The Life of the Party," *Newsweek*, June 23, 1997, 76; Richard Schickel, "Wedding Belle Blues," *Time*, June 23, 1997, 78; Peter Travers, "My Best Friend's Wedding," *Rolling Stone*, July 10–24, 1997, 128.

9 Peyser, "Life of the Party," 76; John Clark, "He Shines Bright but Oh, So Reluctantly," *Los Angeles Times*, June 23, 1997, F10; Gray, "Everett May Be," D1.

10 Maslin, "Someone Borrowed."

11 Hal Hinson, "The Birdcage: A Wingding of a Show," *Washington Post*, March 8, 1996, B1; David Patrick, "Stage Star Gets His Chance to Soar in Films," *USA Today*, March 8, 1996, D1; Maslin, "Someone Borrowed."

12 Maslin, "Someone Borrowed."

13 Rita Kempley, "The Feel-Bad Hits of the Summer," *Washington Post*, August 3, 1997, G1; Goldstein, "How One Actor Changed a Movie," F1.

14 Stephen McCauley, "He's Gay, She's Straight, They're a Trend," *New York Times*, September 20, 1998, B31; Hinson, "The Birdcage," B-1. The son was played by Dan Futterman.

15 Julia Roberts's love interest in the film is played by Dermot Mulroney.

16 Gary Dretzka, "One Minority Has Managed to Find a Place on Television and in Film," *Chicago Tribune*, August 10, 1999, C1.

17 Peyser, "Life of the Party," 76.

18 "The End of AIDS?," *Newsweek*, December 30, 1996; Andrew Sullivan, "When AIDS Ends," *New York Times Magazine*, November 10, 1996. *The Birdcage* was the only one of the three films to mention AIDS. When the senator's daughter tells her father that she wants to get married, he immediately asks her—with no knowledge of the fact that the boy was raised by a gay couple—if the guy "has been tested," to which the girl responds, "Yes, and so have I." The epidemic is briefly mentioned a second time when Albert, while in his Barbara Bush drag, laments the fact that contemporary society is plagued "by drugs and AIDS."

19 Jack Nichols, "Robin Williams Comes Out (As a Gay Activist)," *Gay Today*, March 18, 2004.

20 John Spelling, "Jerry Zucker Gets Candid," *Gays in the Media*, September 12, 2001 (www.gaysinthemedia.com/interview/jerryzucker).

21 Riccardo A. Davis, "Sky's the Limit for Tour Operators," *Advertising Age*, January 18, 1993, 36; Monique P. Yazigi, "New Yorkers & Co.," *New York Times*, February 5, 1995, M4; Richard Harwood, "Gay Chic," *Washington Post*, November 22, 1995, A19; "Buying Power," *Daily Variety*, April 28, 1995, A4.

11 *Ellen*: Coming Out, On Screen and Off

1 Bruce Handy, "Roll Over, Ward Cleaver," *Time*, April 14, 1997, 78.

2 Shauna Snow, "Stepping Out?," *Los Angeles Times*, September 14, 1996, F2.

3 Brian Lowry, "'Ellen' Gets Ready to Open the Closet Door," *Los Angeles Times*, March 3, 1997, F19; Ruth Ryon, "She's Got Lots of Closet Space," *Los Angeles Times*, March 9, 1997, K1.

4 Lowry, "'Ellen' Gets Ready," F19.

5 On DeGeneres refusing to talk to reporters, see Frederic M. Biddle, "Ellen's Coming Out," *Boston Globe*, April 23, 1997, D1; Rick Marin and Sue Miller, "Ellen Steps Out," *Newsweek*, April 14, 1997, 66. On DeGeneres refusing to grant interviews with *Los Angeles Times* reporters, see Brian Lowry, "So

Ellen Is a Lesbian—What's the Next Step?," *Los Angeles Times*, April 15, 1997, F1.

6 Ellen DeGeneres interview by Diane Sawyer, *20/20*, April 25, 1997; Handy, "Roll Over," 78.

7 "The Puppy Episode" aired on April 30, 1997. The segment's title referred to an inside joke among the show's staff members; at one point, ABC executives were so desperate to come up with something to increase the ratings that they suggested Ellen, who clearly was not interested in dating men, should at least adopt a puppy. The friend was played by Steven Eckholdt, and Susan was played by Laura Dern.

8 The therapist was played by Oprah Winfrey.

9 Howard Rosenberg, "Honesty Is the Best Policy," *Los Angeles Times*, April 30, 1997, F8; Tom Shales, "Ellen's Night Out," *Washington Post*, April 30, 1997, D1; Frederic M. Biddle, "Tonight's Show Makes History," *Boston Globe*, April 30, 1997, C1, C8.

10 "Ellen and 'Ellen' Come Out," *New York Times*, May 1, 1997, A26.

11 Alan Bash, "42 Million Tuned in for a TV Coming-Out," *USA Today*, May 2, 1997, 2A.

12 Lowry, "So Ellen Is a Lesbian," F5. Ellen DeGeneres's manager was Arthur Imparato.

13 "Hello Muddah, Hello Faddah" aired on May 7, 1997; "Moving On" aired on May 14, 1997; "Gay Yellow Pages" aired on October 22, 1997; "Social Climber" aired on May 7, 1997; "Roommates" aired on October 8, 1997; "Emma" aired on November 19, 1997.

14 "Public Display of Affection" aired on November 12, 1997; "Hospital" aired on March 4, 1998; "Escape from L.A." aired on February 4, 1998; "Just Coffee" aired on October 29, 1997; "Like a Virgin" aired on November 26, 1997; "The Break Up" aired on December 10, 1997.

15 Brian Lowry, "Ratings, Not Sexuality, Steer Future of 'Ellen,'" *Los Angeles Times*, March 11, 1998, F10.

16 James Collins, "Yes, She's Still Gay," *Time*, October 27, 1997, 110; Eric Mink, "A 'Gay' Sitcom Learns from 'Ellen's' Fate," *Chicago Tribune*, September 2, 1998, A7; Jess Cagle, "As Gay as It Gets?," *Entertainment Weekly*, May 8, 1998, 26–32.

17 Howard Rosenberg, "Putting Anger Aside for Laughs," *Los Angeles Times*, May 13, 1998, F1, F9. *Ellen* ultimately was replaced by *Two Guys, a Girl and a Pizza Place*.

18 *PrimeTime Live*, May 5, 1998.

19 Howard Rosenberg, "The Thin Line Between. . . Fear and Hate," *Los Angeles Times*, October 21, 1998, F10.

20 A.J. Jacobs, "Out?," *Entertainment Weekly*, October 4, 1996, 23; Larry Gross, *Up from Invisibility: Lesbians, Gay Men, and the Media in America* (New York: Columbia University Press, 2001), 158.

21 Shales, "Ellen's Night Out," D1.

22 "Ellen: A Hollywood Tribute" aired on May 13, 1998. Helen Hunt won an Academy Award for best actress in 1998's *As Good As It Gets*, and Emmy Awards for her leading role in the sitcom *Mad About You* in 1996, 1997, and 1998. Julianna Margulies appeared in "Ellen: A Hollywood Tribute," which aired on May 20, 1998; Demi Moore appeared in "The Puppy Episode," which aired on April 30, 1997. Julianna Margulies won an Emmy Award in 1995 for her role on *ER*.

23 Elaine Dutka, "What's Next for Heche?," *Los Angeles Times*, May 1, 1997, F49. Anne Heche played opposite Harrison Ford in the romantic comedy *Six*

Days, Seven Nights, and opposite Tommy Lee Jones in *Volcano*. Ellen DeGeneres and Anne Heche ended their relationship in August 2000, and Heche later married a man and gave birth to a child.

24 Rosenberg, "The Thin Line," F10. On lesbians being stereotyped as humorless, see, for example, Steve Sailer, "Why Lesbians Aren't Gay," *National Review*, May 30, 1994, 43; Kara Swisher, "We Love Lesbians!," *Washington Post*, July 18, 1993, C1; Suzanna Danuta Walters, *All the Rage: The Story of Gay Visibility in America* (Chicago: University of Chicago Press, 2001), 161.

25 Tom Gliatto, "Outward Bound," *People Weekly*, May 5, 1997, 129. The contest that DeGeneres won was called Showtime's Funniest Person in America.

26 Biddle, "Tonight's Show Makes History," C1; Handy, "Roll Over," 82.

27 "Moving On" aired on May 14, 1997. The boss was played by Bruce Campbell.

28 Rosenberg, "Honesty Is the Best Policy," F8. On DeGeneres's private coming out, see also Gross, *Up from Invisibility*, 82.

29 Lowry, "'Ellen' Gets Ready," F19; Dana Canedy, "Advertising," *New York Times*, April 30, 1997, D8; Handy, "Roll Over," 82; Frederic M. Biddle, "No Commercial Break from 'Ellen' Controversy," *Boston Globe*, April 23, 1997, D6.

30 Canedy, "Advertising," D8.

31 Paul Farhi, "Ads of Steel: Show's Sponsors Firmly in Place," *Washington Post*, April 30, 1997, D1.

32 Brian Lowry, "A Closet Door Opens and 36 Million Watch," *Los Angeles Times*, May 2, 1997, F24; "Sponsors Varied," *USA Today*, May 1, 1997, D3.

33 Canedy, "Advertising," D8.

34 Lowry, "A Closet Door Opens," F24.

35 Rosenberg, "The Thin Line," F11.

12 *Will & Grace*: The Biggest Gay Hit in TV History

1 Dennis Hensley, "Blush with Success," *TV Guide*, February 12–18, 2000, 29. The co-creator quoted in the story was Max Mutchnick.

2 Hensley, "Blush with Success," 28; Hank Stuever, "'Will & Grace' And Gays: The Thrill Has Been Long Gone," *Washington Post*, May 14, 2006, N1. *Will & Grace* became the third most popular sitcom on television, behind *Friends* on NBC and *Everybody Loves Raymond* on CBS.

3 "Pilot" aired on September 21, 1998. Grace was played by Debra Messing, and Will was played by Eric McCormack.

4 "Pilot" aired on September 21, 1998. Jack was played by Sean Hayes.

5 John Carman, "Will Plays It Chaste," *San Francisco Chronicle*, July 22, 1998, D1.

6 "Will Works Out" aired on April 22, 1999.

7 Carman, "Will Plays It Chaste," D1; Paul Brownfield, "When a Kiss Is Just a Kiss," *Los Angeles Times*, February 22, 2000, F1.

8 "Pilot" aired on September 21, 1998.

9 A.J. Jacobs, "When Gay Men Happen to Straight Women," *Entertainment Weekly*, October 23, 1998, 23.

10 "Will & Grace," *TV Guide*, September 12, 1998, 40; William Keck, "It's Not Easy Being Jack," *Los Angeles Times*, December 24, 2000, Calendar section, 6.

11 Michael A. Lipton, "Will Power; Happily Married Eric McCormack Plays a Gay Lawyer," *People Weekly*, October 26, 1998, 81–82; Kristen Baldwin, "Full-Mettle Jack," *Entertainment Weekly*, October 23, 1998, 27.

12 Matthew Gilbert, "'Will & Grace' Odd Couple Evenly Matched in Charm," *Boston Globe*, September 21, 1998, C7.

13 "Pilot" aired on September 21, 1998.

14 "FYI: I Hurt, Too" aired on September 16, 2004.

15 "A New Lease on Life" aired on September 28, 1998.

16 "Sons and Lovers" aired on May 17, 2001; "Past and Presents" aired on October 4, 2001.

17 "Advise and Resent" aired on February 29, 2000; "The Birds and the Bees" aired on February 17, 2005.

18 "Oh, Dad, Poor Dad, He's Kept Me in the Closet and I'm so Sad" aired on February 15, 2000; "The Third Wheel Gets the Grace" aired on September 20, 2001.

19 "The Unsinkable Mommy Adler" aired on February 9, 1999.

20 "Pilot" aired on September 21, 1998; "Three's a Crowd, Six Is a Freak" aired on December 14, 2000.

21 Brownfield, "When a Kiss Is Just a Kiss," F1.

22 "Acting Out" aired on February 22, 2000.

23 Brownfield, "When a Kiss Is Just a Kiss," F7. The other co-creator of *Will & Grace* was David Kohan, who is straight.

24 "Coffee & Commitment" aired on January 4, 2001. Joe was played by Jerry Levine, and Larry was played by Tim Bagley. On *Will & Grace* subtly supporting same-sex marriage, see Wright, "Was It Good for the Gays?," *The Advocate*, May 9, 2006, 53.

25 "Husbands and Trophy Wives" aired on October 19, 2000. On *Will & Grace* subtly supporting gay adoptions, see Wright, "Was It Good for the Gays?," 53.

26 Jacobs, "When Gay Men Happen," 24. The NBC executive was Warren Littlefield.

27 Stephen McCauley, "He's Gay, She's Straight, They're a Trend," *New York Times*, September 20, 1998, B31.

28 Hensley, "Blush with Success," 28.

29 Steve Murray, "Oh, My Gay Stars!," *Atlanta Journal*," June 30, 2002, L1.

30 "I Love L. Gay" aired on February 2, 2006. Ellen Gray, "'Ellen' Is Gone, But Not Gays on TV," *Chicago Tribune*, August 6, 1998, 11.

31 Carman, "Will Plays It Chaste," D1; *Prime Time Live*, May 5, 1998.

32 Tracy L. Scott, "GLAAD applauds 'evolution' of gay characters on TV," *Los Angeles Times*, November 29, 2003, E29; Dick Polman, "Gays' Wins Met by Line in the Sand," *Philadelphia Inquirer*, August 10, 2003, A14.

33 An episode in season seven—"Key Party," which aired on October 14, 2004—showed Will and his boyfriend at the time exchanging a kiss that could best be described as "a peck."

34 On lesbians being absent from *Will & Grace*, see Suzanna Danuta Walters, *All the Rage: The Story of Gay Visibility in America* (Chicago: University of Chicago Press, 2001), 108.

35 Bernard Weinraub and Jim Rutenberg, "Gay-Themed TV Gains a Wider Audience," *New York Times*, July 29, 2003, A1. James, played by Taye Diggs, dated Will in "Von Trapped," which aired on January 5, 2006; "I Love L. Gay," which aired on February 2, 2006; "The Definition of Marriage," which aired on February 9, 2006; and "Grace Expectations (2)," which aired on February 16, 2006.

36 Paul Brownfield, "As Minorities' TV Presence Dims, Gay Roles Proliferate," *Los Angeles Times*, July 21, 1999, A1.

37 Brownfield, "As Minorities' TV Presence Dims," A16.

38 Brownfield, "As Minorities' TV Presence Dims," A16.

39 Judith Michaelson, "Straight Talk on a Gay Role," *Los Angeles Times*, December 15, 1998; Brownfield, "As Minorities' TV Presence Dims," A16.

40 *Friends* aired from 1994 to 2004; *Dawson's Creek* aired from 1998 to 2003; *Frasier* aired from 1993 to 2004.

13 *Queer as Folk*: "An Unvarnished Treatment of Gay Life"

1 The premier episode aired on December 3, 2000. The man, Brian, was played by Gale Harold; the boy, Justin, was played by Randy Harrison.

2 Robert Bianco, " 'Queer' Clears the Way for Candid Look at Gay Life," *USA Today*, December 1, 2000, E15; John Levesque, "Showtime Leads the Way in Depicting Homosexuals," *Chicago Tribune*, July 22, 2000, A27.

3 Episode 3 of the third season aired on March 16, 2003.

4 Tom Shales, " 'Queer as Folk,' " *Washington Post*, January 5, 2002, C1; Alan James Frutkin, "The Return of the Show that Gets Gay Life Right," *New York Times*, January 6, 2002; Gail Shister, " 'Queer as Folk' Could Use More Straights, a Star Says," *Philadelphia Inquirer*, February 26, 2004, D6.

5 Frutkin, "The Return of the Show"; Bianco, " 'Queer' Clears the Way," E15; Tom Shales, " 'Queer as Folk,' Still Daring to Be Different," *Washington Post*, April 17, 2004, C1.

6 Michael was played by Hal Sparks, Emmett by Peter Paige, and Ted by Scott Lowell.

7 The premier episode aired on December 3, 2000.

8 The premier episode aired on December 3, 2000.

9 The premier episode aired on December 3, 2000; episodes 2, 3, and 13 of the second season aired on January 13, January 20, and April 14 of 2002.

10 Episode 6 of the second season aired on February 10, 2002.

11 Episodes 4 and 22 of the first season aired on December 17, 2000, and June 24, 2001.

12 The premier episode aired on December 3, 2000; episode 5 of the third season aired on April 6, 2003.

13 Episode 1 of the second season aired on January 6, 2002; episode 12 of the third season aired on June 8, 2003. Debbie was played by Sharon Gless.

14 Marc Peyser, "Gay All the Way," *Newsweek*, November 27, 2000, 78.

15 Episodes 16 and 17 of the first season aired on April 8 and 15 of 2001.

16 Episode 22 of the first season aired on June 24, 2001.

17 Episode 1 of the second season aired on January 6, 2002.

18 Tom Shales, " 'Queer as Folk': Soap Trots Out Its Old Tricks," *Washington Post*, January 5, 2002, C1. Episode 1 of the second season aired on January 6, 2002.

19 Hunter was played by Harris Allan, and Vic was played by Jack Weatherall. Vic died in episode 6 of the fourth season, which aired on May 23, 2004.

20 Episode 7 of the second season aired on February 17, 2002.

21 Episode 9 of the second season aired on March 10, 2002. Ben and Michael struggling with the HIV issue recurred in episodes 6, 7, and 9 of the second season, which aired on February 10, February 17, and March 10 of 2002.

22 Episode 13 of the fourth season aired on July 11, 2004; episode 9 of the second season aired on March 10, 2002.

23 Bernard Weinraub, "Cable TV Shatters Another Taboo," *New York Times*, November 20, 2000, E1; Tom Shales, "Showtime's Shockingly Bold 'Queer as Folk,' " *Washington Post*, December 2, 2000, C1; James Poniewozik, "It's Here, It's Queer, Get Used to It," *Time*, November 27, 2000, 79.

24 Episode 16 of the first season aired on April 8, 2001; episode 7 of the second season aired on February 17, 2002.

25 Ralph H. Major Jr., "New Moral Menace to Our Youth," *Coronet*, September 1950, 103.

26 Episodes 3, 18, 19, 20, 21, and 22 of the first season aired on December 10 of 2000 and April 22, April 29, June 10, June 17, and June 24 of 2001. Blake was played by Dean Armstrong.

27 Episodes 10 and 12 of the third season aired on May 18 and June 8 of 2003.

28 Episodes 11 and 12 of the third season aired on May 25 and June 8 of 2003.

29 Episode 14 of the third season aired on June 22, 2003.

30 Anthony Tommasini, "Looking for a Breakthrough? You'll Have to Wait," *New York Times*, January 14, 2001, B33.

31 Brian Moylan, "Gasp! I Don't Want my QAF!," *Washington Blade*, February 22, 2002, 45; Tray Butler, "What the 'L'?," *Washington Blade*, May 13, 2005, 62; Brian Moylan, "Queerly Emotional," *Washington Blade*, August 12, 2005, 50.

32 Carman, "Will Plays It Chaste,"D1; Craig Wilson, "A Tale of Two Very Different Cities," *USA Today*, January 25, 2001, D1; Joyce Millman, "The Gayest Story Ever Told," *Salon*, November 29, 2000; Howard Rosenberg, "Sex and the Steel City," *Los Angeles Times*, December 2, 2000, F1. The quote was by Don Hammond, who was identified in the story as a gay newspaper editor.

33 Lynn Elber, " 'Queer as Folk' Appeals Not Just to Gays," *Chicago Sun-Times*, January 8, 2002, A34; Millman, "Gayest Story Ever Told."

34 Millman, "Gayest Story Ever Told"; Daryl H. Miller, "Return of Showtime's Gay Soap," *Los Angeles Times*, January 5, 2002, F32. On criticism of the lack of diversity on *Queer as Folk*, see Suzanna Danuta Walters, *All the Rage: The Story of Gay Visibility in America* (Chicago: University of Chicago Press, 2001), 123.

35 Shales, " 'Queer as Folk': Soap Trots Out," C1.

14 *Queer Eye for the Straight Guy*: The "Fab Five" as Gay Reality TV

1 Greg Braxton, "Nice Gays Finish First," *Los Angeles Times*, December 21, 2003, E40; Nicholas Fonseca, "They're Here! They're Queer! And They Don't Like Your End Tables," *Entertainment Weekly*, August 8, 2003, cover, 24–28. On the success of "Queer Eye," see also Michael Giltz, "Queer Eye Confidential," *The Advocate*, September 2, 2003, 40–44; Tom Shales, "Reality TV: Nobodies' Home," *Washington Post*, December 28, 2003, N1, N4; Bruce C. Steele, "The Gay Rights Makeover," *The Advocate*, September 2, 2003, 42–43. *Queer Eye for the Straight Guy* premiered on July 15, 2003.

2 Edward Rothstein, "In the Democracy of Design, Even Bad Taste Is OK," *New York Times*, October 25, 2003, B9.

3 Marco R. della Cava, "Queer Eye Has Keen Eye for Sales," *USA Today*, February 26, 2004, D5; Jonathan Storm, "Rampant 'Reality,' " *Philadelphia Inquirer*, July 4, 2004, H4; Ted Allen, Kyan Douglas, Thom Filicia, Carson Kressley, and Jai Rodriguez, *Queer Eye for the Straight Guy: The Fab 5's Guide to Looking Better, Cooking Better, Dressing Better, Behaving Better and Living Better* (New York: Clarkson Potter, 2004); Kyan Douglas, *Beautified: Secrets for Women to Look Great and Feel Fabulous*; Carson Kressley, *Off the Cuff: The Essential Style Guide for Men—And the Women Who Love Them* (New York: Dutton, 2004); Jura Koncius, "Clear Eye for

Design," *Washington Post*, February 26, 2004, H5. *What's That Sound? Music from Queer Eye for the Straight Guy* was released in 2004 by Capitol Records.

4 Koncius, "Clear Eye for Design," H5; Giltz, "Queer Eye Confidential," 44.

5 Brian Lowry, "It's Profitable to Be a Little Bit Gay," *Los Angeles Times*, August 27, 2003, E2; Bernard Weinraub and Jim Rutenberg, "Gay-Themed TV Gains a Wider Audience," *New York Times*, July 29, 2003, A1. The executive director of the Traditional Values Coalition was Andrea Lafferty.

6 The Bravo Web site (www.bravotv.com) assigns numbers and titles to the various episodes of *Queer Eye for the Straight Guy*, all of which have aired numerous times. The one featuring Brian Schepel was episode 101, which was titled "Hair Today, Art Tomorrow."

7 Wesley Morris, "Beyond 'Queer Eye' Is a Vast National Sex Change Underway?," *Boston Globe*, August 3, 2003, E4; John Sellers, "Queen for a Day: My Gay Makeover," *New York Times*, July 13, 2003, B1; Mike Thomas, "When Gay Men Attack," *Chicago Sun-Times*, July 11, 2003, 41.

8 Robin Givhan, "'Queer Eye' Gives Unblinking View of Trendsetters," *Washington Post*, July 18, 2003, C2.

9 Richard Goldstein, "What Queer Eye?," *Village Voice*, July 23–29, 2003, 48. Episode 101 was titled "Hair Today, Art Tomorrow."

10 Episode 153 was titled "A Home to Come Home to."

11 John Bartlett, "Straight Eye for the Queer Guy," *New York Times*, September 21, 2003, F86; Givhan, "'Queer Eye' Gives Unblinking View," C2.

12 Episode 109 was titled "My Big Fat Greek Haircut"; episode 133 was titled "Refining New York's Finest"; episode 115 was titled "Mr. Clean Comes Clean."

13 Sellers, "Queen for a Day," B1. Episode 155 was titled "An American Straight Guy in London."

14 Sellers, "Queen for a Day," B1.

15 On retailers giving their products and services to the straight men, see, Koncius, "Clear Eye for Design," H5.

16 Episode 107 was titled "He's a Little Bit Country."

17 Episode 151 was titled "A Pigskin Proposal"; episode 148 was titled "An Overdue Reunion"; episode 133 was titled "Refining New York's Finest."

18 Sellers, "Queen for a Day," B20.

19 Episode 133 was titled "Refining New York's Finest."

20 Jeff Weinstein, "Hold the Stereotypes, Cue the Style," *Philadelphia Inquirer*, July 19, 2003, E1; Goldstein, "What Queer Eye?," 48. Episode 147 was titled "The Best Little Fraternity House in Texas"; episode 133 was titled "Refining New York's Finest."

21 Tom Shales, "Bravo's 'Queer Eye' Heads Straight for the Stereotypes," *Washington Post*, July 15, 2003, C8; Martha Irvine, "Peculiar Thing Occurs to 'Queer,'" *Philadelphia Inquirer*, November 5, 2003, C6.

22 Paul Brownfield, "'Queer Eye' Spinoff Lost in Gay Shtick," *Los Angeles Times*, January 11, 2005, E5. The first episode of *Queer Eye for the Straight Girl* aired on January 12, 2005, and the final episode aired on May 8, 2005.

23 Bruce Mohl, "Websites Seek Gay Travelers," *Boston Globe*, October 31, 2004, M7; della Cava, "Queer Eye Has Keen Eye for Sales," D5; Frank J. Prial, "Marriage (Well, Domestic Partnership) of Food and Fun," *New York Times*, November 24, 2004, F5.

24 Ronald Alsop, "Are Gay People More Affluent than Others?," *Wall Street Journal*, December 30, 1999, B1; Andrew Barker, "Same-Sex Ads Swim into the Mainstream," *Daily Variety*, April 13, 2007, A5.

15 Notes on Gay Visibility vs. Lesbian Visibility

1 Suzanna Danuta Walters, *All the Rage: The Story of Gay Visibility in America* (Chicago: University of Chicago Press, 2001), 161; Larry Gross and James D. Woods, "Up From Invisibility: Film and Television," in Larry Gross and James D. Woods, eds., *The Columbia Reader on Lesbians and Gay Men in Media, Society, and Politics* (New York: Columbia University Press, 1999), 293. On gay men being more prominent in the media than lesbians, see also R. Brian Attig, "The Gay Voice in Popular Music," in Michelle A. Wolf and Alfred P. Kielwasser, *Gay People, Sex, and the Media* (New York: Harrington Park, 1991), 186; Peter Blauner, "Trying To Live with the AIDS Plague," *New York*, June 17, 1985, 52; Steven Capsuto, *Alternate Channels: The Uncensored Story of Gay and Lesbian Images on Radio and Television* (New York: Ballantine, 2000), 340–51; Larry Gross, "Out of the Mainstream: Sexual Minorities and the Mass Media," in Wolf and Kielwasser, *Gay People, Sex, and the Media*, 21; Larry Gross and James D. Woods, "Introduction: Being Gay in American Media and Society," in Gross and Woods, *Columbia Reader*, 7; Erik Meers, "Hunky Business," *The Advocate*, April 1, 2003, 39.

2 On lesbians not having a presence in the media because of stereotypes of them being physically unattractive, see, for example, Mark Steyn, "Everybody Out!," *American Spectator*, June 1997, 50; Steve Sailer, "Why Lesbians Aren't Gay," *National Review*, May 30, 1994, 43; Kara Swisher, "We Love Lesbians!," *Washington Post*, July 18, 1993, C1.

3 On lesbians not having a presence in the media because of stereotypes of them being humorless, see, for example, Sailer, "Why Lesbians Aren't Gay," 43; Swisher, "We Love Lesbians!," C1; Walters, *All the Rage*, 161.

4 Stuart Elliott, "The Media Business: Advertising," *New York Times*, June 9, 1994, D1.

5 On sexism being one explanation for the lack of prominence of lesbians in the media, see, for example, Blauner, "Trying To Live with the AIDS Plague," 52; John D'Emilio, "Capitalism and Gay Identity," in Gross and Woods, *Columbia Reader*, 51; Walters, *All the Rage*, 161.

6 Alfred C. Kinsey, *Sexual Behavior in the Human Male* (Philadelphia: W.B. Saunders, 1948), 651; Alfred C. Kinsey, *Sexual Behavior in the Human Female* (Philadelphia: W.B. Saunders, 1953), 488. Kinsey defined adults as men and women between the ages of sixteen and fifty-five.

7 On the strong reaction against physical affection between men being an explanation for the relative prominence of gay men in the media, compared to that of gay women, see, for example, Meers, "Hunky Business," 39; Tom Shales, "Giving Them 'L': Gay Channel Plans Are Still Closeted, but Showtime Is Opening a Door for Lesbians," *Washington Post*, January 18, 2004, N1; Rodger Streitmatter, *Sex Sells!: The Media's Journey from Repression to Obsession* (New York: Westview Press/Perseus Books Group, 2004), 151.

8 Paul Brownfield, "As Minorities' TV Presence Dims, Gay Roles Proliferate," *Los Angeles Times*, July 21, 1999, A1, A16. On more gay men than lesbians working in the entertainment industry, see also Larry Gross, *Up from Invisibility: Lesbians, Gay Men, and the Media in America* (New York: Columbia University Press, 2001), 5; Tracy L. Scott, "Gay Characters Gaining TV Popularity," *Washington Post*, November 30, 2003, Y6; James M. Wall, "Stereotypes In and Out," *The Christian Century*, October 15, 1997, 899; Suzanna Danuta Walters, "Who Let the Dogs Out?," *Images* (Gay & Lesbian Alliance Against Defamation magazine), Summer 2001, 5.

16 *The L Word*: Lesbians Move into the Spotlight

1 Booth Moore, "Dressed-Up Diversity," *Los Angeles Times*, February 8, 2004, E4.
2 Roberet Bianco, "The L Word," *USA Today*, January 16, 2004, E9.
3 Bette is played by Jennifer Beals.
4 Tina is played by Laurel Holloman; Shane is played by Katherine Moennig; Dana was played by Erin Daniels; Jenny is played by Mia Kirshner.
5 Dennis Hensley, "L Is for Leisha," *The Advocate*, February 17, 2004, 41, 53.
6 Alessandra Stanley, "TV Weekend," *New York Times*, January 16, 2004, E1; Devra First, "Women Say 'The L Word' Is Worthy," *Boston Globe*, January 24, 2004, C1; Ariel Levy, "Lipstick Lesbians," *Slate*, February 18, 2005. On the characters being highly attractive, see also Carina Chocano, "Looking for Love," *Los Angeles Times*, January 9, 2004, E46; Jeff Weinstein, "Kudos to 'The L Word' for Making an Invisible Group Visible," *Philadelphia Inquirer*, January 18, 2004, H3.
7 *Los Angeles Times*, Laurie K. Schenden, "The L Words: Lives, Loves. . .Oh, and Lesbians," January 9, 2004, E46; Moore, "Dressed-Up Diversity," E4.
8 *Washington Blade*, K. Pearson Brown, "'The L Word' vs. Reality," May 20, 2005, 31; Tray Butler, "What the L?," May 13, 2005, 62.
9 Luisita Lopez Torregrosa, "'L Word' Star Basks in an Erotic Mystery," *New York Times*, April 5, 2004, E1.
10 Kera Bolonik, "Not Your Mother's Lesbians," *New York*, January 12, 2004, 20, 23; Tom Shales, "Giving Them 'L': Gay Channel Plans Are Still Closeted, but Showtime Is Opening a Door for Lesbians," *Washington Post*, January 18, 2004, N1.
11 Bianco, "The L Word," E9.
12 Meghan Daum, "Making Straights Flush," *Los Angeles Times*, February 20, 2005, E30. Episode 13 of the first season aired on April 4, 2004.
13 Episodes 5 and 6 of the first season aired on February 8 and 15 of 2004. Tim was played by Eric Mabius.
14 Episode 1 of the first season aired on January 18, 2004.
15 Episodes 1, 2, 9, and 12 of the third season aired on January 8, January 15, March 5, and March 26 of 2006. Carmen was played by Sarah Shahi.
16 Kit is played by Pam Grier.
17 Marina was played by Karina Lombard; Candace was played by Ion Overman; Tasha was played by Rose Rollins.
18 Marlee Matlin won the Academy Award for best actress in 1986 for her role in *Children of a Lesser God*.
19 Episodes 1, 5, and 11 of the first season aired on January 18, February 8, and March 21 of 2004.
20 Matthew Gilbert, "'Word' Has It Jenny Set to Take Her Lumps," *Boston Globe*, February 17, 2005, D1; Torregrosa, "'L Word' Star Basks," E1.
21 Episode 9 of the third season aired on March 5, 2006. The father, Henry, is played by Steven Eckholdt.
22 Episodes 4, 6, and 9 of the third season aired on January 29, February 12, and March 5 of 2006; episode 4 of the fourth season aired on January 28, 2007. Moira/Max is played by Daniela Sea; the woman who screamed at Max was played by Chelsea Hobbs.
23 Episode 1 of the first season aired on January 18, 2004.
24 Episodes 1 and 14 of the first season aired on January 18 and April 11 of 2004; episode 9 of the third season aired on March 5, 2006.

25 Episodes 6, 10, 11, and 12 of the third season aired on February 12, March 12, March 19, and March 26 of 2006.

26 Episodes 5 and 12 of the first season aired on February 15 and April 4 of 2004; episodes 3, 5, and 13 of the second season aired on March 6, March 20, and May 15 of 2005; episodes 7 and 10 of the third season aired on February 19 and March 12 of 2006. Lara was played by Lauren Lee Smith, and Tonya was played by Meredith McGeachie.

27 Stanley, "TV Weekend," E1; "The L Word," *People Weekly*, 13 February 2006, 39; Weinstein, "Kudos to 'The L Word,'" H3; Joy Press, "Sapphic Lights," *Village Voice*, January 7–13, 2004, C101; Bianco, "The L Word," E9.

28 First, "Women Say 'The L Word' Is Worthy," C1; Moore, "Dressed-Up Diversity," E4.

29 Hensley, "L Is for Leisha," 48; Moore, "Dressed-Up Diversity," E4; Laurie K. Schenden, "Something for the Girls," *Curve*, February 2004, 34.

30 "The L Word," 39. Episode 9 of the third season aired on March 5, 2006.

31 Julie Smith, "How Does Girl Meet Girl?," *San Francisco Chronicle*, July 1, 1969, A17; Stacey D'erasmo, "Lesbians on Television: It's Not Easy Being Seen," *New York Times*, January 11, 2004, B1.

32 Elise Harris, "Women in Love," *Mademoiselle*, February 1993, 182; Laura Weinstock, "Lame-duck Lesbians?," *The Advocate*, April 26, 2006, 72. The seven major characters in the original cast were Bette, Tina, Shane, Dana, Jenny, Alice, and Kit. From the beginning of the series, Kit was straight and Alice was bisexual. By the beginning of the fourth season, Tina and Jenny were accurately identified as bisexual, as they had both had sex with men as well as women on numerous occasions. Dana was dead. So only Bette and Shane were accurately identified as lesbian.

17 Same-Sex Marriage: A Journalistic Love Fest

1 *60 Minutes II*, March 10, 2004 (the segment was titled "Marry Me!" and was reported by Bob Simon).

2 "The Merits of Gay Marriage," *Washington Post*, November 20, 2003, A40; "Same-Sex Semantics," *Boston Globe*, November 25, 2003, A14; "A Victory for Gay Marriage," *New York Times*, November 20, 2003, A30.

3 Michael Getler, "Was This News for Kids?," *Washington Post*, March 21, 2004, B6; Christine Chinlund, "A Bias in Favor of Gay Marriage?," *Boston Globe*, December 15, 2003, A19; Daniel Okrent, "The Public Editor: Is The New York Times a Liberal Newspaper?," *New York Times*, July 25, 2004.

4 In October 2005, Connecticut became the second state to legalize same-sex civil unions; New Jersey and New Hampshire followed in December 2006 and April 2007, respectively.

5 The Massachusetts Supreme Judicial Court handed down its ruling, by a 4–3 vote, in November 2003, but agreed not to put the new law into effect for six months in order to give local officials time to prepare for the large number of same-sex couples who were expected to be requesting marriage licenses.

6 *USA Today*, Fred Bayles, "Same-Sex Marriage Begins in Mass.," May 17, 2004, A1; Maria Puente, "Much Ado About Gay Commitment Ceremonies," May 17, 2004, D5.

7 Philip Kennicott, "Altared States," *Washington Post*, May 18, 2004, C1.

8 Catherine Saillant, "Same-Sex Marriage: Around the State/Bakersfield," *Los Angeles Times*, June 18, 2008, A11.

9 Charisse Jones and Fred Bayles, "First Weddings Intensify Gay-Marriage Debate," *USA Today*, May 18, 2004, A2; Jonathan Finer, "Gay Couples Line Up for Mass. Marriages," *Washington Post*, May 17, 2004, A2.

10 Rona Marech, "Gay Couples Can Be as Stable as Straights, Evidence Suggests," *San Francisco Chronicle*, February 27, 2004, A19.

11 "Weddings/Celebrations; Hillary Goodridge, Julie Goodridge," *New York Times*, May 23, 2004, I15. It was front-page news in 2006 when Julie and Hillary Goodridge ended their relationship.

12 *60 Minutes II*; Laura Gunderson, "Gay Marriage: Who Did, Didn't and Why," *Portland Oregonian*, March 28, 2004, B1; Carol Beggy and Mark Shanahan, "The Ultimate Wedding Gift," *Boston Globe*, July 6, 2004, D2.

13 Ginia Bellafante, "Two Fathers, With One Happy to Stay at Home," *New York Times*, January 12, 2004, A1; Denny Lee, "Neighborhood Report: New York Up Close," *New York Times*, February 11, 2001, N8; Rachel Gordon, "O'Donnell Ties Knot at City Hall," *San Francisco Chronicle*, February 27, 2004, A1.

14 Richard Higgins, "Vermont Licenses First Civil Unions," *Boston Globe*, July 2, 2000, B1.

15 *ABC World News Tonight*, May 17, 2004 (the newscast was anchored by Peter Jennings; the segment was reported by Ron Claiborne).

16 CNN, May 17, 2004 (the newscast was anchored by Aaron Brown; the segment was reported by Maria Hinojosa).

17 *CBS Evening News*, May 17, 2004 (the newscast was anchored by Dan Rather; the segment was reported by Mika Brzezinski); *NBC Nightly News*, May 17, 2004 (the newscast was anchored by Tom Brokaw; the segment was reported by Rehema Ellis); *Fox Evening News*, May 17, 2004 (the newscast was anchored by Shepard Smith; the segment was reported by Alisyn Camerota).

18 *60 Minutes II*, March 10, 2004 (the segment was titled "Marry Me!" and was reported by Bob Simon).

19 Eun-Kyung Kim, "Gay Marriage Would Make Their Families Official, Kids Say," *St. Louis Post-Dispatch*, April 7, 2004, A1. The sociology professor quoted in the story was Tim Biblarz of the University of Southern California.

20 Kim, "Gay Marriage Would Make Their Families Official," A1.

21 *New York Times*, Patricia Leigh Brown, "For Children of Gays, Marriage Brings Joy," March 19, 2004, A14; Bellafante, "Two Fathers," A1.

22 Brown, "For Children of Gays," A14.

23 Bellafante, "Two Fathers," A1.

24 Laurie Goodstein, "Gay Couples Seek Unions in God's Eyes," *New York Times*, January 30, 2004, A1.

25 Anne Hull, "Just Married, After 51 Years Together," *Washington Post*, February 29, 2004, A1.

26 "Civil Unions Granted in Vermont," National Public Radio, July 8, 2000 (the anchor for the segment was Laurie Howell, and the reporter was Tovia Smith); "CNN Worldview," CNN, July 1, 2000 (the anchor for the segment was Brian Nelson, and the reporter was Bill Delaney).

27 See www.pollingreport.com.civil.htm. In the poll, 36% of respondents supported same-sex marriage and 9% of respondents were unsure.

28 See the Marriage Law Project at Catholic University (http://marriagelaw. cua.edu/Law/states/doma.cfm).

29 Richard Harwood, "Gay Chic," *Washington Post*, November 22, 2004, A19.

30 Cynthia Cotts, "The Media and the Moguls," *Village Voice*, August 14–20, 2002. On the Gay Mafia extending to the *New York Times*, see also Paul

Brownfield, "Critic's Notebook; No Longer Hiding," *Los Angeles Times*, May 19, 2006, E2; Jennifer Harper, "New York Times Eyes for Bias," *Washington Times*, August 20, 2002, A6; George Rush and Joanna Molloy, "Ovitz: I Didn't Fail, Gay Mafia Killed Me," *New York Daily News*, July 2, 2002, A18.

18 *Brokeback Mountain*: "A Breakthrough Gay Romance"

1 Anne Thompson, "'Brokeback Mountain' Charts New Territory," *Chicago Sun-Times*, November 20, 2005, D12; "A First for Gay-Themed Movies," *Entertainment Weekly*, May 7, 2006.

2 Joanna Weiss, "'Brokeback Mountain' Turns a Short Story into a Hollywood First," *Boston Globe*, December 11, 2005, N13; Anthony Lane, "The Current Cinema: New Frontiers," *The New Yorker*, December 12, 2005; Jose Antonio Vargas, "Gay Moviegoers Tip their Hats to a Love Story," *Washington Post*, December 14, 2005, C1.

3 The best director award went to Ang Lee, the best adapted screenplay award went to Larry McMurtry and Diana Ossana, and the best musical score award went to Gustavo Santaolalla.

4 Stephen Holden, "Riding the High Country, Finding and Losing Love," *New York Times*, December 9, 2005; Peter Hartlaub, "Tips for Getting over 'Brokeback' Hump," *San Francisco Chronicle*, February 5, 2006, D1. The actresses who expose their breasts are Michelle Williams and Anne Hathaway.

5 Ken Tucker, "The Final Frontier," *New York*, December 5, 2005.

6 Annie Proulx, Larry McMurtry, and Diana Ossana, *Brokeback Mountain: Story to Screenplay* (New York: Scribner, 2005), 1–2; Kenneth Turan, "The New Frontier of 'Brokeback' Is Vast and Heartfelt," *Los Angeles Times*, December 9, 2005, E1. The short story, written by Annie Proulx, was published in *The New Yorker* on October 13, 1997.

7 Lane, "Current Cinema."

8 Turan, "New Frontier of 'Brokeback,'" E1.

9 Ty Burr, "'Brokeback' Is an Affecting Study of Stifled Passion," *Boston Globe*, December 16, 2005, D1.

10 David Ansen, "The Heart Is a Lonely Hunter," *Newsweek*, December 19, 2005, 72.

11 Holden, "Riding the High Country."

12 On the scenes being a plea for an end to homophobia, see Maria DiBattista, "Can Movies Change Our Minds?," *Los Angeles Times*, February 5, 2006, M2; Karen Durbin, "Cowboys in Love with Each Other," *New York Times*, September 4, 2005, B2; Owen Gleiberman, "Brokeback Mountain," *Entertainment Weekly*, May 7, 2006; Lane, "Current Cinema."

13 Durbin, "Cowboys in Love," B2.

14 Gleiberman, "Brokeback Mountain."

15 Robert W. Welkos and Elaine Dutka, "Can 'Brokeback Mountain' Move the Heartland?," *Los Angeles Times*, December 14, 2005, A1; Tom Long, "Breakthrough 'Mountain,'" *Detroit News*, December 16, 2005; Rene Rodriguez, "'Brokeback' Is a Timeless Love Story—with a Twist," *Miami Herald*, December 16, 2005; Frank Rich, "Two Gay Cowboys Hit a Home Run," *New York Times*, December 18, 2005, D13.

16 Chris Crain, "No Losers in 'Brokeback' Showdown," *Washington Blade*, March 17, 2006, 26 (www.imdb.com/title/tt0388795/business).

17 Rachel Leibrock, "'Mountain's' Time: A Changing Society Lays the Groundwork for the success of the 'Brokeback' Gay Love Story," *Sacramento Bee*,

January 11, 2006, E1. On other publications discussing the public only being ready for such a film in 2005, see Thompson, " 'Brokeback Mountain' Charts," D12. Larry McMurtry won a Pulitzer Prize in 1986 for his novel *Lonesome Dove*.

18 Claire Hoffman, "Wal-Mart Sells 'Brokeback' Amid Conservative Protest," *Los Angeles Times*, April 4, 2006, C1.

19 Tim Maher, "Voices from Brokeback Mountain: Heath Ledger," *Gays in the Media*, December 12, 2005 (www.gaysinthemedia.com/interview/heath ledger).

20 Noah Schweitzer, "Voices from Brokeback Mountain: Anne Hathaway," *Gays in the Media*, December 12, 2005 (www.gaysinthemedia.com/interview/ annehathaway).

21 George Archibald, "Moguls, Actors Support Gore," *Washington Times*, May 15, 2000, A1.

22 Tim Maher, "Voices from Brokeback Mountain: Ang Lee," *Gays in the Media*, December 12, 2005 (www.gaysinthemedia.com/interview/anglee).

Conclusion: From "Perverts" to "Fab Five"—Progress in Three Stages . . . and Waiting for a Fourth

1 Lucretia Mott, "National Convention at Cincinnati, Ohio," in Elizabeth Cady Stanton, Susan B. Anthony, and Matilda Joslyn Gage, eds., *History of Woman Suffrage* (New York: Fowler & Wells, 1881), 164.

2 Jerry Lisker, "Homo Nest Raided, Queen Bees Are Stinging Mad," *New York Daily News*, July 6, 1969, B6.

3 Corey Kilgannon, "Just Off a Park's Playing Fields, Another Game Thrives," *New York Times*, September 21, 2005, B1, B2.

4 Christopher Lisotta, "Broadcast TV a Little Less Gay," *Television Week*, August 21, 2006, 7. Marc is played by Michael Urie.

5 Jane Applegate, "Gay Households," *Chicago Sun-Times*, April 28, 1993, Financial 54.

6 Jack Nichols, "Billy Crystal: Interview with A Gay Icon," *Gay Today*, January 26, 2004.

7 Paul Brownfield, "As Minorities' TV Presence Dims, Gay Roles Proliferate," *Los Angeles Times*, July 21, 1999, A16; Cynthia Cotts, "The Media and the Moguls," *Village Voice*, August 14–20, 2002.

8 Lydia Saad, "Tolerance for Gay Rights at High-Water Mark," May 29, 2007, www.galluppoll.com/content/?ci=27694.

9 "Tidings of Job," *Time*, December 27, 1993, 71; Larry Kramer, "Lying About the Gay '90s," *Washington Post*, January 9, 1994, G1; Saad, "Tolerance for Gay Rights at High-Water Mark."

10 Mark Peyser, "The Life of the Party," *Newsweek*, June 23, 1997, 76; Saad, "Tolerance for Gay Rights at High-Water Mark."

11 Dick Polman, "Gays' Wins Met by Line in the Sand," *Philadelphia Inquirer*, August 10, 2003, A14; John Sellers, "Queen for a Day: My Gay Makeover," *New York Times*, July 13, 2003, B1; Saad, "Tolerance for Gay Rights at High-Water Mark."

12 "Move to Bar Perverts from ECA Beaten," *Washington Times-Herald*, April 1, 1950, A2; Lawrence K. Altman, "New Homosexual Disorder Worries Health Officials," *New York Times*, May 11, 1982, C6. The premier episode of *Queer as Folk* aired on December 3, 2000.

13 Peter Hartlaub, "Tips for Getting over 'Brokeback' Hump," *San Francisco Chronicle*, February 5, 2006, D1.

14 Laurie Goodstein, "Gay Couples Seek Unions in God's Eyes," *New York Times*, January 30, 2004, A1.

15 Bill Carter, "The New Season/Television," *New York Times*, September 12, 2004, B81.

Index

20/20 (TV show) 104–105, 108, 111
60 Minutes (TV show) 159

ABC (TV network) 37–49, 54, 60, 66, 68, 73, 75–77, 80, 91, 104–114, 124, 183, 187–188
ABC World News Tonight 68, 163
Academy Awards 2, 75, 84–85, 93, 95, 98, 102, 108, 115, 154, 169, 175, 177–178, 184
actors as gay rights activists 48–49, 92, 102, 114, 125–126, 177–178, 184
actors playing gay or lesbian characters 34–35, 41, 47–49, 94, 118, 123, 130, 151
Adair, Carol 159, 162, 164, 168
advertising and gay and lesbian content 32, 75, 77,104, 111–114, 123–124
Advertising Age 103
Advocate, The 50, 157–158
AfterEllen.com (Web site) 157
AIDS 3–4, 50–64, 71, 83–86, 89–91, 101–102, 119, 128, 131–132, 135, 165, 168–169, 180, 186
Allen, Ted 139, 141
All in the Family (TV show) 4
All the Rage: The Story of Gay Visibility in America (book) 34, 45, 63, 146
Alternate Channels: The Uncensored Story of Gay and Lesbian Images on Radio and Television (book) 45
Alwood, Edward 54
American Family Association 111
American Psychiatric Association 40
anti-sodomy laws 138

Arnold, Roseanne 73, 76, 80, 112–113
Atlanta Journal 124
Atmore, Bill 162
Auger, Marie 165
Austin, Dorothy 162

Bailey, Gloria 161, 167
Baldwin, Alec 108, 115
Ball, Lucille 13
Baltimore Sun 77
Banderas, Antonio 86–87, 91, 101, 161
Bargeman, John 141–142
Basic Instinct (film) 73–75, 77, 79–81, 83, 112–113, 147, 149, 157–158, 182
Bazell, Robert 54
Beals, Jennifer 151
Bernhard, Jusak 165
Birdcage, The (film) 2, 93–95, 97, 100–103, 112, 114, 120, 126, 164, 178, 180–181, 185, 187
bisexuals 79–80, 151, 154–155, 158, 182
Bishop, Jerry 52
blackmail of homosexuals 9–10
Blick, Roy E. 8, 13
Boston Globe 8–9, 32, 60, 75–77, 83, 106, 110, 119, 139, 145, 151, 154, 156, 159–160, 162–163, 169, 172
Botas, Juan 86
Boys in the Band, The (film) 2, 26–36, 41, 46–47, 66, 85–88, 94, 114, 119–121, 153, 165, 168–169, 171, 179, 183
Bravo (cable TV channel) 137, 142, 143

Bridges, Fabian 60, 63
Bridges, Styles 7
Brokaw, Tom 54
Brokeback Mountain (film) 2,
    169–178, 180–181, 186–187
Brooks, Shane 162
Brown, Michael 64
Buckley, Declan 166
Bush, George W. 166

Cahill, Elizabeth 162
Cammermeyer, Margarethe 70, 71,
    72
Capsuto, Steven 45
Carpenter, Kelli 162
CBS (TV network) 13, 53–54, 66, 68,
    72, 105, 159, 162, 164
CBS Evening News 68, 163
Celluloid Closet, The (book) 34
Centers for Disease Control 51, 54
Chancellor, John 69–70
Cher 115
Chicago Sun-Times 20, 32, 92, 135,
    169, 184
Chicago Tribune 9, 60, 64, 66–67,
    71, 74, 99, 107, 124, 127, 139
Cleveland Plain Dealer 9, 92
Clinton, Bill 5, 65, 67, 68, 71–72,
    109, 113
Clooney, George 117
Close, Glenn 115, 125
CNN (TV network) 66, 68, 163, 166
Cole, Nat King 48
Collins, David 137, 148
*Columbia Reader on Lesbians and
    Gay Men in Media, Society, and
    Politics, The* (book) 146
coming out as a gay man or lesbian
    95, 99, 104–105, 107, 110–111,
    113
Compton, Robert 163, 167
Congress, U.S. 14, 65, 71, 181
Coronet (magazine) 8, 9, 11–12,
    14–15
Cosmopolitan (magazine) 77–79
couples
    gay male 31–32, 40, 83, 90, 99,
        101, 129, 160, 161–178, 187
    lesbian 23, 150–151, 153,
        155–156, 158–162, 164–168,
        187
*Covering the Plague: AIDS and the
    American Media* (book) 53, 60
Cox, Bill 61–63

Crane, David 126
Crawford, Cindy 108, 113, 158
Crystal, Billy 2, 38, 41, 47–49, 92,
    102, 163–164, 182, 184
Cummings, Bernie 165
Curve (magazine) 157

Daily Variety 103, 145
Dallas Morning News 9
Damast, Gabriel 164
Damon, Matt 115, 125
Davies, Linda 161, 167
Dawson's Creek (TV show) 126
Day, Doris 57
DeGeneres, Ellen 104–114, 124, 147,
    149, 160, 163, 181, 187
D'Emilio, John 63
Demme, Jonathan 86, 91
de Rossi, Portia 160
Depp, Johnny 109
Dern, Laura 106, 108
Desperate Housewives (TV show)
    188
Detroit News 176
Diaz, Cameron 95, 102
diversity in gay and lesbian
    community 26, 33–36, 91, 100,
    125, 135, 144, 149, 153–154,
    156, 181
"don't ask, don't tell" policy 65
Douglas, Kyan 138, 143
Douglas, Michael 74–75, 80–81, 115,
    125
drag queens 23, 25
Drake, Donald 59

Early Frost, An (film for TV) 4
Eaton, Catherine 78–79
Eck, Diana 162
Ellen (TV show) 2–3, 104–114,
    117–118, 123–124, 135, 144,
    146, 149, 158, 168, 180–181,
    185, 187
Emmy Awards 2, 108, 123, 134, 142
Entertainment Weekly (magazine)
    107–108, 118, 123, 137, 169,
    175
Epstein, Joseph 22
ER (TV show) 117
Esquire (magazine) 8–9, 12, 20, 21,
    90, 139
Evans, Linda 57
Everett, Rupert 93–96, 98–99,
    101–102, 147, 187

Falwell, Jerry 111
families of gay men or lesbians 31,
  83, 87, 90, 172–174
Filicia, Thom 138–141
Ford, Harrison 109
Fox News Channel 3, 164
Foxx, Jamie 188
Frasier (TV show) 126
Friends (TV show) 126, 143

Gant, Robert 130
Garland, Judy 17–18, 26–27
Gato, Kevin 166
gay and lesbian buying power 92,
  102–103, 114, 125–126, 145,
  147, 161, 184
gay and lesbian parents 42, 46,
  122–123, 130, 153, 160,
  164–165, 180
gay bashing 128, 130–131, 135,
  170, 173–175, 177
Gay Mafia 126, 148, 168, 184
gays in the military 3, 5, 65–72,
  146, 168, 180
Glamour (magazine) 78–79, 81,
  87
Goldwater, Barry 69
Goodridge, Hillary 162–163,
  167
Goodridge, Julie 162–163, 167
Gorman, Cliff 35
Graziano, Lisa 78
Grey's Anatomy (TV show) 188
Groff, Diane 162
Gross, Larry 34, 45, 53, 146
Gyllenhaal, Jake 170

Hackman, Gene 95, 102
Haffner, Kate 79
Hailey, Leisha 151
Hanks, Tom 84–85, 87, 92, 99,
  101–102, 161, 180, 184–185
Harper's (magazine) 20, 22
Harrison, Randy 130
Harris, Susan 47
Harwood, Richard 167
Hathaway, Anne 172, 177–178
Hayes, Sean 116, 118
HBO (pay-cable TV channel)
  188
Heche, Anne 108–109, 113
Hemingway, Mariel 73, 76, 79–81,
  112–113, 147, 158
Holloman, Laurel 151

Hollywood supporting gay rights
  48–49, 92, 102, 114–115,
  121–122, 124–126, 148,
  177–178, 184
Holms, Sally 54
homophobia 56, 59, 63, 69–70, 84,
  88–90, 170, 174–175, 177
Honolulu Star-Bulletin 61–62
Hudson, Rock 52, 57–59, 63
Humphrey-Keever, Parke 165
Hunt, Helen 108, 113–114, 158

illness, homosexuality as 12–13, 15,
  20, 23, 40, 64, 82
I Love Lucy (TV show) 13
In & Out (film) 93–101, 103, 114,
  169, 180, 185, 187
*I Now Pronounce You Chuck and
  Larry* (film) 183

Johnston, Ernie 165
Joint Chiefs of Staff 65
Jones, Tommy Lee 109

Keenan, Joe 126
Kidd, Tom 166
Kinsella, James 53, 60
Kinsey, Alfred C. 13, 148
Kinsey Report 13
Kirshner, Mia 152
Kline, Kevin 93, 95–9, 101–102, 187
Kressley, Carson 140–141, 143, 181,
  183
Kutcher, Ashton 188

Lane, Nathan 93, 94–95, 97–101,
  112, 187
Lauren, Ralph 140
Ledger, Heath 170, 177–178
Lee, Ang 178
Lee, David 126
Lerner, Max 12–13
"lesbian chic" phenomenon 74,
  77–80, 158, 182
lesbian invisibility 6, 22, 24, 35, 63,
  72–73, 78–81, 91, 100,
  112–113, 125, 135, 146–148,
  156, 168, 176–177, 186
Letterman, David 104
Lewis, Anthony 69
Life (magazine) 61, 64
Look (magazine) 26
Los Angeles Times 3, 7, 9, 32, 43,
  50–51, 53, 59–60, 67, 69–70,

73, 75–77, 83, 89, 96, 98,
104–107, 111–112, 118,
121–122, 124–126, 134–135,
137, 144, 148–149, 152, 156,
161, 168, 171–172, 175, 184
Luckinbill, Larry 35
L Word, The (TV show) 2, 149–159,
165, 168, 182, 185–186, 188
Lyon, Phyllis 166

McCarthy, Joseph R. 7
McConnell, Jamie 162
McCormack, Eric 116, 118, 123
McDonald's 111
Mademoiselle (magazine) 77, 79, 158
Madonna 115, 125
Mandel, Lisa 164
Manley, Jeffrey 165
Margulies, Julianna 108
Martin, Del 166
Martin, Steve 108
Matlin, Marlee 154
Mayoni, Paul 166
Media Research Center 76
Messing, Debra 116, 119
MGM Studios 94, 103
Miami Herald 9, 176
Miller, Arthur 14
Miller, Bill 163
Moore, Demi 108, 113–114, 158
Moore, Mary Tyler 48
Morgan, Diane 78
Mott, Lucretia 15, 25, 179
Mullally, Megan 116, 119
Mulryan, Dave 112
Mutchnick, Max 122, 126, 184
My Best Friend's Wedding (film) 2,
93–96, 98–103, 114, 120, 126,
147, 168, 178, 180, 185, 187

National Federation of Decency 39
National Public Radio 166
NBC (TV network) 54, 56, 66,
68–70, 105, 115–126, 129, 134,
143, 186–187
NBC Nightly News 68–70, 163
New York (magazine) 54, 78–79, 88,
152, 170
New York Daily News 18, 19,
23–25, 32, 42, 168, 182
New Yorker, The (magazine) 8, 32,
169, 171–172, 176
New York Herald 15
New York Native 53–54

New York Post 10–14, 18–19
New York Times 1, 5, 7, 9–10, 15,
18, 20–21, 23, 34–35, 39, 47,
50, 52–55, 59, 61–62, 64,
67–72, 74–77, 82, 97–98, 101,
103–104, 106, 111–112, 123,
125, 128, 132, 134, 137–142,
145, 147, 151–152, 154, 156,
159–160, 162, 164–165,
168–169, 173, 176, 182, 185,
187
New York World-Telegram 9, 10–11,
14
Newsday 75, 77
Newsweek (magazine) 19–20, 39,
51–52, 63, 74–5, 78, 84, 96,
100–101, 130, 173, 185
Novak, Robert 68
Nyswaner, Ron 84

O'Donnell, Rosie 162
Oregonian 162
Orlando Sentinel 76–77

Paige, Peter 130
Paramount Studios 94, 103
Pasieniti, Jim 21
Pearce, Martin 162
Pegler, Westbrook 10
People (magazine) 84, 95, 156–157
"Perverts on the Potomac" scandal
6–16, 24, 35–36, 46, 50, 63–64,
71, 146, 167
Peurifoy, John 7, 9
Philadelphia (film) 2, 83–92, 94, 99,
101–103, 114, 135, 153, 161,
169, 180–182, 185, 187
Philadelphia Inquirer 3, 59, 124, 143,
156, 185
physical contact between gay people
42, 47, 73–7, 80, 87, 91, 107,
112–113, 115, 121–122,
124–125, 127, 134, 143, 148,
163
Potter, Chris 130
Premiere (magazine) 84, 86–87
*Prime Time Closet: A History of
Gays and Lesbians on TV, The*
(book) 45
Public Broadcasting Service 60

Queer as Folk (TV show) 2,
127–136, 142–144, 149, 152,
158, 165, 173, 180, 186–188

Queer Eye for the Straight Girl
  (TV show) 144
Queer Eye for the Straight Guy
  (TV show) 1–2, 137–145, 148,
  153, 162, 168, 176, 180–181,
  183, 185, 187
Quindlen, Anna 69

Roberts, Julia 95–96, 98–99, 102
Rodriguez, Jai 139–141, 144, 153
Rolling Stone (magazine) 54
Roseanne (TV show) 73–81, 113,
  115, 121, 147, 149
Ruark, Robert C. 10–11
Russo, Vito 34
Ryan, Kay 159, 162, 164, 168

Sacramento Bee 176
safe sex 128, 132, 135, 180
Salon (magazine) 134–135
same-sex civil unions 122, 124, 160
same-sex couples adopting children
  122–4
same-sex marriage 132, 158–168,
  180, 187
San Diego Union 43
Sandler, Adam 183
San Francisco Chronicle 9, 22–24, 32,
  50–51, 62, 81, 117–118, 124,
  134, 157, 161, 169, 187
Sarelle, Leilani 74, 79, 81
Saturday Evening Post (magazine) 8
Schepel, Butch 139
Seagren, Bob 42
Selleck, Tom 93, 95–99, 102, 187
Senate, U.S. 6–9, 94
Sex and the City (TV show) 188
sexism 147
*Sexual Behavior in the Human
  Female* (book) 148
Sexual Behavior in the Human Male
  (book) 12, 148
Shaw, David 53
Shilts, Randy 62, 63
Showtime (pay-cable TV channel)
  127–128, 135, 143, 149–150,
  180, 185–186, 188
Simms, Sylvia 161
Simon, Bob 164
Slate (magazine) 151
Soap (TV show) 2, 4, 37–49, 55,
  91–92, 102, 118, 120, 135, 137,
  144, 164, 179–180, 182, 186
Springsteen, Bruce 84

Stanton, Elizabeth Cady 15
State Department, U.S. 6–8, 10–11,
  32, 63
Steele, Maria 140
Steele, Ray 140
stereotypes of gay men, negative
  bitchy and mean-spirited 27–29
  child predators 11, 14–15, 22, 24,
    35, 66–7, 71, 131
  drug abusers 128, 133, 135, 180
  effeminate 10, 19, 25–26, 32–33,
    35, 37, 86, 138, 171
  immoral 11–12, 15, 24, 58, 60–61,
    63–64, 67, 71
  isolated from straight people 35,
    130
  narcissistic 26, 28, 30, 35, 37, 171
  overly emotional 10–11, 15, 26,
    30–31, 35, 46, 171
  overly sexual 13–15, 20–22, 24,
    26, 31–32, 35, 51, 55, 66–68,
    71, 86, 127–129, 133–135, 143,
    156, 165, 171, 180, 186–187
  sad and pathetic 26–28, 35, 86
  self-loathing 26, 28–29, 35, 85
  suicidal 28, 35, 41, 46
  villains 58, 60–61, 63
  violent 20, 23–24, 63
stereotypes of gay men, positive
  charming 85, 93–96, 100, 147,
    171, 185
  chaste or monogamous 94, 99–100,
    117–118, 134, 165
  close bonds with straight women
    93–94, 115, 119, 124
  endowed with good taste 93–94,
    97–98, 100, 139, 171, 185
  fun 85, 93–94, 115, 139–141, 143,
    147, 160, 163
  high achieving 71, 41–42, 85–86,
    93–94, 98–100, 160, 162–163,
    171, 185
  heroic 58, 61–63, 83, 85–86, 119
  narcissistic 115, 120–121, 124
  physically attractive 41, 85, 86,
    93–94, 96–97, 124, 147, 171,
    185
  witty 115, 120, 124, 139–141, 143,
    147
stereotypes of lesbians, negative
  alcoholic 23, 82
  humorless 109, 147, 186
  man hating 24, 81, 113, 147
  masculine 22, 24, 81–2, 147

overly sexual 22–23, 74–75, 81,
113, 149, 152–153, 155–158,
165, 180, 186–187
suicidal 23, 82
unattractive 147, 186
violent 22, 74–75, 81, 112
St. Louis Post-Dispatch 164
Stone, Sharon 74–5, 79, 80–81,
112–113, 147, 157, 158
Stonewall Inn 17–19
Stonewall Rebellion 3, 17–25,
35–36, 46, 50, 63–64, 71,
81–82, 113, 146, 157, 168,
171, 179, 182, 185
*Straight News: Gays, Lesbians, and
the News Media* (book) 54
Strait, George 60
"Streets of Philadelphia" (song) 84
Streisand, Barbra 94
Supreme Court, U.S. 138

Taylor, Elizabeth 57–58
Time (magazine) 8, 13, 20–21, 23,
26, 39, 43, 54, 59, 61, 75, 81,
82–85, 92, 95, 104–105, 107,
110, 132, 185
Traditional Values Coalition 138
transgender people 38, 42–43, 46,
154, 157–158, 182
Tripplehorn, Jeanne 74, 79
TriStar Pictures 75, 80, 91–92,
94, 103
Tropiano, Stephen 45
Truman, Harry 11
Trzcinski, Dolores 165
Turner, Chuck 163
TV Guide (magazine) 115, 118,
123

Ugly Betty (TV show) 183
*Up from Invisibility: Lesbians, Gay
Men, and the Media in America*
(book) 34, 45, 53

USA Today 4, 57, 60, 69–70, 76–77,
83, 91, 96–97, 127–128, 134,
145, 150, 152, 156, 161

Village Voice 18, 19–20, 22–23, 144,
156, 168, 184
Vogue (magazine) 74, 77, 80, 82

Wall Street Journal 52, 56, 68, 85, 145
Walters, Barbara 137–138
Walters, Suzanna Danuta 34, 45, 63,
146
Washington Blade 134, 151
Washington Daily News 11
Washington, Denzel 84, 88, 90–91,
102
Washington Post 19, 24, 39, 59,
62, 69, 73, 75, 77, 79, 82, 86,
95, 97–99, 103, 106, 108, 111,
128, 131–132, 135, 139–140,
144, 152, 159–161, 165–167,
169, 185
Washington Times 168, 178
Washington Times-Herald 7, 9, 11,
13–14, 186
WB (cable TV channel) 126
WCCO (TV station) 60
Weddell, Tracy 161
Wilde, Oscar 3
Will & Grace (TV show) 2–3, 47,
115–126, 129, 134–135, 137,
142–144, 147–148, 171, 176,
180–181, 184–187
Williams, Michelle 172
Williams, Robin 93, 97–102, 112,
164, 178, 184, 187
Williamson, Kevin 126
Wilson, David 163
Winfrey, Oprah 110, 114
Women's Liberation Movement 147
Woods, James D. 146

Zucker, Jerry 95, 102, 178